Editors on Editing

FOR FAR TOO LONG America's editors have been concealed under a cloak of undeserved anonymity. Midwives to the book and the magazine, their "deliveries" gain fame while they remain in obscurity.

At last, here in the pages of EDITORS ON EDITING, the editors come out from behind the scenes and into their own. At last the twin questions: What is an editor? What does he do? are answered fully and with authority.

To achieve this necessary unmasking of the editor's personality and his multi-faceted role in the creation of the book and the magazine, Gerald Gross, editor of PUBLISHERS ON PUBLISHING (published by Grosset & Dunlap in 1961), has drawn upon the memoirs, correspondence, articles, speeches and original comments of a score of the best-known, most influential and articulate editors of our time.

Each of these editors tells of his or her personal approach to his particular editorial specialty: children's literature, copy editing, textbooks, paperbacks, magazine fiction and non-fiction, editorial ethics and philosophy, etc.

One section of the anthology is devoted to the editor-to-author correspondence of such illustrious editors as John Farrar, Henry Simon, Harold Strauss and a candid woman editor who prefers to be known as "Anonymous." These selections make their debut in this anthology. A group of Maxwell E. Perkins' correspondence rounds out this especially valuable section of EDITORS ON EDITING.

There is something for everyone interested in the creation of books and magazines in the pages of EDITORS ON EDITING – for editors of all specialties and years of experience, for novice and established authors, and for all those who love books and want to know how they come into being.

Editors on Editing

SELECTED AND EDITED WITH COMMENTARY AND INTRODUCTION BY

GERALD GROSS

The Universal Library

GROSSET & DUNLAP

NEW YORK

A UNIVERSAL LIBRARY ORIGINAL

FIRST EDITION, 1962

PRINTED IN THE UNITED STATES OF AMERICA

For My Daughter

Alison

ACKNOWLEDGMENTS

ANONYMOUS for a selection of editor-to-author correspondence. By permission of the Author.

JEAN P. COLBY for selections from *Children's Book Field* by Jean Poindexter Colby, printed by Farrar, Straus & Cudahy. First edition out of print. Second edition to be published by Hastings House in 1963.

COLUMBIA UNIVERSITY PRESS for "Copyediting" by William Bridgwater and "Securing and Selecting the Manuscript" by John Farrar. Reprinted with permission from Chandler B. Grannis, Editor, *What Happens in Book Publishing,* New York, Columbia University Press, 1957.

EDMUND L. EPSTEIN for "Editing Quality Paperbacks" by Edmund L. Epstein. By permission of the Author.

JOHN FARRAR for a selection of editor-to-author correspondence. Letters by John Farrar have been reprinted by permission of the Author.

HELEN HARTER for "Textbook Editing" by Helen Harter. By permission of the Author.

L. RUST HILLS for "Editing: or Arguing, Procuring, Tinkering and Sending Things Back" by L. Rust Hills. By permission of the Author.

MRS. BERNARD DE VOTO for "The Constant Function" by Bernard De Voto from the Centenary Issue of Harper's Magazine. By permission of Mrs. Bernard De Voto, owner of copyright.

LITTLE, BROWN AND COMPANY for selections from *The Happy Profession* by Ellery Sedgwick. Copyright 1946, by Little, Brown and Company and selections from *In Friendly Candor* by Edward Weeks. Copyright, 1946, 1947, 1951, ©, 1955, 1956, 1957, 1958, 1959, by Edward Weeks.

Russell Lynes for "Confessions of an Author-Editor" by Russell Lynes. This article originally appeared in The Bulletin of The New York Library (citation). By permission of the Author.

Harry E. Maule for "The Objective View" by Harry E. Maule. By permission of the Author.

Ken McCormick for "Editors Today" by Ken McCormick from *Collected Bowker Lectures* published by R. R. Bowker Co. Article and Postscript by permission of the Author.

Ken Purdy for "The Fruit of the Bittersweet" by Ken Purdy, from *The Writer's Craft* edited by Frederic C. Birmingham. By permission of the Author.

M. Lincoln Schuster, President and Editor-in-Chief of Simon & Schuster, Inc., for "An Open Letter to a Would-Be Editor" by M. Lincoln Schuster. By permission of the Author.

Charles Scribner's Sons for a selection of editor-to-author correspondence. The letters from *Editor to Author: The Letters of Maxwell E. Perkins,* edited by John Hall Wheelock (Copyright 1950 Charles Scribner's Sons), are used by permission of Charles Scribner's Sons.

Henry Simon for a selection of editor-to-author correspondence. This correspondence is published with the permission of its authors.

George Stevens for "Editing for Sense and Effect" (Authors Nursemaid) by George Stevens. From *Bookmaking and Kindred Amenities,* edited by Earl Schenck Miers and Richard Ellis. Copyright 1942 by the Trustees of Rutgers College in New Jersey.

Harold Strauss for a selection of editor-to-author correspondence. By permission of the Author.

Helen K. Taylor for "What Is an Editor" by Helen K. Taylor. By permission of the Author.

Mrs. James Thurber for selections on Wolcott Gibbs and Harold Ross from *The Years With Ross* by James Thurber, © 1960 Estate of James Thurber. Originally published by Atlantic Monthly Press — Little, Brown and Company.

University of Toronto Press for selections from *The University as Publisher* by Francess Halpenny. Reproduced by permission from *The University as Publisher* edited by E. T. Harman (1961 University of Toronto Press).

DONALD A. WOLLHEIM for "Editing the Mass-Market Paperback" by Donald A. Wollheim. By permission of the Author.

A special, personal acknowledgment is due to John Farrar for the kindness and cooperation he extended to me during the preparation of this anthology. Thank you again.

A careful effort has been made to trace the ownership of selections included in this anthology in order to secure permission to reprint copyright material and to make full acknowledgment of their use. If any error of omission has occurred, it is purely inadvertent and will be corrected in subsequent editions, provided written notification is made to the publisher, GROSSET & DUNLAP, Inc., 1107 Broadway, N. Y. 10, N. Y.

CONTENTS

INTRODUCTION

I was sixteen years old when I decided to become an editor. Shortly after making my decision I went out to look for a book that would tell me all about how editors functioned. There was none. I went on to become an editor despite the absence of such a book, but I had always thought that such a book was definitely needed, and always hoped to create one.

Editors on Editing is that book, and I hope it will provide today's young aspirants to a career in editing with an introduction to the multifaceted responsibilities and pleasures of the working editor.

Two other audiences will find the book of value: the many young authors who will one day work with editors, and the general reading public who would like to know something about how books come into being.

In compiling *Editors on Editing* I followed much the same principles and general format used in my previous anthology *Publishers on Publishing.*

Editors on Editing attempts to give a rounded, clearcut portrait of the editor as a man and as a skilled professional. I have tried to reveal the particular types of personality and temperament of the editor: his attitude toward literature, his educational background, his involvement and/or detachment with the author he works with, ways of approaching the manuscript he edits, etc. And, in addition, I have tried to show many of the areas in which an editor functions: obtaining and selecting manuscripts, criteria used in ascertaining the quality of a manuscript, dealing with authors, agents, revising the manuscript, "packaging" the manuscript, etc.

Again, as in *Publishers on Publishing,* I went directly to the men and women who knew their craft best—the editors themselves. These top professionals write freely and frankly on many different aspects of their work in the pages of *Editors on Editing.* Their comments and experiences should provide valuable background, insight and first-hand information for the would-be editor.

Unlike *Publishers on Publishing, Editors on Editing* does not attempt to provide a definitive review of the history of editing. The "history" is, for one thing, quite short. The editor has only just about come into his own as a power in the publishing world. As the old-fashioned publisher—the man who selected, backed and "personalized" his books—grows fewer in number, the editor supersedes him in power and influence.

I would suggest that in the next ten years there will be many additions to the literature of editing written by editors. Until now they have been comparatively inarticulate in print, being content to remain behind the scenes. The day is changing, however, and as publishing companies lose their identity through one merger or amalgamation after another, the individuality of the editor will develop and he will find a new voice.

To compile *Editors on Editing,* I queried nearly fifty of America's leading trade publishing and magazine editors for information on their published or unpublished articles and speeches. The response, on the whole, was extremely gratifying in terms of interest in and approval of the idea of a book coming into being whose theme was editors on editing. I would have preferred many more selections in *Editors on Editing,* but what has gone into the volume represents, I believe, the very best of what editors have said about themselves and their profession.

A portion of *Editors on Editing* has been first printed elsewhere, but usually in small-circulation periodicals or out-of-print books. There is much, however, that is in the anthology that appears here for the first time.

Harry E. Maule has contributed an original essay on editing today's "far-out" writers; Ken McCormick has sent in a timely postscript to his famous 1948 Bowker Memorial Lecture "Editors Today"; Edmund L. Epstein has composed a witty and provocative essay on editing quality paperbacks; Donald A. Wollheim writes knowingly on the origins of the mass-market paperback and how to edit them; L. Rust Hills confides in us his esthetic theory concerning the choice of fiction for *Esquire.* And there are other such stimulating pieces making their debut in these pages.

One of the most interesting and valuable sections of the anthology is devoted to the never before published editor-to-author correspondence of John Farrar, Henry W. Simon, Harold Strauss and a candid woman editor who prefers to remain "Anonymous." A selection of the correspondence of Maxwell E. Perkins rounds out this group of noted editors.

It is my hope that this volume will attract many bright, creative men and women to the profession of editing. It is not a career for everybody. "Of that," to quote from Mr. W. S. Gilbert, "there is no possible shadow of doubt whatever." For the frustrated writer, editing other writers could prove to be excruciating torture and a damper on one's own creative efforts. For the dilettante "who just loves good books" but who has no little knowledge of or concern for the reading trends and tastes of the book buyers themselves, editing can prove to be a most traumatically disillusioning experience. For the young man or woman who believes editing means a round of glamorous cocktail parties, access to unlimited expense accounts, and the warm companionship of literary lions day after day, one month in the profession will disabuse him or her all too quickly. And as for getting rich by being an editor . . . well, just ask the man or woman who is one!

So much for what editing is not. It is, for one attuned perfectly to its demands, responsibilities and often tedious tasks, a most rewarding career—fully as creative, imaginative and satisfying as being a writer. And some editors might even go so far as to say—"more so."

I compiled this book with a tender loving care that I hope indicates my deepest feelings about the profession of editing. I loved it from the beginning and love it more now after nine years full of joys, griefs, achievements and frustrations. I hope that this volume will inspire all would-be (and currently practicing) editors to similar heights of dedication and delight.

GERALD GROSS

New York City
May 1962

BOOKS

PART ONE: *Aspects of the Editors' Craft*

Helen K. Taylor

Helen K. Taylor, now a Senior Editor at the Viking Press, has been in New York book publishing for over three decades, starting in advertising and publicity at Harcourt, Brace and Company (now Harcourt, Brace and World), then joining Henry Holt and Company (now Holt, Rinehart & Winston), and next becoming a founder and Editor-in-Chief of William Sloane Associates (now merged with Morrow) before going with Viking in 1949.

WHAT IS AN EDITOR? *was written for a series of* SATURDAY REVIEW *institutional advertisements for Holt while she was Advertising and Promotion Manager as well as an editor.*

There have been many definitions of just what an editor is, but Helen Taylor's remains one of the freshest and wittiest of them all. She has caught in remarkably few words the temperament and personality of the editor with vivid humor and quiet wisdom——his addiction to books of all kinds, his wide range of interests, his abiding concern for people, his responsibility to himself as a professional man and to the society he serves.

WHAT IS AN EDITOR?

A SHORT time ago we wrote an SRL page about our manufacturing man and how he designs books. We doubt now that it gave you any real information (that's what he says), but anyway we were trying to convey the general idea of how good things get done by a good designer. That's just the trouble, said our M.M. We didn't say anything much except that he put his feet on the desk and let things occur to him. Didn't we know about sleepless nights with drawing boards dancing in the dark, about the dozen or more no-good trys at a title page, about figuring costs on twenty new books in one day, about jams in pressrooms, proofs going astray, bindings warping, engravings biting too deep—detail, detail, detail?

Yes, these are the unsung heroisms of a good job. In repentant thinking about our manufacturing man, we reflected on the work of some other important people on our staff. One of them just went by the door with a bulging brief case, probably going home to get two days' work done in one night. We'll tell you the whole truth, if we can, about what an editor in a publishing house is, and what he does.

An editor is a man with a finger to the wind. He reads all important periodicals and newspapers and when he thinks a book on a certain subject is needed he tries to find the best person to write it. This might entail anything from a telephone call to a series of investigations resembling the work of the FBI.

An editor is a man who likes to read, and a good thing too. He must be on speaking terms with all notable and all best-selling books currently published. He can only read a few hundred of these books a year; therefore he scans all book review sections carefully.

An editor is a man of hope. He reads from ten to fifty manuscripts in a week; less than one per cent of them is ever published by his house. He is also courageous and tactful, for he must reject the rest of those manuscripts, often face to face with the author, and give the honest reasons.

An editor is a man with a gregarious mind and a tender regard for human nature. He works sympathetically with any number of his firm's authors, no two alike, writers being more individualistic than most people.

An editor is a friend to all literary talent and thereby leads a haunted life, for his friends' friends and all their merest acquaintances besiege him with mistaken ideas of their own creative powers. But that doesn't stop him. Let him get his hands on a manuscript "with promise," or a "great" manuscript, and he is a humble and happy man. He will rack his brain to help a writer out of a dilemma with a character or a situation. He will "style" it for the printer with great care; or he will throw all style to the winds if the material demands it.

An editor is a plastic surgeon to books by "unprofessional" writers. Book writing these days, unlike a century ago, isn't limited to people trained in literary matters. Let someone devise a new way of erecting chicken houses, or let him live six months in a Persian village, and the result is a book—full of facts, true—but not always too well written. That's where the editor comes in. It is he who cuts thousands of words of dead wood, organizes and tightens, reshapes sentences, puts in the grammar and punctuation, and still retains the author's book too, though the author often doubts it while the process is going on.

An editor is a businessman. He arranged contracts with authors and authors' agents. He has a sharp eye for second-serial and reprint possibilities for his firm's books. He wrestles with Hollywood for a good price. He has to predict sales of books, too, and when he is off by the thousands, as he often is, people accuse him of being a visionary or a liar, and not a good businessman.

An editor is a gambling man. He will recommend that his firm publish the first, the second, and even the third book by an author, knowing full well that they will lose money. The editor is putting his chips on the books this author will write a decade or more hence, and you couldn't get any side bets in Wall Street on a proposition like that. The editor must also steel himself for the author's disappointment; whatever form of reviling or despair it may take, he must comfort and encourage him.

An editor is a denizen of the reference room. He verifies all dates, quotations, and name-spellings in every book his firm publishes. He sees to it that copyrighted material is never used without formal permission. He checks bibliographies, indexes, sources of illustrations. It would be fine if he were sometimes clairvoyant, there being in every manuscript passages that could read two ways, and the editor, therefore, has only two chances. If he guesses right, the author admires his own smooth-flowing prose. If he guesses wrong, the author bemoans the ravages of the blue pencil.

An editor is something of a legal man. When writers put real people into books and then invent a story about them, it is apt to come out libel, and the editor somehow has to scent this out. There's the case of the fiction writer who called a cafe and a waitress therein by their right names but embroidered the waitress' extracurricular activities. This crime slipped past the editor in a busy season, and the book is still under injunction.

The editor is a detail man. When he isn't on the job, the heroine's eyes can change color in the course of a novel, and characters can change their names without benefit of court decision, and the *New Yorker* can add to its voluminous files testifying to the danger of infatuation with one's own words. Why, then, be an editor? There are only a few whose patient and often inspired work with talented writers has brought then, the editors, out of the anonymity of their common lot. There are more hazards, disappointments and weary hours to this job than one likes to count.

Editors have their compensations. When our friend the manufacturing man comes upstairs with the first copy of a book that's just off the press, he's always going to the editor whose baby it is and saying, "How do you like it?" The editor reaches for it with a glint in his eye and says, "Let's see it." And they stand there, both of them admiring it, like a couple of fools.

M. Lincoln Schuster

M. Lincoln Schuster, along with the late Richard L. Simon, founded Simon & Schuster in 1924. They gambled everything on their first book and won! The book was Margaret Petherbridge's first book of cross-word. That kind of imagination and daring has remained an invisible trademark of Essandess for these nearly forty years. Mr. M. Lincoln Schuster, the President and Editor-in-Chief of Simon & Schuster, is the personification of that trademark, being an astute, dramatic and inventive publisher-editor.

Mr. Schuster's article, written especially for this anthology, is, as can be expected, refreshingly and provocatively different in theme and format. Really a collection of pensées, *their sum total is a distillation of Mr. Schuster's nearly four decades as one of trade publishing's most creative and challenging editors. In just twenty-four trenchant comments he offers a lifetime of advice to any young editor ready to read them, remember them and, when he can, act upon them.*

AN OPEN LETTER TO A WOULD-BE EDITOR

I

THE great danger in applying for a job is that you might get it. If you are willing to take that as a calculated risk, I will set down some possibly helpful suggestions in the form of a few *short sentences* based on *long experience.**

II

You ask for the distinction between the terms "Editor" and "Publisher": An editor selects manuscripts; a publisher selects editors.

* *I wouldn't exaggerate if I said thirty-eight years.* M.L.S.

III

An editor's function doesn't begin with a *complete* manuscript formally submitted to him, all neatly packaged and ready to go to press. Almost the first lesson you must learn is that authors (or their agents) frequently submit not manuscripts, but ideas for manuscripts, and give you the privilege of "bidding blind." You are lucky if you can see an outline and a sample chapter first. Sometimes you *don't even see a single word.*

IV

A good editor must think and plan and decide as if he were a publisher, and conversely a good publisher must function as if he were an editor; to his "sense of literature" he must add a sense of arithmetic. He cannot afford the luxury of being color-blind. He must be able to distinguish between black ink and red.

V

It is not enough to "like" or "dislike" a manuscript, or an idea or blueprint for a book. You must know and be able to tell convincingly and persuasively *why* you feel as you do about a submission.

VI

Don't pass judgment on a manuscript *as it is,* but *as it can be made to be.*

VII

Forget all clichés and myths about a "balanced list." If you think in such terms you will soon be stricken with *hardening of the categories.*

VIII

The greatest joy and the highest privilege of a creative editor is to touch life at all points and discover needs *still unmet*—and find the best authors to meet them.

IX

There are times whey you must finally say: "Although this is a bad idea, it is also badly written."

X

Learn patience—sympathetic patience, creative patience—so that you will not be dismayed when you ask an author how his new book is coming along, and he tells you: "It's finished—all I have to do now is write it."

XI

Master the art of skimming, skipping, scanning and sampling—the technique of reading part of a manuscript all the way through. You will have to learn when you can safely use this technique, and when you *must* read every single line, every single word.

XII

Learn to read with a pencil—not simply to note possible revisions and corrections—but to indicate both to yourself and to your colleagues ideas for promotion and advertising which may be activated many months later. Such ideas will be infinitely better if you spell them out while you are excited and inspired with the thrill of discovering the author or the book.

XIII

Deliberately practice the art of reducing to a short sentence or two the basic theme or impact of a book. You will have to learn to put the quintessence of the book on the back of a visiting card. This will later give you the nucleus for your editorial report, your jacket copy, your publisher's preview, your letters to reviewers, opinion-makers, salesmen and book-sellers.

XIV

Don't worry too much about mistakes you make deliberately; that is, disappointments and failures that may come from taking a calculated risk. Editing and publishing are risk-taking professions—sometimes they are wild gambles.

XV

Don't follow current vogues and fads, and never think of doing "another" book imitating the best-seller of the moment. Start trends, don't follow them.

XVI

Give great weight to an author's potential for growth—and to the long-life "survival value" of a given book for your back list—a criterion far more crucial than immediate sales appeal.

XVII

If you are prepared to cast your affirmative vote for a book because of its prestige value—treating it realistically as a *succèss de fiasco* or a *flop d'estime*—spell out the *reasons* for your enthusiasm, and calculate the fiscal arithmetic, so that you know just how much you are willing or prepared to lose.

XVIII

If you feel you must enlist the aid and advice of a recognized authority or specialist on a given subject, remember that an expert frequently avoids all the small errors as he sweeps on to the grand fallacy. A truly creative editor must become an expert on experts.

XIX

Don't be dismayed or disheartened if you learn that another publisher is getting out another book on the same subject. Far more important than being the first, be willing to settle for the best.

XX

Welcome suggestions and recommendations from your sales staff and your promotion and advertising colleagues, but resist any pressures that will be exerted by them for "sure things" and easy compromises.

XXI

Forget or disregard any glib over-simplifications about "the reading public." There is no such thing as one reading public.

XXII

Learn to win the confidence of your authors *before* the book is published, *during* the publication process, and *after* the book is released. Unless you inspire and enlist such confidence and cooperation, you will find yourself going back to the early days when the book-sellers were also publishers, and the relationship between an author and a publisher was a relationship between a knife and a throat.

XXIII

For an editor the moment of truth comes when you ask yourself the $64 question: Would you buy this book if it were published by some other firm? This challenge, this test, can be expressed in many rule-of-thumb formulas, such as these: Stab any page and see if it bleeds. Do you feel that if you skip a paragraph you will miss an experience? Does it make the hair on the back of your neck stand on end (this test was suggested by A. E. Housman). But all these criteria come back to the two basic questions: Would you put your own money on the line to buy the book you are considering and, even more important, would you want to keep it in your own library—so much so that you will be happy to find it there years later, and look forward to the joy not only of reading it but re-reading it?

Always remember that you are being watched and judged by your colleagues and by your publisher, by authors, agents, book-sellers, critics and reviewers. They will rate you not on any single success or failure, but on your overall batting average. Babe Ruth, Ty Cobb, Mickey Mantle and Roger Maris became world-famous champions by batting between .300 and .400—or somewhere between three and four hits for every ten times at bat. Therefore, within reasonable limits, you can luxuriate in integrity by acting with courage, with imagination, and above all, with the creative motivation that means fulfillment.

XXIV

Editing can, and should be, not only a life-enhancing profession but also a liberal education in itself, for it gives you the privilege of working with the most creative people of your time: authors and educators, world-movers and world-shakers. For taking a lifetime course for which you would be willing to pay tuition, you are paid, not merely with dollars, but with intellectual and spiritual satisfactions immeasurable.

Ken McCormick

Ken McCormick began with Doubleday as a salesman in their stores in the Pennsylvania Terminal and in Philadelphia. In the 1930's he entered the publishing department, serving first as a reader in the Crime Club. After many advancements he became, in 1942, editor-in-chief of the company.

"The most important change in an editor's job today is that he has slowly acquired the publisher's responsibility . . . In the United States editors have come to know a sort of new freedom in which editorial decisions are more and more in their hands. The publisher now concerns himself far more than ever before with business management."

Mr. McCormick's article is a wide-ranging discussion of the increasing number of decisions now in the editor's hands.

In a short postscript, Mr. McCormick brings his reflections on publishing up-to-date, bringing a new timeliness to the body of his remarks, which originated as a R. R. Bowker Memorial Lecture delivered in 1948.

EDITORS TODAY

WE SALUTE Richard Rogers Bowker tonight. It would not be easy to forget him and his tremendous influence on the book business. No greater memorial could stand for Mr. Bowker than one which he helped erect: the international copyright law. He was instrumental, along with a half-dozen other publishers and several authors, in bringing about the enactment of the copyright law of 1891 and its revision in 1909. This is his great monument.

As an editor Mr. Bowker knew a world of publishing not unlike the one we know today. There were old problems in his day; perennial problems; and new problems. It's the same today. I intend to outline some of the editor's responsibilities in this decade.

The worst editorial problem of the nineteenth century was lack of international copyright protection. Thanks to Mr. Bowker and his associates, this is so well solved today that only two people are required to handle all the copyright work for Doubleday & Company and its various subsidiaries. Once, however, the black flag of piracy was in evidence everywhere. The battle of infringements raged most furiously across the Atlantic: both England and the United States printed each other's books with abandon, without authority or acknowledgment. It is much less of a problem today and flourishes only in Asia, where steps are being taken to control it.

In the nineteenth century, as now, the two bad words of publishing were "libel" and "plagiarism." Editors have always had legal worries but never more than now. To libel anyone intentionally is obviously a criminal act. In the book world there is comparatively little of it. There is a certain type of reader who prays that he'll be libeled, or seem to be libeled, so that he may sue. Nuisance suits brought by those who imagine themselves libeled cause more legal expense and professional worry than any other aspect of our business. A recent example is all too familiar a pattern in outline: Miss Ilka Chase wrote a novel called *In Bed We Cry*. She called one of her minor characters Madeleine Valdane. The character in the book was twenty-eight years old, gay and disposed to quick romance. In Philadelphia a woman of impeccable character, but over fifty years of age, whose name was Adelina Patti Valdane, chose to assume that Miss Chase had written about her and that she was being libeled. Her reputation had been damaged and she required $50,000 to make up for the loss of her friends' esteem.

Lawyers for Miss Chase and Doubleday worked for months preparing a case which ran its weary length for one week in a local court. It cost Miss Chase about $15,000 to prove not only that she had not libeled Adelina Patti Valdane but that she'd never heard of her. As one witness after another went to the stand it became evident that the only safe way to write a novel would be to number the characters rather than name them. This sort of suit calls for constant vigilance on the part of the editor to be sure that his author understands the nature of libel laws and the danger of using a name which might be associated with someone of similar character in a locale which might resemble that of the one in the book.

Editors are less worried by plagiarism suits because there are fewer of them. Again the copyright laws were made to protect writers, and any editor would be a fool not to use them for his own protection. Intentional plagiarism is extremely rare because, aside from any ethical or moral point, it is bad business. In the past twenty-five years there have been two or three notable trials in which similarity of theme has led a writer to believe that he has been plagiarized. The most recent case was one brought against Lady Browning, Daphne du Maurier, author of *Rebecca.* The estate of the author of a book entitled *Blind Windows* sued Lady Browning and Doubleday & Company for a sum of money in astronomical figures. The case was based on certain similarities in theme. The story of *Rebecca* in its barest theme outline is as old as the story of the Prodigal Son and as available to all to write about as that parable. In this case the judge found Lady Browning innocent but not until it had cost her $25,000 in legal fees and a trip across the Atlantic to prove that she did write *Rebecca.*

As for the plaintiff, in the Chase libel suit the settlement was far below the probable cost of the suit while in the Du Maurier case the plaintiff received nothing for his pains.

Editors are haunted by the ghosts of books they may never have read which may hover over the book of the hour, ready to drop like hawks to accuse it of imitation.

Occasionally a publisher is sued for the loss of a manuscript. No manuscript is so valuable as the lost manuscript. It may be trash but it is worth $10,000 lost; found, it's worth ten cents. Few manuscripts are lost, and most writers have come to follow the editors' advice, which is never to send to a publisher a manuscript of which he does not have a carbon.

Editors aren't infallible and accidents do happen, though rarely. I remember one "lost" manuscript which almost sent the author to jail. We approached him with the regretful news that his manuscript had been lost and a request to have his carbon so that we could have a new original typed for him at our expense. He immediately countered with a suit for $10,000 because we'd lost his only copy. The insurance lawyers pointed out that of course he had damages coming because we *had* lost his manuscript. But, since our testimony in court about the value of the contents of the manuscript would be considered prejudiced, the insurance lawyers suggested that we check other publishers to see if they had previously rejected the manuscript. On the basis of several rejections we might establish the fact that the manuscript was unpublishable and worth little more than the author's time to write it.

I wrote every editor in New York City and got an answer in twenty-four hours from almost everyone. They all lived in fear of losing a manuscript and my letter was like an SOS signal; they might need help someday too! I wrote to twenty-four editors, sixteen of whom replied that they had considered and rejected the manuscript. But four replied that the manuscript or copy of it was under consideration at the very time we had lost it. The author had withdrawn the manuscript in each of the four cases on the day he received our letter advising him that his manuscript had been lost. The man had perjured himself, of course; and, very much chastened, retired from the case, although a modest settlement was made to forestall further trouble. This case became doubly offensive when we found the author's manuscript had been copied on a co-operative basis with the understanding that when it was sold the typist would be paid. She, we discovered, had never been advised that he was suing Doubleday.

I'm glad to say that this type of behavior among authors is the exception and not the rule. But it has always added to the troubles of the editor who tries to deal fairly and honestly with writers.

I'm sure that there are many more old problems which have been handed down to contemporary editors but this sampling will suffice to acknowledge the fact that we still have many of the same old problems with us.

Perennial problems abound by the score, and to these we give the most attention because they bridge the rich past of publishing with what we hope will be a richer future.

Where to find potential writers is a quest which has engaged editors for generations. The editorial scout has never been so active as today and it is almost inconceivable that a talent could go undiscovered. Actually scouting is now being carried to a point near absurdity. We scout magazines for new talent, keep track of writers' conferences and college writing laboratories. It's hard for a man to write a short story for the *New Yorker* and not have at least one offer for a collection of his future short stories once he's written them. If he then goes on to write a novel, that is reward indeed for the lucky publisher. Baseball clubs are being penalized for drawing players from high school teams, and I expect any day to see that the Authors' League has fined one of our publishing houses for invading high school English classes in search of talent.

Certainly this scouting is healthy and has produced an atmosphere of importance in which the writer's ego can breathe. It would not be possible today, for instance, to have a contemporary Frank Norris arrive on the scene as fully developed as he appeared to the world of books in 1898. He had written and published dozens of short stories in Western literary magazines, had written three novels, *McTeague, Vandover and the Brute,* and *Moran of the Lady Letty,* before Johns Phillips of Doubleday, Page & Company read the first part of *Moran* as a serial in *Overland Magazine* and made him an offer for book publication. In the next eighteen months Doubleday published three of his novels, all written before he had had a book contract. Today he'd have had an advance against his royalties after the first chapter of *McTeague,* and his short stories would have been published long before that.

There are fewer unsolicited manuscripts accepted by publishers today because it is almost impossible for any talented individual to write much without being observed. He is approached by the publisher, an agent, or a friend who *knows* a publisher or agent. It's a strange talent that goes unsolicited today. Or any day, for that matter. Genius discovers itself first and I doubt that any great writer in recent years has gone unpublished.

In fact it isn't even necessary to be a writer at all to be published. The world is so full of people with something to say and with no means to say it, and other people who speak beautifully but have nothing to say, that publishers have effected a union between these two groups. Ghosting and collaborating have been responsible for many fine books which might never have been written. The editor who brings the right man of ideas in contact with the right man of expression has effected something of a creative process in so doing.

The economics of publishing is an increasing problem to the editor. Advance royalties and general payments to the author present the editor with an economic responsibility to his authors not to bankrupt them by encouraging them to think that they can support themselves by writing. Although more writers are now living from royalties than ever in the history of publishing, many are doing second-rate work to maintain themselves. In some part this is the fault of the editor. Book writing is a full-time occupation for comparatively few of the thousands who write for profit. It is very easy for an editor to tempt a writer who has done a couple of short stories to free himself sufficiently to write a novel. If he writes that novel on an advance against royalties he is living on a precarious future. Having finished the novel, he must live, and by this time the idea of writing each day has come to appeal to him. It is then the editor's job to keep him alive until the book is published. Even then the writer is not in the clear because he must earn more than his advance payment.

There is much to be said for the week-end writer who does his best writing as an avocation rather than mediocre writing as a vocation. Until a writer is fairly well developed the editor must encourage him to maintian economic security in some other field so that he won't do his writing out of desperation. Certainly some literature has been produced by the starvation route but I've never been sure that it wouldn't have been better if the man had eaten regularly.

I knew one writer who began his first novel on the subway traveling to and from night school. He supported himself as an accountant while he went to night school to study law. His accountancy job in the garment district supplied him with endless material for the novel he wished to write in addition to guaranteeing him a weekly wage. His law school work was a side bet on the future on the chance that his writing did not materialize. He went through a writing apprenticeship of several years during which he wrote short stories which were published here and there but never in a profitable medium; he wrote two novels which were turned down and was at work on the third novel when it was signed for publication. During that time he had taken care of himself, his family, and his education. He had confidence in his ability to earn a living if his fountain of ideas dried up, and as he worked he stored up material for more and more books. No editor can be given credit for guiding this writer; he knew what he should do.

Too often, however, editors do assume a responsibility which is not advisable. Writers who should be encouraged to stay at home and keep up their writing are encouraged to come to New York City, where they lose the one thing they had to offer: a feeling for their own grass roots. In a day when earning a living is a matter of amassing a small fortune it is the responsibility of editors to protect their writers from stranding themselves.

By so restricting writers the editor can keep the author who has very little to say from glutting the market with second-rate stuff. After all, editors must protect the reader from boredom and the market from saturation. Unfortunately, the present-day contract system does little to alleviate this tendency. We're somewhat the victim of the three- or four-book contract in the same way that the movies are victims of the star system. Once you have a writer you must publish him to keep him.

To ease the life of the successful author, many avenues of payment have been opened. Spreading royalties over a long period of years has helped to alleviate the writer's burden of income taxes. The occasional outright sale of a whole property has given him the right to enjoy a capital gains tax rather than an income tax. Both of these methods have produced their own evil as far as the editor is concerned, however, and that's the unearned advance. This loss is being viewed more and more casually by the author and his agent as part of the risk of publishing.

It is not entirely the authors' fault that 1947 was a generally colorless publishing year in which little of distinction appeared. Editors have encouraged mediocrity by publishing too many undistinguished books. In some respects this is an outgrowth of the war and days when almost anything sold. We're in a period in publishing not unlike the early lumbering days, when areas were cut over indiscriminately. Later came intelligent, selective cutting. It isn't too wild a stretch of the simile to say that we must save *some* people to be readers.

However, every age is beset with too many books, and ours will survive along with others. It is a little disarming to discover that in 1842, when so much that was written, viewed in retrospect, seems to have been a gem, the editor of an American magazine called *Brother Jonathan* remarked, "Literature is a drug. All the markets are overstuffed." Later, in 1890, when a new world of novelists was rising, an anonymous American journalist paused to note: "There is too much of the modern novel everywhere. It is hawked in the street, it crowds the El stations, until I am conscious of a feeling of nausea at the mere sight of a row of paperbacks." Today I think we have a more intelligent attitude toward the printed word. It doesn't carry quite the frightening authority that it once did, and books are not quite such sacred objects as they once were. Yet it is still hard to get readers to throw books away. Who among us keeps bound volumes of *Redbook* on our shelves? But a novel, a hard-bound book—it's almost impossible to part with it. The control of this flood of print, which is no greater in ratio to the population than it was a century ago, is, as far as books are concerned, the responsibility of the editor and the writer.

World War II ended our literary provincialism and we have had to stand on our own feet through necessity. The twice-yearly trips to London which used to be the automatic duty and pleasure of editors have now become less pertinent. The fact that English publishers are more consistently coming to the United States than we are going there is testimony to the fact that America has come of age in letters and that her literary provincialism is ended. But the end of any bondage instantly imposes new responsibilities. If indeed this country is leading the world of arts in general, and in literature in particular, the editor has the new and terrible task of finding and evaluating this talent; of helping to mold it in the direction of global concepts; and of passing on to authors the sense of importance that must be theirs. It means less experimenting for experimentation's sake. It means more solid directions and more healthy convictions. It means that authors and editors alike must realize that the eyes of the literary world are upon them as certainly as they were once on the Asiatics, later on the Greeks, the Romans, the Spanish, the English, the French, the Germans, the Russians, and now finally on us.

The shortest route to a new provincialism born of self-satisfaction is to ignore the translation of foreign literature. The pioneers who first published translations are still alive in two of the three primary cases and have taught their fellow editors much about the need for it. Mr. Benjamin Huebsch, later Mr. Horace Liveright and Mr. Alfred Knopf among them began the work of bringing to American audiences translations of great European books. The problem of the editor today is to find intelligent and perceptive readers to evaluate books in foreign languages, and once having done that, to keep from using so few translators that the rich field of foreign books may not appear in translation to have been written by a half-dozen men.

The Russian classics sound much alike because of the energetic translating of one person. It is as if the Russians had gained the impression from translations into their language that Wolfe, Fitzgerald, Hemingway, and Faulkner all wrote alike. Translation is a creative art and one practiced much less devoutly than it should be. There have been a few giants in the field, but not enough. Translations are most successful when the translator is rendering a book into his native tongue. Americans should translate books for Americans. Vincent Sheean's remarkable translation of Eve Curie's life of her mother is a perfect example.

No editorial problem is so basic and so recurrent as censorship. The denial to the public of several books in the past few months calls attention to the fact that considerable ground has been lost in the direction of a free press. The censor has been with us since Roman days but it remained for the invention of printing to bring the full impact of previous restraint to the printed word. In Europe and England, Church and State soon imposed controls. In England, Mary forbade all printing except by license and it was not until Milton wrote his *Areopagitica* in 1644, proclaiming that a man's conscience should be his final and only guide in reading, that prepublication control was seriously attacked in England. Except for certain fields in which it still persists, it was abolished in 1695.

Even here in America we have the same heritage of prepublication censorship: the first printing presses in Massachusetts were licensed by the Massachusetts theocracy. "Published by Authority" appeared on newspapers until 1725. It was not until the First Amendment in 1791 that previous restraint was abolished in America. Every member of an editorial department is grateful for the sentence in that amendment which reads: "Congress shall make no law abridging freedom of speech or of the press."

But this was a broad freedom which allowed opportunity for censorship of movies and radio. The fear that this censorship may spread to books is beginning to worry publishers.

The threat of censorship, of course, has always been with us but it was never more firmly put down than during the 1920s. O'Neill, Dreiser, Mencken, Bodenheim among writers; Huebsch, Liveright, and Knopf among publishers; and Ernst and Hays among lawyers all understood that the writer and the publisher were the chief creators of a common consciousness in people. They knew that it was the writer's obligation to try to tell "how people feel about things." The 1920s closed with books freer than any other medium. Radio and movies had each submitted to heavy restriction but books were free because everyone concerned was ready to fight to keep them that way. By being free in a way that other media were not, books had changed American metabolism in a dozen important respects.

A depression and a war have intervened since that time and we've lost some ground. The most immediate and glaring example of how much ground has been lost is the action of the Thomas Committee and the resultant milk-toast defense of the movie magnates who abandoned their writers in a sudden, frightened gesture of "*We* didn't do anything!" Whether the Thomas Committee has so outraged the respect for civil rights of Americans that its own effectiveness will be qualified remains to be seen; but meanwhile it is the responsibility of editors and publishers to fight any such abrogation of the rights given by the First Amendment as seem to be in danger.

It is so easy to lose hard-won ground that it is in order to review a little of what censorship implies.

Vincent McHugh, who has recently been a victim of John Sumner's guillotine, has indicated three or four types of censorship which have crept in on us in the years since 1930. Censorship by accommodation between 1929 and 1948 accounted for a dangerous uniformity of thinking and expression. Conformity was rewarded, and in many cases enforced.

Censorship in wartime is praiseworthy in intent but not in effect. It invites a habit of censorship, an accommodation to it. When the emergency is over it is the editor's job and the writer's to throw off the habit and again give vent to free expression. A writer's primary obligation is to speak all the private truth that is in him, even against his own party or his own interest. Only consensus of such ruthless private truths can be melted down into a useful social truth. In this way the writer, and the publisher as well, can discharge their common social function.

During the war American writers caught the habit of conformity and, not dissuaded by their editor, became vulnerable to a subconscious or public censorship which they themselves practiced against their own enemies. Certain kinds of accommodation became virtually automatic, and this accommodation in itself has constituted censorship.

Censorship by commercial compromise is more apparent in radio, movies, and the magazines than in the book field, although even in our bailiwick certain combines have begun to suggest it. The problem is to keep books from becoming less and less a matter of free imagination, rather than a presumptive adaptation to the tastes of the customer. Mr. McHugh points out that the present condition of Hollywood is an excellent example of a calculated product beginning to euchre itself out of the market.

It is under such conditions, which are apparent in the book business, that the editor must face the tremendous responsibility of retaining enough acknowledged money earners on his list to keep the publishing house alive while he explores new fields to vent new talent. Experimentation as an end in itself, however, is a vacant room with so many doors leading into it, in the name of poetry, essay, criticism, and narrative, that an editor can easily lose himself chasing in and out of the same room by a variety of doors, convinced by the speed of his motion that he is opening the way to new vistas.

Special groups bringing special pressures make it harder and harder for the editor to resist them. Since we live by the sales of our product and not by advertising, we are freer of such pressures than the magazines, but both Catholic and Calvinist restrictions are such that editors must constantly evaluate and evade them.

Shaw's terrible question in *St. Joan*—"Must there be a Christ in every generation to save those without imagination?"—applies so endlessly in our business that it might well stand as the guide for editors. Without being too dramatic about it, apparently it *is* necessary.

The censorship feared by many in the growth of book-clubs need never develop if in editing and choosing books for mass circulation we do not underrate the public taste. It is too easy to assume that the words will be too difficult for the mass audience; the ideas too involved; the subject matter too limited in appeal. The public has long revealed itself as singularly discerning, with an eye more intent on finding food for growth than weeds for narcotics. As editors we can't throw the responsibility on the public. It is ours.

The perennial problem of scientific, religious, and political books requires that an editor concern himself with the new ideologies. H. M. Tomlinson recently remarked that "never before in history have men known so many facts about this mysterious universe as they know now, nor so little what to do with them; never such an unquestioned belief in science nor so empty a care for the value of life and personality."

Scientists have developed a world in which they must live and survive along with the rest of us. They've got to help us live with what they've created. Atomic power has finally forced a philosophical point of view upon them. The editor must find the articulate among scientists so that the layman can be educated to the philosophical concepts and realities of the scientist's new and frightening world.

Scientists themselves have progressed as if the frontier of science were limitless. There are those who believe that the field of scientific research is not infinite; that it is definitely finite and that we are within perhaps a thousand years of a terminal point in such research. If that is so, science has an even greater need to project its stark realities into the philosophical and help adjust the individual to its growing world. It's the editor's job to find the writers who can translate scientific wonders to the reader.

Novelists can play a great part in this adjustment by helping to educate the reading public. I don't refer to the interstellar-space boys but we need Dreisers and Upton Sinclairs of this generation to write about scientific advances and relate them to everyday life. Where is the man today who can write a novel about atomic power and relate it as certainly to our daily life as Dreiser brought the financial world within the lay readers' grasp in *The Financier* and *The Titan?* These writers must be found and encouraged. Fiction, after all, far more than fact, can arouse men to worthy ends, partly because fiction appeals to man's emotions, his most vulnerable and unconsciously idealistic point of access.

An editor must be concerned with the evaluation of man's religion. The need for clarification of faith is always with us. Whether it is an appeal to reason by Jean Paul Sartre or a "blue sky" exposition by Rabbi Liebman or a concern with human destiny by Lecomte du Noüy, the editor must be aware of the audience which awaits such utterances and must form an opinion of their worth. There is no field in which so much claptrap is written nor any branch of editorial work which is so subject to the intense assault by authors who are ordained by God to speak. I was once approached by a Hard-shell Baptist from Florida who rejoiced in the name of Buzzacott. He wanted me to publish his book on self-impregnation, in which he proved to his satisfaction that God had provided a special Darwinianism which called for the ultimate bestowal of both sexes in one body, that man might propagate himself alone. The fact that this manuscript arrived in a large trunk packed in with red flannel underwear always seemed to me to have its own Freudian significance.

An editor must be concerned with the evaluation of politics, national and international. The world is bursting with commentators but few authorities. No big voice dominates. Perhaps this is just as well, but it is the editor's responsibility to search for and single out those who speak with truth and understanding.

So much, then, for perennial problems, of which there are scores and only a few of which I've mentioned. Our new headache today is one which should not concern editors at all. The editor faces mechanical difficulties as never before. For some time, as this complication was activating itself, authors and authors' agents looked with boredom on our business problems and were of the opinion that we were crying because the honeymoon of wartime sales was over. However, with all credit to them, they have come to realize that editors more and more reflect publishers' worries and that with the help of authors and agents the editors and publishers can whip this new problem of manufacturing.

It is not news that the cost of manufacturing has risen largely because of wage increases in composition, plating, presswork, and binding. If there had to be an increase in the cost of manufacturing there couldn't be a better reason. But the result has been to double the cost of composition and plating and to triple or quadruple the cost of paper, printing, and binding. These increases have, of course, affected the price and design of books. In many instances publishers have been forced back into wartime economies of design. But in order not to lose the beauty of format we have economized in the length of books, which has made cutting an essential part of an editor's job. Old German publishers abhorred cutting and rarely tampered with a writer's work in this regard. We can't afford that luxury today.

This need to cut may be the ill-wind department which blows somebody good. We have fewer sprawling books as a result, although *House Divided* and *Raintree County* belie the fact. At Doubleday we have recently cut a travel book by 45,000 words and a novel by 30,000 words. In each case, of course, with the author's consent and co-operation. I'm glad to say that in both instances the authors feel that the work has been improved.

It is not too much of a problem to cut manuscripts but the real problem is to keep in print books already published. We can't cut fifty pages out of *Lydia Bailey* by Kenneth Roberts. Bennett Cerf can't excerpt two hundred pages from the Nonesuch Edition of Thomas Aquinas. And so we've been forced in many instances to increase the price or ask the author's indulgence in the matter of a royalty curtailment during this emergency. Authors in general have been quick to grasp the predicament and have co-operated so that their books can remain in print. The most important change in an editor's job today is that he has slowly acquired the publisher's responsibility. This is particularly true in the United States. In England the head of the house, the publisher, still chooses his own list, keeps track of all the authors, and gives little credit to others. Editors and readers are seen but not heard. In the United States editors have come to know a sort of new freedom in which editorial decisions are more and more in their hands. The publisher now concerns himself far more than ever before with business management.

Giants in the field like Maxwell Perkins have helped the publisher to gain confidence in his editors and to delegate a great deal of responsibility to them. One of the first responsibilities is to understand that the author belongs to the house, not to the editor, and that he, the editor, in this part of his work is a steward. Rarely do editors leave one publisher with a stable of authors to take to another house (although it has happened). Authors have editorial preferences and shift their allegiance with or without editors, so the fact that an occasional author leaves with an editor is no more surprising than that many more stay on. An author's loyalty is rarely used for bargaining for advancement in the field.

An editor, of course, has a responsibility to his employer, to the publisher who makes it possible for him to employ his talents, whatever they may be. His primary responsibility is to publish the best books possible and to make a reasonable profit. Somehow this latter point is evidence of a contract with the devil in many authors' eyes and the editor is faced with a running warfare over his right to exploit subsidiary rights. His need to exploit these rights comes from the fact that no publisher can make money today simply by publishing books. His margin of profit lies in the subsidiary rights. His right to exploit those subsidiary rights lies in the fact that the editor and the advertising man and the sales manager have worked together to make a property of the book and thus makes the subsidiary rights more valuable. The publisher therefore feels that he has a right to share in some small percentage of the profits derived from these rights. For instance, a movie treatment sold directly to the movies will bring a modest price. This same treatment written as a novel and published as one will immediately command a higher respect in the eyes of the movies. If it has stopped on Broadway as a play en route to the movies its value is doubled or tripled. So the editor too often finds himself a bargainer as well as an editor. Maxwell Perkins took the position that an editor had no interest in anything but the book itself; that his responsibility lay solely with the author and that once he had discharged that responsibility his part of the work ceased. For the generation to which he belonged he was right; but the fact remains that publishing is not that simple today. Editors must have some business sense, which should be directed to the benefit of the author and the publisher alike.

The last ten years have provided an atmosphere of gloom which has cast a considerable blight on the writer's creative process. In the depression there was much fine writing born of desperation and survival. But with the beginning of World War II this spirit was lost, and ever since that time editors have had the new problem of trying to make writers *write*. The peak of this blight came between 1939-41, when the young writer said: "How can I write when I don't know that there will be a world tomorrow?" This was not surprising among young writers, but when a seasoned writer like Stewart Edward White told me in 1940 that he could not possibly finish the second book of his two-volume novel, Volume 1 of which was *Wild Geese Calling,* I knew that something had attacked the creative spirit and had felled a real oak among writers. Certainly if a man who was a master at avoiding the distractions which keep a man from writing had succumbed, then indeed a blight was upon us. As the war progressed, as it became evident that the lights would go on again this part of the editor's job lessened, but with the bursting of the atomic bomb it began all over again.

Writers have been sterilized and it is the editor's job to try to revitalize them. One of the ways that he can do it is to make writers aware of the fact that we must break away from the '20s and '30s. Hemingway, F. Scott Fitzgerald, Wolfe, and Dos Passos are all giants whose influence may well become negative if a creative school does not appear.

The history of art has been that great writers tend to throw a pall over a decade or two ahead. New composers find it hard to initiate new forms in music after a great composer has seemed to say all that there is to say. Piano composition was blanketed by Chopin and the literature of the piano seemed to have been written for generations until composers pulled away from his influence.

Jean Paul Sartre is quite firm on this point. For him the absolute is the thing we see and feel and taste; to eat a banana grown in South America is eating a dead banana, not the real thing. Anyone today reading a book written a hundred years ago may not be reading a dead book, but the experience of reading it is not the same as that had by a contemporary reader, for a book's meaning changes with the times. Therefore, argues Sartre, writers must be passionately interested in the problems of today; they must write of and for today and take their wistful eyes from posterity. It is the editor's job to help inspire a revolution and yet retain the strength of the old school to add it as a basic measure to the new school. There is a new generation of writers and they are showing their strength tentatively. Gore Vidal's *In a Yellow Wood,* John Horne Burns's *The Gallery,* Calder Willingham's *End as a Man,* Robert Lowry's *Casualty,* Thomas Heggen's *Mr. Roberts,* and Truman Capote's *Other Voices, Other Rooms* are all possible forerunners of the new direction, the "new look," in fiction.

The desperate search today is for writers who really have the new approach. It is not entirely the fault of the writers that the renaissance of letters which was expected after the war has failed to materialize or to send up more than its first shoots. Reporting during the war, both in words and movie newsreels, was so good, so expert, that it is harder for a writer to bring something new to the reader than it was after the last war.

The writers of the 1920s were speaking to a world that had not been educated throughout the war by expert radio broadcasts, who had not been treated to some of the finest reporting in the history of journalism, and who had received no inkling of the war from the documentary films and movie combat reports. The new audience, quite well versed and ready to meet an author on semi-expert ground, provides a considerable challenge to the young writer who intends to interpret the war. When the war fiction comes I think it will be more philosophical and less a matter of action than war fiction in the past. However, war is war in any generation and it breeds adventure. Of course, there will be war fiction of this war as before, but I think the implications of this fiction will be on a far higher level than they were after the last war. Editors are searching for these interpreters.

Doubleday published the work of sixty such impressionists in a book called the *Purple Testament.* It was not literature but it challenges the editor and writer to realize what a vast, experienced audience awaits war fiction; what a terrible responsibility the writer assumes in declaring himself to an audience of readers who know from experience what he wishes to tell and who have made a fumbling attempt to express it themselves. There could be no better audience than that which participates, and for this vast group the editors today are looking to find writers who can interpret the war. This interpretation must be above the first stultifying influence of the atomic bomb. The editor must somehow free his writers from the psychological effect it has had.

I discussed the possibility of a novel along these lines with a literary editor who aspires to write fiction. His was a completely negative attitude and he seemed stopped before he had started. The fact that almost everyone in the editorial field experienced the war in fact, or vicariously through collateral organization which aided the war effort, will make this guidance of writers by editors more intelligent.

Editors must constantly resist one set of impulses and help generate another. In resisting the temptation to slant every novel toward Hollywood, toward a book-club, and yet do his duty to the author by giving him full opportunity to express himself (the author may *want* to write a novel for a book-club *and* Hollywood), the editor is trying to win the battle against standardization. But even there he finds himself stymied in his ideal because standards do not necessarily stultify—standards, like everything else, can rise.

This again is a new problem. It has been only in the last ten or fifteen years that Hollywood has recognized that the publishing business has an impact on the movie audience; that editors should be wooed and drawn into the world of mass markets. The Metro-Goldwyn-Mayer Novel Contest was the first overt act which indicated that movie companies realized the part publishers play in making a book attractive as a movie to the public. This contest has been followed by numerous tie-ups in which editors have been encouraged to accept movie money to help finance the writing of novels. This can hardly be called an evil but it is a new temptation toward a short cut to big sales.

With all credit to the book-clubs, I know of no single case where their editors or judges have made an effort in any way to influence the direction of the writing of a book, or any single evidence of financing an author. Their function has been held at a rigid level: to select books from among those contracted for and published by publishing houses.

Whatever the temptation to slant a book toward the movies or a book-club, when its natural growth is in another direction, the editor must keep his sights clear and know his responsibility to the author. With all the mutations of the book business today, with all its problems, mechanical, legal, ethical, political, and otherwise, it is very easy to lose track of the fact that the entire business is founded on one man: the author. The editor who for an instant loses track of this fact is not doing his job.

Certain bellwethers of the publishing business like Dr. Henry Seidel Canby and Alfred McIntyre on the publisher's side and Louis Bromfield on the author's have expressed themselves as fearful of the fate of the new writer, the writer of subtle values whose books may not have wide circulation. At present the reason for dismay is twofold: the broad effect of book-club distribution and the high cost of manufacture. In the former instance it is felt that mass distribution will smother the sales of books of more permanent value. This is an old despair and Cassandras of many periods in publishing history have moaned over the fate of good books.

I quote again, this time from *A Publisher's Confession,* written in 1905: "The present fashion of a part of the writing world to squeeze the last cent out of a book and to treat the publisher as a mere manufacturer and 'boomer' cannot last. It has already passed its high period and is on the decline. The writer of romances for kitchen maids and shopgirls, whose measure of a book's values are by dollars only, will disappear. Such fashions always pass. For, if novel writing be so profitable an industry, a large number of persons naturally will take it up . . . and ruin the market by overstocking. Fast passing then . . . thank God . . . is the 'boomed' book, which, having no literary merit, could be sold by sheer advertising in several editions of one hundred thousand each!"

Publishers aren't going to drop the publishing of good books today any more than they did in 1905. There was never a time when young men with young and vital ideas were so much in control of the publishing business. These men are as anxious as their seniors to leave their mark as true publishers. They're trying to find new writers and revive the faith of old writers.

There is much editorial tightrope walking as to what is first- and second-rate. Editors recognize the fact that there is a thoroughly informed audience for whom *Inside U.S.A.* is a waste of time, and a nominally informed audience for whom it is meat and drink. How to appeal intelligently to the nominally informed without outraging the intelligence of the well-informed is a problem for every age but an acute one today.

To continue the Gunther illustration (without malice), who now reads *Inside Europe?* Many of the author's points have been proved wrong but the book added to the sum total of intelligence and query. Who can point to the direct result of a meal eaten five years ago? The slow storing up of energy in eating is certainly not unlike the slow endowment of knowledge and the whetting of intelligence which comes from wide reading. *Inside U.S.A.* is the *kind* of book which made Lafcadio Hearn say: "When a new book comes out I read two old ones."

This is a nihilistic point of view if I ever heard one, because it is the daring publisher who accepts many books and the daring public who screens them who provide the fertile field in which literature grows and in which the Lafcadio Hearns of this world can flourish.

The editor must try to keep some contact between these two worlds—the intolerant world of the artist and the amazingly tolerant world of the reading public. If he can act as a catalytic agent and bring these two together he has more than served his purpose in the scheme of publishing. If he can at least relate the two he has accomplished part of his mission.

It is at this point that he becomes aware of the need to satisfy and direct the diet of an increasing appetite for fiction. Critics have long been irritated with the fact that the best books of the year are not always book-club selections and conversely that the most successful book-club selections are often critically unheralded. The editor must ask himself whether the public has a right to satisfy its appetite fully. How far should he, the editor, go in yielding to a cry for more of the same? Isn't there a danger that he will allow the new readers to exhaust themselves and stray away from the world of books to other forms of entertainment?

A critic of considerable standing, Diana Trilling, has said that in our democracy leaders have moved away from their constituents, leaders of labor unions have lost touch with the rank and file, and that in our literature there is no longer any natural association between writer and audience. This is only a partially true statement. The really great and inspired political leaders, the Lincolns, the Roosevelts, the Churchills of history, have always had the common touch. Their greatness as leaders depended on their knowledge of the pulse of their people. Leaders of our great and well-run unions are of and for the rank and file, and have never had anything to fear from them. And our really great writers and poets have seldom lacked a great and catholic audience. Shakespeare, Milton, Dickens, Mark Twain all wrote for and appealed to tremendous numbers of people in every walk of life. Poets and philosophers, students and bricklayers, secretaries and executives all have been touched and changed by what they have read.

There is a trend today, fostered by our intellectual writers, unable to be sufficiently universal in their language and message to appeal to more than a limited part of our reading public, to condemn those readers they cannot reach as a popular and, therefore, contemptible audience. On the other side the writer who can easily reach this large and so-called popular audience is considered definitely lacking, to have definitely sold himself out artistically for the proverbial thirty pieces of silver. The idea that subtlety, insight and artistic distinction in writing can be only for the intelligent, chosen few is tiresome intellectual snobbery; that the ability to communicate to large numbers of readers automatically means undistinguished writing and indiscriminate detail and subject matter is entirely specious. It has permeated the ranks of editors as well, to the extent that in many publishing houses there is at least one editor who handles only esoteric and so-called high-brow literature.

There are divisions and castes growing in our American life today, and to assist in preventing their growth is one of the major tasks of the editor. This trend can be nourished or gradually starved, and an editor can do a great deal toward turning it one way or another. I believe the time has come for the editors of the United States to enter upon something akin to a holy crusade to convince our intelligent, but frequently unintelligible, poets that great poetry should be understood, deeply felt, and loved by many. It's time to impress our many fine writers that ideas, to attain true vitality, must be clearly understood; that distinctive writing and clarity can go hand in hand; that the deliberate obscurantism frequently indulged in is a poor goal indeed, shrinking the horizons of the writer and his audience.

To bring the intellectual writer out of his ivory tower on one hand and to raise the standards of the glib writer on the other is the dual task of the editor today.

POSTSCRIPT: 1962

Many problems are the same today as they were in 1948, when "Editors Today" was written. Plagiarism and libel are still the two bad words of publishing. The translation problem is improving but is far from solved. Censorship is always with us in a series of brushfires, although perhaps less serious now than at any point in the last fifteen years with the adult acceptance of publications of such books as *The Tropic of Cancer* by Henry Miller, a circumstance which would have been impossible in 1948, when Doubleday recently had been enjoined for publishing the comparatively innocent *Memoirs of Hecate County* by Edmund Wilson.

Costs were continuing to rise in 1948 as they are continuing their upward spiral in 1962; but there are in 1962 two or three exciting prospects that were not apparent in 1948. For one thing, 1961 was far from a colorless publishing year. More particularly, the quality paperback book has enormously broadened the book reading market in high school, college, and particularly in the adult reading field. Adult education, which was beginning to feel itself mature in 1948, is now an enormous, sweeping cultural movement over the United States, involving millions of people. Quality paperbooks in every field, particularly the most serious scientific, philosophical, and sociological books, are selling to an audience who are reading them for what they can get out of them, not as requirements in school.

Television in the last ten years has begun to do for books what radio three decades earlier began to do for phonograph records: educate the broad public to a taste it didn't know it had. Public library withdrawals, which had begun to take a serious dip downward in the last years of the 40's, have made a striking comeback and are now way beyond their former high. Subjects which are suggested and lightly, or seriously, treated on TV have driven viewers to a further curiosity about them, and books are sold, rented, and withdrawn from public libraries as a direct result of TV programs that pique public curiosity.

The 60's present a new outlook with lively new publishing houses, and mergers of old publishing houses to bring together educational and trade departments in a new harmony.

The 60's offer a rosier future than any other decade in this century.

John Farrar

John Farrar entered trade publishing in 1925, at the age of 29, as an editor for George H. Doran Co. while still serving as Editor of THE BOOKMAN. *Since 1929 he has headed his own publishing firm, now known as Farrar, Straus and Cudahy.*

If you've ever believed even for a moment that editors just sit at their desks and do nothing but read books all day, Mr. Farrar, in his illuminating review of the duties of a trade publishing editor at work, will disbelieve you quickly. "The answer is he usually does it nights and weekends," Mr. Farrar says.

What he does *do during the office day—from the conception through delivery of the completed manuscript—is discussed with the acuity, dry wit and bedrock business sense that has enhanced Mr. Farrar's reputation for over three decades.*

SECURING AND SELECTING THE MANUSCRIPT

THE securing and selecting of manuscripts in book publishing is an editorial function. The distribution of authority and of particular duties in connection with this delicate and vital performance varies among publishing houses, so much so that perhaps no single pattern emerges. A discussion of the perfect pattern would be highly controversial and I hope, to avoid contentiousness, to present as simple a picture as possible of what this editorial function is in today's publishing—to make clear how things are, not how they ought to be.

WHAT IS AN EDITOR?

In splitting up editorial duties, particularly in large firms, there may be many types of editors with various titles bestowed upon them. There may be special editors such as juvenile editors, religious editors, business editors, garden book editors, and so on.

In some firms the partners themselves enjoy both managerial and editorial duties. Many firms have an executive or managing editor whose duties are usually planning and scheduling the list, coordinating details, and integrating the creative side of the process with the production and business side.

The copy editor's functions of preparation for the printer, house styling, and the handling of proofs are discussed elsewhere in this book. I refer to the copy desk because many people think of all editing as copy editing. The copy editor is usually not the same person as the general editor. In my experience the gift of meticulous care in the correction of punctuation, spelling, and so on does not usually combine with the abilities of an editor who concerns himself with the earlier problems of an author's creative period.

Assume, however, that every publishing house has a principal editor, no matter what his title, with assistants varying in number with the size of the firm. It is obvious that there would be no publishing whatsoever without manuscripts, and that for this precious metal to exist at all there must be authors. It is the author, therefore, his nurture and welfare, that is in a very real sense our chief concern here.

The word "editor" once actually meant "publisher," and *éditeur* is so used on the cover and title pages of books in France today. The word derives from the Latin "*editus,* past participle of *edere,* to give out, put forth, publish." In early days authors wrote their books, delivered them to printers, and the printers were the booksellers. The modern middlemen, the publisher and his editors and the various distributors, are the refinement of this simple process.

It is my own pleasure to think of the editor as, primarily, the friend and advocate of the author. I have often quoted Stephen Vincent Benét when he was once called upon to debate with a publisher on the subject of editing. Mr. Benét, it seems, liked editors, the editor liked authors, so the debate became an exchange of compliments. Mr. Benét pointed out that every author *must* have an editor, that writing is a lonely business and that the author must talk over his work with someone, that the someone does not necessarily have to be a publisher, however, but can be teacher, brother, librarian—even a wife or a literate, knowledgeable friend. When this friend turns out to be his publisher, so much the better; it is neat, it is convenient. He did point out, however, that he thought it dangerous for an author to have too many advisers.

During my own lifetime in publishing there have been many

fine editors. There are still. Among those who have died in recent years and whose reputations are even so soon somewhat legendary are Eugene Saxton, Maxwell Perkins, T. R. Smith, Rutger Jewett, Guy Holt, John Woodburn, Ray Everitt, and Nicholas Wreden. All of them were strongly individualistic in their characters and methods, yet all had certain things in common. Although they had a deep appreciation of the finest things in literature, they were not literary snobs; all of them liked authors as friends and all liked to read and enjoyed a good story; they worked night and day and loved publishing even as it became more and more a business and less a profession. Naturally preferring to work with books they admired, they were willing to undertake more routine jobs.

As we proceed with this description I think it wise to remember that only a small percentage of the books on any list are by any test works of literature. Many titles are, indeed, not produced by seasoned professional writers. Much of the editor's work would be eliminated if all manuscripts aimed at the publisher's desk were perfectly executed. Yet here we are considering all sorts and conditions of manuscripts, from the works of a great artist to a frankly ghost-written opus.

In closing these opening paragraphs I should point out that there is a growing feeling among authors that editors have become too possessively meddlesome with manuscripts, that editors increasingly want to change for the sake of change and override the author's prerogatives. I will not discuss this problem but only point out that the exigencies of today's publishing and the increasing hazards discussed elsewhere in the book have made this natural, if not inevitable. To illustrate the rigorous attitude and to highlight the controversial point without discussing it, I quote here with her permission a letter which that fine writer and wise woman, Marchette Chute, recently wrote me. She says: "I take a rather stern, old-fashioned point of view on the subject of writing. I think the good writers all have a period of struggle and defeat and probably need it, like the fight to get out of a chrysalis, and they end in control of themselves and their material. The other kind, the ones that chase around everywhere looking for help and support and advice, very seldom amount to anything and are mostly not worth the trouble they cause. A first-rate writer is usually stubborn and self-reliant, and the limp ones are seldom of value."

As you meet editors, and I believe this applies to all types of editors, you will find them men of affection, industry, and enthusiasm, and most of them dedicated to their job. That all editors are frustrated writers is a myth; but were it true, I believe it would make them better and more understanding editors. As I attempt to describe this business of editing, I hope you will feel that after lo! these many years, it is a business I cherish.

SECURING MANUSCRIPTS, DEVELOPING IDEAS

How are manuscripts secured? What brings authors to a publisher's door? Do they come neatly to the editor while he waits at his desk or does he go out with a dredge or a butterfly net? He and his various associates do both.

The most important factors in luring a parade of authors to any publisher are the distinction and attractiveness of the books published by a firm and its performance in presenting, advertising, and selling them. One might call this the personality of the house, and part of this is the personality of the members of the firm, the editors and the rest of the staff including the office boy and, of great importance, secretaries, receptionists, and telephone operators. Here we mustn't forget the business department. It must provide the promise of fair dealing and efficiency.

Given such a pleasing frame, the editorial department must work both within and outside it. Its members must be grounded in the history of writing and be aware of current writing in all its aspects. The ideal editor would be a superman, with world events as well as literatures at his fingertips. Many editors, even the most scholarly, read widely and with catholicity of taste. They must if they are to keep their jobs. They are aware of fads and fancies as well as of world events, politics, and philosophies. Editorial departments watch for good writers wherever they appear. They read other publishers' books and catalogues. They read newspapers and magazines—all sorts of magazines. They follow the theater, the radio, and television. They must follow, too, not only creative writing but critical writing, and watch closely the publications of their own trade, the reviews, the book announcements. They often follow writing in the colleges, the work done at writers' conferences. And all this, of course, not only on the domestic scene and in English-speaking countries but over the globe. Interest in translated works has greatly increased in the last twenty years, and is now rapidly extending from Europe to the Far East.

The editor searches for writing talent wherever he can find it, gets in touch with promising new writers, asks to read their work, nurtures them. Prizes are often offered by publishing houses, some of them grants to writers while they are creating their books. As times have become more stringent, this type of fellowship is less usual than it was soon after the Second World War, but the practice still continues.

The editor must keep an open door to all who come to him with ideas. Ideas for books may come from the most unexpected places. The editor may be bored by the next door neighbor's suggestion, but it sometimes turns out to be a good one. He may dislike cocktail parties or gatherings of authors and their friends, but they are part of the job. Of course, the tavern-hopping aspects of publishing are overemphasized in fiction and among the columnists. An editor, or someone representing him, must have feelers out in all directions. To be sure, he must know what to do with ideas when they come to him, but that is another part of the chapter. It is usually one of the editors who makes trips to England, the Continent, and, increasingly, all over the globe to interview publishers and authors and to seek out books.

Anyone following publishing even casually knows that authors change from one publisher to another. A whole book could be written on the ethics and complications of this fact. Suffice it to say that one source of authors for any publisher is a source for all the rest of the publishers, friend and foe alike.

Ideas for books are often generated within the publishing house itself. It is said of one highly modern firm that a rolling wall-screen is kept with such ideas graphically represented. If an author enters with an idea for a book on, say, "Games My Grandfather Played," the proper scroll is pulled down to display the fact that the editor himself had that inspiration long ago. The practice of developing ideas in editorial departments, then finding writers to do them on assignment has, I should think, doubled since the twenties. Some of our most successful books are developed in this manner, and it is doubtful if many successful publishers' lists could exist without them.

A publisher is perhaps interested in biography. He feels that a study of some titan, past or present, would ornament his list. He selects a writer known for his biographical writing, or perhaps a brilliant unknown. Often the writer has no current enthusiasm of his own and is happy to accept the assignment. Or a publisher has an idea for a certain type of book in psychology, medicine, history, or what-not. He may want a game book, or a special anthology. He may design a series of books of a certain type. Following the news, some personality may appear whose story, told by himself or ghost-written, may appeal. Current best-seller lists are studded with these.

Here the fertile imagination of the editor combines with his knowledge of available writers to produce much profitable merchandise and, indeed, occasionally a piece of real literature. Often the process is reversed and an author, barren for the moment, will come to a publisher seeking an idea. In some houses, editorial meetings are held frequently to dream over such imagined volumes and to produce lists of them for experimentation. Such books are not always ordered; often authors are prevailed upon to produce outlines, a few chapters, as an experiment, usually with some payment for the endeavor. The project may end there.

While an editor does occasionally present a writer with a plot or a theme for a novel, most of his own planning of books is done in nonfiction. Specialized nonfiction lists need much more inside-the-house planning than the general trade list.

Another source of books developed largely since the Second World War is the so-called package book presented to publishers by various individuals and a few concerns. A package book is usually, although not always, the sort of book that would be developed by the publisher himself as a house-idea book. But in this case, the outside idea man has produced the book entire, dealt with the author, secured illustrations, and so on, and delivers the completed product. There are several clever groups of editors working outside publishing houses who produce such books. They receive special fees or a share in the royalties or both—sometimes from the publishers, sometimes from the authors. Some printing firms have special individuals or departments that produce package books, requiring the *quid pro quo* that the printing be done by them at their price.

A profitable phase of publishing for many years has been the publishing of books on great industries or industrial figures or on some phase of business of use for commercial distribution—books often heavily financed by the industries themselves. This type of book is very often initiated and brought to completion by the package book firms.

With the development of the paperback book business, book ideas and completed books are now increasingly offered to publishers of hard-cover books by the houses dealing with the paperback books. This is a reversal; in former days the original publisher almost always offered books complete to the reprint houses, although occasionally he discussed an idea with them.

Of all outside aids in the securing of books, the most important are the literary scout and the agent (paid or unpaid) and I shall discuss each of them now.

LITERARY SCOUTS

A literary scout of one sort or another is responsible for bringing to the attention of a publisher almost 100 percent of the manuscripts accepted for publication. He is, of course, an extension of the scouting duties of the editor. The percentage of manuscripts accepted from those that come in "unsolicited," "unattended," or "over the transom" is appallingly slim. One reason for this is that most writers know someone who knows someone in a publisher's office.

Scouts are, first, the good friends who bring the editors advice, assistance, and manuscripts. They are also the publisher's own salesmen on the road. And friendly booksellers. They are legion and they are often unpaid. They become scouts in fact when they are paid, sometimes by outright fees, sometimes by royalties paid by the publisher. Some publishers have elaborate and far-flung scouting systems with representatives all over the world. They are to be found on college campuses, in various cliques, literary and otherwise, in special areas such as business, medicine, the sciences. In any milieu where the background is rich and someone might write something entertaining about it, you may find the literary scout. A few New York publishers have offices in Chicago, in San Francisco, in London, and so on. While these are usually business offices, they also perform scouting duties. Scouts are, perhaps, most useful in securing foreign authors and often specialize in one foreign country or a group of foreign countries.

In a sense, the literary agent is the publisher's most important and active scout. The difference, however, lies in the fact that, in a material and contractual sense, the scout is working for the publisher and is paid by him, the agent is working for and is paid by the author.

Some well-known literary scouts have worked for more than one publisher at a time, but it is usually understood which of several publishers they serve *first*. If this is clearly understood, the seeming division of loyalties has proved manageable.

Scouts have been known to attempt to persuade authors to leave one publisher for another. This may be dangerous procedure and often results in unhappy relations all around, but it is nonetheless a cold fact. The literary scout is not so dramatically active as the talent scout in the entertainment or sports world. Please do not visualize a huge network of well-organized publishers' spies. This would be a misconception. However, the literary scout does exist and is valuable.

LITERARY AGENTS

The literary agent since the First World War has risen with increasing rapidity to become one of the two or three most important factors in publishing. An author who does not employ an agent these days is rare, and the publisher who does not advise an author to use an agent is even rarer.

Literary agents in foreign countries are important both in their scouting and business capacities. They often represent specific publishers in placing translation rights. Literary agents in England or in other countries are usually represented by a specific American literary agent if they do not have their own branch office in the United States.

The business functions of the literary agent will be discussed elsewhere in this book. My concern here is with his relation to the editor. When I first came into publishing in the early twenties there were relatively few agents in the United States. There were more of them in England. They dealt largely with matters of finance then, but there were men and women among them who were advisers in literary matters as well. So closely are the two allied that several good editors have become agents, and vice versa.

Literary agencies vary in size, as do publishers, from the small, highly personalized organization with a handful of people on the staff, to huge corporations dealing in the various ramifications of the literary and entertainment world. The large agencies, as well as the publishers, have their own scouting systems. Some authors use their lawyers as agents, some lawyers specialize these days in literary matters. Some of these lawyers like to fancy themselves as editors—some are good ones, too!

Today a number of the best editors in publishing are among the literary agents. The functions of securing manuscripts, nurturing authors, editing, and the like, are done in varying degree and intensity by these able and hard-working folk. Usually the author's agent and the publisher's editor work together very closely. The extent to which a publisher works directly with an agented author depends entirely on the personalities and desires of all concerned. Some agents carry on practically all contacts with the publisher in the case of certain authors, while with others on their roster exactly the opposite may be true, except in business matters.

The agent is often the author's advocate in questions of disagreement between author and editor. He is, too, adjudicator. If he is good at his job, he does not, of course, always agree with his client. He must sometimes persuade him.

Moreover, the agent's duty to his author is to consider his work from an overall point of view. The agent may think it wise for an author to write exclusively for the magazines, to accept motion picture contracts, and so on. In this proportioning of what time the author is to spend on writing books there is room for much consultation and real disagreement.

The entire career of the author, the long view of his writing and publishing life, is the true duty of both agent and editor. For example, an author's career can be endangered by too frequent publication. He can be unwisely advised to follow too closely the pattern of former success, or to venture into projects beyond his special talents. Myriads of problems arise in this overall picture and, in my experience, it is here that the author most often really needs advice given with wisdom and integrity because his own eyes fail to see too clearly.

Both publisher and agent find that they are often deeply involved in the personal lives of their authors. Much has been written, some of it in rather impish terms, of this fact. In any profession or business is one not involved with one's friends? Are one's friends not temperamental? Aren't bankers temperamental? Aren't bus drivers temperamental? Aren't editors temperamental? So it goes. However, I must say that when arguments arise, as they do now and then between editor and author, it is extraordinarily comforting for the publisher, and the author as well, to have the agent around to pick up the pieces.

RECEIVING AND CONSIDERING MANUSCRIPTS

Receiving and considering manuscripts are of first importance. A loose system of entering and controlling manuscripts while they are in the house can be both time-consuming and hazardous for public relations. Most houses have found that, no matter to whom the manuscript is addressed, immediate carding and acknowledgment of a manuscript at a central point, with notations also as to accompanying illustrations and directions if any for return, is wisest, and that whenever a manuscript is moved, whether to a department or an individual, a notation be made. It is wise to keep relating correspondence with the manuscript, although this is a difficult problem and an expensive one to solve if, as is sometimes the case, folders on all incoming manuscripts are kept. Lists of incoming manuscript are usually circulated among those concerned, so that all responsible people know what manuscripts are in the house, and frequent check-ups must be made to see that manuscripts have not strayed or been under consideration too long. A recurrent editorial nightmare is of a strayed or lost manuscript.

Some publishers reject manuscripts with great speed and, in this case, an acknowledgment of receipt is not always made. While many authors resent speedy rejection, I have always felt that it was professionally fairer to make this process as swift as possible, and not to hold a manuscript for the sole purpose of convincing its writer that it has been read from first page to last, as, indeed, it often is not. I like these two paragraphs from the English publisher Michael Joseph's warm book *The Adventure of Publishing*.

"Publishers will tell you, with their tongue in their cheek, that every manuscript which reaches their office is faithfully read, but they are not to be believed. At least fifteen out of twenty manuscripts can be summarily rejected, usually with safety. There may be a masterpiece among them, but it is a thousand to one against. . . .

"Most authors are born to be failures, and the publisher knows it. He makes his living out of the few successes and if he is indulgent with less successful writers it is not only because there is always the possibility that today's failure may become tomorrow's best-seller. Unless he has a genuine sympathy with the author's problems no one can hope to make an enduring success of publishing."

Since authors do not always make clear how they wish manuscripts returned, an involved correspondence is often necessary. Authors occasionally do not even notify publishers of a change of address. It is necessary to hold manuscripts and, unbelievable as it may seem, manuscripts often are held for weeks or even months to be called for. This necessitates a careful recording and filing of manuscripts being held after rejection, and personnel who are aware of all of the details of this complicated process of reception, logging in, distribution within the office, mailing or expressing, the financial details of the operation, and so on.

I have detailed this operation with some care for two reasons: first, to emphasize the necessity of some central and tactful control; and second, to persuade such authors as may read this book that patience is a great help in a process which is so filled with pitfalls and frustrations. After all, manuscripts are brain-children and, no matter what their quality, are precious to their parents; and, in a not so very different sense, precious to the publisher. Because they are so precious, an author must make and keep at least one, preferably more, copies of his manuscript. To send the sole existing copy of a manuscript to a publisher is dangerous and unfair to all concerned.

The question of rejections and their handling is a troublesome one. Printed rejections, post cards, and letters are used by many publishers for many manuscripts. Editors write most carefully to any author who shows promise. It is considered by some unfair to criticize a manuscript in a letter of rejection unless there is a strong possibility that the publisher would seriously consider a revised manuscript. However, when a publisher writes a gracious letter of rejection and says that he would like to see more of an author's work, he usually means it.

Many authors feel that they do not get fair treatment from publishers. I think they are mistaken, but I have never found any way of persuading them of the fact.

HOW MANUSCRIPTS ARE JUDGED

The consideration of book ideas, the reading and judging of manuscripts, leading to the acceptance of a book, are of course the primary concern of a publishing house.

To accomplish this readers are employed, from one to dozens, some working on salary inside the house, some who take manuscripts home to read, some who are specialized experts in various fields. In some houses a so-called "first reader" (there may be more than one) winnows all manuscripts, although usually a manuscript from a known author or one arriving with an impressive endorsement goes directly to an editor.

As I have pointed out, few unsolicited manuscripts are accepted for publishing. Publishing houses, nonetheless, treat them, and at considerable cost, with care, with varying degrees of care, to be sure. How much of a manuscript is read depends partly on the experience of the reader. There are some editors who prefer to weed out these manuscripts themselves, rather than to leave the matter to inexperienced readers. With experience behind him, and a knowledge of the needs of his own house, he can perform this operation with speed and with less chance of error.

Whether it is unsolicited or not, a manuscript that shows promise is passed on with a report to a second reader or to an editor. Reports may consist of a sentence or of many pages. A number of houses provide printed forms for their readers which list the various aspects on which an opinion is desired. Spaces are left for a plot outline in the case of a novel or a digest of content for nonfiction, for a discussion of style, and for notation of various types of appeal. When I was first an outside reader for a publishing house in 1919 (Henry Holt & Co.), the form was a several-page masterpiece in which the most careful instructions were given. I have even seen forms which required the reader to give his estimates of percentages of appeal. For example, 5 percent sex, 10 percent adventure. The more informal report, however, of a very simple printed form, is now the general custom.

The easiest thing in publishing, as a rule, is to reject a book. But the hard work and the rewards, in spiritual as well as fiscal satisfaction, are in acceptance. I believe it is not generally understood what we publishers mean by the phrase, "It does not fit the list," but this is the reason why many books can be quickly rejected. A manuscript may conflict in many ways with books already accepted. The list may already be crowded. The subject matter of the book may be one which has proved unsuccessful for that publisher in the past. A book on playing bridge or an inspirational book might be born only to die on one publisher's list and become a national best seller on another's. Some of these facts an editor knows by instinct, some by training, but he must have a sense of the necessities and possibilities of the "complexion" of his own list. This does not stop him, alas, from reading many a manuscript he enjoys although he knows from the first page it is not for him. This only proves he is not so cold a fish as some would suppose. Moreover, there is always the exception. The editor may get so all-fired excited that he breaks all his own house restrictions.

The first delight that happens in the acceptance of a book is when someone, be it first reader or editor, is set afire. He likes the book. It is as simple as that. Not so simple, you say, and ask an editor, what makes *you* like a book?

Ellery Sedgwick, for many years the great editor of *The Atlantic Monthly,* once said that he published many different kinds of articles but never anything that did not please him, and that he had found that if something pleased him it appealed to many people. The late George Horace Lorimer of *The Saturday Evening Post* told me the same thing. They were magazine editors and their publications were very different—but it is a good rule for any kind of editor, provided, naturally, that he doesn't live in an ivory tower.

Not long ago I was talking with a group of my best friends, all of them editors, of varying ages and experience, all of them still excited by their jobs. What was it that made them want to publish a book? I asked. In what frame of mind did they sit down to read a manuscript? All were agreed that their first consideration was the book as a writing performance, as a book, that a consideration of sales possibilities came later.

One of them said that he always had three things in mind when he was reading any kind of manuscript: first, literary quality; second, topical value, and third, the future possibilities of an author. Another claimed that his rule was much simpler. His first judgment came when he got up and left the manuscript, went off for a walk in the woods. If he *had* to go back to the manuscript, he knew that it was worth going on. Then, he'd put it away for a week. If he still remembered it vividly, he was reasonably sure.

There are no rules except that one must be excited. I do not believe in successful editors who maintain calm. To be very personal but to make my meaning, I hope, clearer, wouldn't you have felt the magic if you had picked up, before they were published, T. E. Lawrence's *The Seven Pillars of Wisdom,* DuBose Heyward's *Porgy,* Stephen Vincent Benét's *John Brown's Body?* If you wouldn't have, then the publishing business is not for you!

After this adventure into magic, we become more practical again.

How is the actual decision to publish made after the enthusiasm from one or more readers?

Many successful publishers have made their decisions on the basis of a set of readers' reports, never having read the manuscripts themselves, usually after consultation with the sales department.

A good many publishers have editorial meetings at which editors present the books they wish to publish to the management and members of various departments—sales, promotion, publicity, business.

In some houses, principal editors have unlimited powers of decision, although they restrict these powers by many methods of checking and must exercise a large amount of personal self-control.

It is very important to consult the sales department. Many books are accepted without their enthusiasm and support, but this is unwise, and the closer an editor works with the salesmen, the sounder his decisions are likely to be.

Last, but in some ways most important, a manuscript's production costs, an estimate of the book, should be made, before its acceptance, in cooperation with the business department. The editor should know, before negotiations are started with author or agent, what the so-called "get out" point for a particular book is. In other words, how many copies a specific book must sell before it pays for itself and starts to make some profit for the firm. With these figures before him, he may decide to take chances, but it is very foolish not to know what chances he is taking.

The firm has now decided that it wishes to publish the book. What are the editor's responsibilities from this point on?

EDITOR AND AUTHOR

After the acceptance of a manuscript for publication, the first duty of the editor is to establish the friendliest and most cooperative relation possible with the author. The more mutual trust there is, the happier their whole publishing life together will be. Often this relation has been established long before acceptance. Together, they will now be sure that the manuscript is as perfect in all ways as it can humanly be before it is presented to the copy editor. A whole book could be written about this mutuality of the editor and author. I have already said as much about it as can readily be told in this book. The relation has been compared to marriage and to that of the psychoanalyst and his patient. At any rate it is delicate and difficult but it can be most rewarding.

The final selection of a title, for example, might seem a simple problem but often becomes a matter of bitter argument among author, editor, salesmen, and promotion and publicity men. A given title must be cleared, to be sure that it has not been used too recently or too often. That a book title cannot be copyrighted is true, but there are certain legal problems in relation to repeated titles. It has been my experience that a sales department seldom likes a title when it first hears it, and often not until it has become a best seller. The more original the title, the more discussion is likely to eventuate. I well remember that Carl Carmer's *Stars Fell on Alabama,* Hervey Allen's *Anthony Adverse* and Carlo Levi's *Christ Stopped at Eboli* were all considered too odd by most of the salesmen, and that the argument over the Samuel Leibowitz-Quentin Reynolds *Courtroom* went on for weeks. Sometimes the author becomes stubborn about a change. Often both editor and author must call a halt to discussion and say "This is it!" but if a sales department really can be persuaded to like a title it is the healthiest situation. It is they who must first sell the book to the booksellers.

The editor and the copy desk are responsible for the front matter of the book, the list of the author's previous works, the dedication, the introduction or preface, if any, and, in cooperation with the production department, the captions on any illustrations. If the book is to be indexed, this is sometimes done by the author, or by a professional indexer under the supervision of the editor or copy desk, and is usually paid for by the author.

To have more than one manuscript available is wise, one to be the setting manuscript, others for the use of departments other than the design and production department. From this point on in the publishing life of a book, various operations can be carried on simultaneously, and speed is most valuable. How long the process now is from manuscript to publication date—ideally from four to six months for books that are fairly uncomplicated and routine—is not generally realized. Other chapters will emphasize this point but I make it strongly here because an editor is usually primarily responsible for the coordination that is necessary if time is not to be wasted, and the success or failure of a given title often lies exactly here.

The contract for the book is signed at some point before the manuscript starts on its way. It may have been signed long before the book was written, and financing of the author undertaken while the work was in progress. These business arrangements will be discussed elsewhere but I mention them here because many editors are responsible for contract negotiations with author and agent. Some of the best editors of the past have negotiated *all* contracts with authors, interpreting the author's needs and demands, so to speak, to the rest of the publishing house. Other editors have never discussed money matters with authors or, indeed, matters of promotion, advertising, sales, and so on. Which is the better system probably cannot be decided. It depends, in part, on the size of the publishing house and, in part, on the special abilities and characters of the authors and editors involved. Some fine editors cannot add a column of figures. Some editors, and authors too, are surprisingly good businessmen. Some merely fancy themselves as such.

However, the editor knows best the personal problems of the author. He understands the author's intent in regard to a specific work, and his enthusiasm and belief must light up all departments and individuals concerned. I believe that the success of a publishing house lies in the strength of the unity it achieves in its presentation of a single title, as well as in the selection and planning of the whole list. The smaller publisher obviously has less difficulty in achieving this unity, but he also finds it more difficult to stay in business these days.

Since the Second World War, assigning a particular author to a particular editor has become more and more the practice. "Mr. Jones is *my* editor," the author says with a certain possessive satisfaction. This editor is charged with seeing a book through all its operations or at least with advising and assisting in them. However, in many publishing houses several editors still work closely with one another on various projects and titles.

COOPERATION WITH OTHER DEPARTMENTS

Most of the processes discussed from here on are covered in other chapters, and I shall only indicate what the editor's connection with them is. He may actually do the job, or it may be done by other individuals or departments, but it is done, at best, always with the editor's cooperation, especially when consultation with the author is necessary or wise.

The problem of possible libel may be involved in a manuscript and, if there is such danger, the editor is responsible for consulting with lawyer and author.

One word of caution on libel from the editorial point of view. I have often found that if an author becomes too involved in a consideration of libel danger while his is writing, a dangerous block can result. The safer way is for the author to plunge ahead and let the editor and lawyer worry. However, the author must confess to his editor if his characters come close to living people, or most unpleasant situations can result.

Permission for the use of quoted material and the taking out of copyrights are sometimes handled by the editorial department, but usually not.

In the designing of a book the editor's responsibility is first to interpret an author's ideas or prejudices and then to contribute any of his own ideas as to the jacket or the actual physical make-up of the book.

Without such cooperation the book can be designed right out of its market. For example, an old-fashioned romantic story, if given a modernistic treatment in type selection and arrangement of title page, chapter headings and so on, may displease potential readers before they ever buy the book. The responsible editor should approve jacket sketches and sample pages before the book actually goes to press. My own feeling is that only for the most special and even experimental types of books should highly modernistic designing be used. From the editor's point of view anything that distracts the reader from his actual reading of the book is an error. The editor, too, should take great care in the numbering methods of sections and chapters, also the selection of titles. Some books demand chapter titles; others should have none. Very often, descriptive material before parts or chapters is an effective method of leading the reader on.

The handling of proofs is the responsibility of the copy desk or production department but the editor sometimes prefers actually to send the author's proofs to him or, to be entirely safe, also to check galley proofs or pages himself before the book is finally printed.

The writing of copy for the jacket of a book, the preparation of biographical material on the author, securing of photographs, catalogue copy, the preliminary steps toward sales promotion and publicity are sometimes undertaken by the editor. In the case of jacket copy, most publishers believe that the editorial department should be closely involved, if not the actual producers of the copy. Here, again, the author and the editor know best the fundamental idea that lies back of the book. And in the first slanting of copy lies the germ of future plans for exploitation.

Just how much part the editor plays from the time the completely produced book arrives on his desk varies greatly. As the author's representative in the publishing house, he must follow the whole operation closely. He sometimes shares with the publicity department the presentation of the list in advance to reviewers. He often chaperons the author in his progress through the tortuous mazes of personal appearances and literary entertainment. At least, he is a kindly parent when he sees signs of failure leading to despair, or the even more perilous effects of huge success.

The need for meetings, for frequent consultation among different departments of a publishing house, must have become apparent to you from these discussions. Formal meetings of personnel engaged in the various departments are, therefore, essential, although they can be overdone, and at most of these meetings, whether they concern business, sales promotion, publicity or advertising, or simple publisher's housekeeping, the editor should be present. He can also be useful in advising those concerned with the sale of supplementary rights and reprints. How does he ever get any editing done, you ask? The answer is he usually does it nights and weekends.

In many ways the most important meeting of all is the full-dress sales meeting held twice, sometimes three times, a year, and discussed elsewhere. However, one of the editor's most important duties is to present the books on which he has been working to the salesmen and others gathered at these meetings. Cleverness in doing this can make or break a book. The editor must not only be prepared to make clear what the book is about, but why and to whom he thinks it will sell. He should be as brief in his talks as possible, but never too casual. By using all the wit and strength he possesses, he must see to it that he *never* bores those who are to sell the books. He must be ready to answer questions and to parry negative reactions. I have never known an editor who looked forward to sales meetings. But unless he is at least vigorous about them, he and the authors he represents are lost. Authors sometimes appear at sales meetings and it is usually the editor who coaches them beforehand.

The editor, then, is the man who is supposed to know what's in the book and what its potentialities are. He, therefore, under the guidance of management, must make the strongest effort to secure the unity in operation that will realize the potential.

PLANNING THE LIST

The planning and scheduling of a list is, of course, the concern of the entire publishing house. The editor, however, is the one who knows from what direction and when the books are coming. The business department tells him what volume of sales is necessary to make a profit. He knows with terrible clarity that maximum sales with a minimum number of titles is the goal. He must bring his knowledge and prophetic powers into play to advise as to the number of copies to be printed in a first edition, and hazard guesses as to probable sales, for a budget is necessary. This is the chief reason why publishing is considered a business only for those with a gambling instinct. In spite of all hazards, a list must be produced every year that will not fall behind calculations. There must be books that are sure of a wide, quick, immediate sale and those which, with a smaller original sale, will become established and, perhaps, sell for many years. No publishing house can really be successful without building such a treasure house of backlist books.

The human factor, the author's ability to produce on time, is a perilous one. You have counted on a book, you have included it in your budget, and through various unforeseen accidents it must be postponed. Such a hole is sometimes impossible to fill. The inability of a writer to finish his book on schedule is unfortunately too usual. One of the most valuable efforts of an editor is his aid in helping such a writer extricate himself from his writing block. The psychologists have written much about mental blocks of various kinds. They can be very serious indeed. I knew one writer who, after a great success, was so overcome by fear that she was never capable of producing another book. The editor must be the understanding counselor. Sometimes only brief encouragement is needed; sometimes it takes long hours and much study before the work again begins to flow. Sometimes a psychoanalyst is actually consulted.

This has always been a fascinating study to me, but one which is haunting, for if one's greatest best-selling author suddenly finds that he cannot write it is easy to see that this violently dislocates one's professional pride as well as the budget.

The great worth of steadily producing authors of quality must be apparent here. The greatest prize for any publisher would be several authors each one of which was sure of producing one book apiece every year that would sell fifty thousand copies or more.

Perhaps because I entered publishing as a magazine editor (a magazine about books, to be sure), I find it useful and comforting to think of a publishing list as two issues of a magazine (spring and autumn). The magazine must have variety. It has special departments. It must have important, known writers and new faces. It must not have conflicts of too similar material within the same issue. All this is true of book publishing. To maintain a reserve of material in magazine production is, of course, easier than in book publishing, and the time between acceptance and publication is not so great.

Editors of the specialized departments of publishing are often tempted to schedule too many titles for one season. Sometimes it is necessary to become stern with authors whose books must be postponed, or even to lose an author, rather than have too many garden books, religious books, and so on, in one season.

The editor, then, must dream his ideal list, work and hope to make his dream a reality and, above all things, coordinate details so that preventable accidents do not stop or delay the production of any book; but the seemingly impossible does happen: the perfectly planned and executed list appears; the authors keep to schedule; production and all the other departments function smoothly. The best sellers arrive. It has been a successful season. The editor may relax, but only briefly, for he must begin to dream of the next season and the next.

AUTHOR AT THE HELM

Should any author or would-be author read these pages, my hope is that he will not find them too cold or matter-of-fact.

Describing the complexities of editing in today's publishing factually and at the same time maintaining a degree of warmth has not been easy. Please keep in mind that I believe firmly in my heart that the author must actually always be at the helm. The publisher, the editor, can be only so great, in spirit and in performance, as the author allows them to be. Great editors do not discover nor produce great authors; great authors create and produce great publishers.

William Bridgwater

William Bridgwater is the Editor-in-Chief of the Columbia University Press and an Advisory Editor of The Dryden Press.

The copy editor does far, far more than just make sure that everything in a manuscript is spelled, parsed and punctuated correctly. Mr. Bridgwater's comprehensive discussion of the wide range and high importance of the copy editor's craft concludes with these solemn yet glorifying words: ". . . upon his shoulders lies the weight of centuries of learning. . . . The little marks he puts on paper are for the betterment of mankind."

The young, apprentice editor who feels burdened with the necessity of learning copy editing would do well to commit those lines to memory and believe in them. They very well can transmute his "drudgery" into a noble "calling."

COPY EDITING

TAKE the manuscript of a book. Set it firmly upon a desk or a table so that it cannot slip or slide. Pick up a pencil. Start reading through the manuscript, and as you read correct typographical errors and note passages that may confuse a reader and usages that may cause trouble for a printer. You are doing copy editing.

THE SCOPE OF THE JOB

If the task sounds easy, you do not understand it. There are many complications, not the least of them being that it is a task without thoroughly set limits. What is called copy editing in one publishing house is almost never identical with what is called copy editing in another. Thus it is in book publishing, which exists solely to provide human communication through the printed word, yet violates principles of communication by using terms vague and multiple in meaning, but triumphantly workable. Everyone in publishing knows what copy editing is, so why define it precisely? It is not editing as such—or general editing as it is called here—for that, as has already been shown in this book, is a supernal occupation concerned with telling an author Yes or No as to whether his book will be published, with admonishing him to alter whole chapters, and with other such high affairs. It is not production work, for that involves familiarity with type, sinkage, the moving of space from one place to another, and other matters shared only with printers. Yet in the spectrum of publishing, copy editing lies between general editing and production. Copy editing is basically the mechanical marking of a manuscript so that it is in literal and literary form ready to go to a printer.

In publishing, the edges within the spectrum are blurred. The general editor may do the copy editing himself. Even the publisher may deign to make all necessary changes on a manuscript (usually in a hand totally illegible to the printer). Sometimes the copy editor is called upon to rise above mere marking and rewrite large portions of a book. Occasionally the bearer of the title "copy editor" has as his only duty the marking of a manuscript with direct instructions to the printer as to matters of typographical style and manufacture, but such workers are more properly called production editors. They are concerned with the manuscript but not with copy.

The fundamental, unavoidable, and not infrequently boring part of copy editing is the discovery in a manuscript of all usages that may hinder the reader or may stop him short and make him leave the book altogether, like a man dragging his feet out of a swamp. And "usages" include not only misspelled words and missing or excessive punctuation, but also more important items, such as meaningless headings and references to nonexistent illustrations. These hindrances the copy editor must find and remove by exercise of his pencil, by suggestion to the author, or by referring the matter back to higher authority (usually the general editor or publisher; in short, the boss). If, for instance, an author persists in writing *quarternary,* the copy editor simply cuts out the offending extra *r* wherever it appears. If in a numbered list, Item 3 and Item 5 are present, but Item 4 is absent, he writes a polite note to the author asking for Item 4. If he comes upon a chapter that he knows to be filled with error—in which, for instance, towns and cities of Australia are persistently misnamed and confused and there is a long description of a journey by boat from one place to another whereas in geographical fact neither place is remotely connected with a waterway—he usually takes the manuscript back to his superior. Such actions would at least qualify as normal copy-editing procedure, though other answers might be found. Copy editing will vary with the practice of the house, the nature of the boss, the character of the book, the attitude of the author, the amiability of the copy editor, and sometimes with the weather. Yet if no action at all is taken in such circumstances, the worker is no copy editor.

Of these forces that control the scope and variation of copy editing by far the most determinative is the character of the book itself. The more creative the writing, the less the copy editor can or should do.

In books of poetry the author is almost entirely responsible for the whole, including the spelling and the physical appearance of the pages; the responsibility of the publisher is purely to translate the author's intention into terms of type on paper, and this responsibility lies almost exclusively in the hands of the general editor and the typographic designer. The function of the copy editor shrinks to measuring and proofreading, and even the measuring is strictly under orders of the designer and the proofreading under orders of the author (who may, if he pleases, scorn all dictionaries). It is true that in anthologies, texts, or quotations of poetry the copy editor has somewhat larger duties, but these are still strictly mechanical: determining whether indentions must be kept as in the original publication, whether Elizabethan spelling may or may not be modernized, and deciding like issues, all of them involving meaning and therefore involving the copy editor, but all of them verging upon the prerogatives of the general editor or the designer or both. For the copy editor the requirement for editing poetry is plain: HANDS OFF!

The requirement for editing plays is a bit less stringent: Hands off the text! The actual words written to be spoken—or, in the case of "literary" plays, written as *if* to be spoken—should normally be regarded as sacred, subject only to proofreading. The acting and stage directions must, however, be tested in detail by the copy editor to be certain that a sane and reasonably intelligent person can follow them. Even this limited function disappears when the author has melded everything into a conglomerate and sometimes deliberately obscure whole. Designer, general editor, and author usually determine what typographical mechanics should be employed, as, for example, whether names of characters speaking are to be in small capitals, in italics, in boldface (rare in these days), or in plain roman. The copy editor gleans the wheatfield after them; he questions inconsistencies, unintelligible abbreviations, and other usages that might trap the reader. Again, as in poetry, he has a greater responsibility in new editons or reproductions of old works. It may fall to his lot, for example, to point out to the author or the general editor that the manuscript contains detailed attempts to "picture" the original in ways that, except in a facsimile edition, are foolish, delusory, or even downright dishonest.

In ordinary prose fiction the scope of the copy editor is less, but not much less, limited. The job of "creative" editing, if it is to be done at all, is within the province of the general editor. Some fiction, such as stream-of-consciousness novels and short stories, even defies the crudest type of proofreading, and here the copy editor's job is almost nil. But the pendulum swings in a wide arc. In most romantic and mystery fiction, the dispassionate eye of a copy editor is of value in checking expression and fact. In one quite distinguished novel, when the author asked that no copy editing be done, none was, and to the disturbance of readers one of the minor characters quite inexplicably changed his name from Bob to Bill in the middle of the book. It is this sort of thing, and not cadence or charm that is supposed to occupy the time of the copy editor of fiction. Occasionally the copy editor is also asked to cut the copy of a story to a predetermined length. He should have sufficient skill at abstracting to perform such a task without doing violence to what the author has created. No matter what the circumstances, the copy editor never has the slightest excuse for trying to preempt even the smallest section of the author's creative job.

It is in works of nonfiction that the copy editor is called upon to do his broadest and most useful work. The classification nonfiction covers all sorts of books, good, bad, and indifferent; cheap in idea and approach or elevated to the point where only the most highly trained can follow what is said; intended to be read to children of two or three years or to be read by graybeards in libraries. Each book varies in its audience and in its demands on the copy editor. Art books, for example, require that copy editors know enough about printing reproduction to be sure that the meaning of the text and captions meshes with the illustrations. Juvenile "fact books" should have copy editors as alert as general editors to the demands of word levels and to the responses of children. Copy editors of textbooks must support the efforts of the publisher to produce books that meet the needs of large groups of students of a particular subject at a stated level; in such books meaning and approach become one with expression and form. The range in nonfiction and in the resultant demands upon copy editors is infinite. Yet in the copy editing of works of nonfiction of all types there are basic procedures and techniques, which must be adapted to the purpose of the publishing house and to the book itself. These principles may be extended to all sorts of copy editing.

FIRST VIEW OF THE MANUSCRIPT

The process usually starts as this chapter does, with a manuscript spread out on a desk. In former days, when printing costs were lower, copy editing was by some publishers permitted to wait until the book was in galley proofs, and in exceptional cases this practice still holds. But the risks of expense for the publisher, exasperation for the author, and frustration for the editor and the printer are great indeed, and copy editing in proofs is inadvisable and rare. Usually the copy editor is handed a manuscript. It is given to him by the publisher, the general editor, the author, or some other agent, with the assurance that there are practically no flaws in it (even if the author is an Eskimo who has just learned to read and write) and almost always with the admonition that it must be edited immediately and in great haste because of the publication schedule.

A good copy editor listens and heeds these words, even if he has heard them in variant form a thousand times. They are a reminder that in a job largely concerned with discovering faults the temptation is always to find too many and not too few; in a job that must be meticulous if it is to be good, attention to detail can easily absorb too much time and painful effort.

With such sobering considerations in mind, he begins a quick inspection of the manuscript as a whole—or at least the whole of what has been given to him. Not all copy editors make this preliminary run-through, but most good ones do. The purpose is twofold: to get the shape and feel of the book, and to uncover major discrepancies in usage and serious copy-editing problems. Such a full view gives the copy editor a better chance to unify his editing and generally improve the book. Therefore, in Utopia a copy editor would always receive the full manuscript at once, including the title page, preface, and other front matter, as well as bibliography and notes, if such there be. Yet in this workaday world schedules frequently make necessary the submission of manuscript in driblets from the editor or the author, and the copy editor must work away on what he has, hoping fervently that there are no large bears behind the bushes in scenery not yet viewed. In some publishing houses the title page, preface, and the like never pass through the hands of the copy editor at all. This practice has the advantage of keeping the copy editor busy at the task in which he is most useful, minute examination of the text. It does, however, have the disadvantage of preventing the copy editor, who necessarily ends by having a more intimate knowledge of the book than anyone else in the publishing house, from detecting in front matter usages and even statements that flatly contradict those in the finished text.

GETTING DOWN TO DETAILS

After the first rapid and informative survey the copy editor buckles down to his real work. He goes through the manuscript chapter by chapter, paragraph by paragraph, sentence by sentence, word by word. He always has in mind how the pages of the manuscript will be in detail translated into pages of type. He is trying at the same time to read the text in terms of the readers expected for that particular book. This judgment is not always arithmetical. Thus, if the book is intended for the wider general public, the copy editor must try to prevent it from containing words, allusions, or tone addressed exclusively to the literati or the cognoscenti. Such editing does not mean eliminating all difficult words, elegant figures, and serious information. Any reader is by definition literate. Most readers, even when they peruse a book for sheer entertainment, are happy to improve their stock of knowledge, for this is, after all, the essence of reading, and they may even from a hard-boiled detective story or a sex-charged historical novel garner an astonishing harvest of exotic and authentic information. In every instance the copy editor must keep in mind the virtues and possibilities of the manuscript in hand. To each book its own copy-editing problems.

Copy Reading. Rudimentary but fundamental is direct proofreading of the manuscript itself. Many authors are proud of their inability to spell and leave such trivial matters as spelling to menials. Copy editors, as those menials, may quietly harbor contrary opinions about the value of spelling, but they must of necessity spend their time in quietly bringing the spelling into line with the pronouncements of the dictionary that the publishing house has chosen as authoritative. To do so is not a simple business of going from manuscript to dictionary and back again, pencil in hand. Always there is the problem of exceptions. The makers of dictionaries must choose among various spellings used and understood by educated English-speaking persons: there is no unanimity in English spelling, and the problem of preference often arises. An author has the right to cling to his idiosyncrasies. If he likes to write *meagre* instead of *meager,* his book should have *meagre,* even though the copy editor must take a note of the exception and watch carefully to change to *meagre* any occurrence of *meager.* Worse, dictionary makers cannot in the nature of things be up to the very last moment in decisions on innovations. New words and phrases are being added almost daily to the English language. They come not only down from science and technology, but also up from popular speech and across from foreign languages. Consider spinors, rock 'n' roll (or rock and roll or rock n roll), and caudillismo. An expression or a word that has become current with the author and his audience cannot be despised. Since dictionaries must follow usages and not create them, the copy editor must be familiar with new words before they enter dictionaries.

Among words proper names occupy a special position. Many authors are just as careless with these as with common nouns, and proper names are harder for a copy editor to check. Most editors develop a certain wariness and caution toward names, both personal and place. Authors who spell by ear can easily create orthographic monstrosities; only too often Nietzsche becomes Nietsche and Khrushchev becomes Kruschev. For this sort of error the good copy editor is ready. He is even able to cope with the fact that the name of the sacred city of Xauen may also be spelled Xexauen, Chauen, Shishawen, Sheshawen, or Sheshauen; he merely finds the form most frequently used by the author and asks if that may not be used throughout the book. The author will usually consent, and that particular name problem is solved. If the author wants to follow the practice attributed to T. E. Lawrence of educating the reader by throwing at him all possible English forms of the name, it is legitimate for the editor to point out that the reader is more likely to be confused than educated. He may even go so far as to hint that an eccentricity which the public found enchanting in T. E. Lawrence may prove only annoying in the works of John J. Jones.

The checking of names is a delicate and many-sided operation. Offhand it would seem that an author using foreign names would be in a position to dictate what forms of names should appear. Generally this is true, but the exceptions cause trouble. An American book that has Roma and Firenze and Bruxelles instead of Rome and Florence and Brussels is pretentious and absurd; an American who tried to say Bruxelles in conversation would be laughed at—and justifiably. A book in English should be in English, proper names and all. A good copy editor tries to steer an author toward name forms that will be usable for American readers.

Even in the editing of an insipid novel names can be an aggravating and complex problem. In considering them the copy editor is always halted by the caution of time. He may look up every American and English personal name in the appropriate *Who's Who,* if the volumes are at his elbow. But he may not devote hours to such checking. A sampling is all that is required. If the samples turn out, on assay, to have small gold content, then the matter must be referred back to the author or the general editor. The copy editor has only a limited number of hours to devote to a particular book.

In the checking of names the copy editor also encounters danger; he may only too easily commit the cardinal sin of copy editing. He may change something that is right into something wrong.

Proofreading and Proper Names. Words, including names, are of prime importance to the copy editor. Facts, as such, are more important to author and general editor and less the concern of the copy editor. One function of the copy editor is, however, to act as watchdog. It is part of his job to be suspicious. The author is responsible for all misstatements, falsehoods, and misapprehensions. He makes the statements, and the copy editor has only a small chance to check them. Yet, so far as a copy editor can review the facts, he must. In every book he edits he brings to bear all his knowledge, derived from experience or from reading. When there is due reason for querying an author's assertion, the copy editor must query all that seems wrong or dubious. He must point out demonstrable errors, giving his reasons for querying. In many cases, disagreement with a reference book is not quite sufficient to justify more than a mild query, for usually the author should know as much or more than the author of an article in a reference book. The copy editor is obliged to bring to bear all the knowledge that he has. As a native of Kansas City, he will not tolerate geographical misinformation about that metropolis. If he does, he is being a knave as well as a fool. He must, further, query facts if he has good reason for doubting their authenticity, even if he is not absolutely certain. Usually such queries are addressed to the author, who will take great satisfaction in declaring his statement right and the query useless, if such is the case. When a copy editor finds the queries growing to a bulk too large for comfort, it is usually time for him to ask the editor or the publisher to intervene and request that the author check and rewrite his material or hire someone else to do so; in rare instances only is it the copy editor's business to talk directly with the author on total revision.

The Phrase and the Meaning. Words, facts, and finally usage. The most troublesome part of an editor's job is the review of a manuscript in search of grammatical and rhetorical vagaries.

It is in making decisions on usage that the copy editor receives most guidance from the house stylebook, if there is one. Such stylebooks vary in an enormous range. They may be glossily written, expensively produced pamphlets intended primarily to impress authors; they may be stodgy collections of decisions about hyphenation (for example, Never hyphenate an adverb ending in *-ly* with a succeeding adjective), word choice (for example, Do not use *implement* as a verb), paragraphing, and chapter division. The prescriptions of stylebooks may be restricted to directions for the author in preparing a physical manuscript: typing in double space on standard-sized paper, with no short pages or random pieces of manuscript; no use of pins, stapling machines, or Scotch tape to fasten inserts to the pages; and reams of other practical advice. On the other hand, the stylebook may be a compilation of exceptions, additions, and expansions of dictionary rulings. If such rulings are prescribed, the copy editor who is trying to trim up the manuscript must hold to them and try to make the author hold to them.

The true danger for a copy editor who is undertaking revision of expression is a sort of overconfidence, especially marked in young editors. The neophyte is sometimes under the mistaken impression that he has been hired as a literary critic. Without long experience he finds it hard to read a typewritten script with the same respect that he gives to the printed word. In a course in copy editing I have made the experiment of giving students sentences written by masters of English prose. Always a large percentage of the students with earnest abandon will "correct" the phrasing of Walter Pater and Virginia Woolf. Perhaps their changes are improvements; I am no more in a position to judge their alterations than they are to judge the original. But clearly the alterations are unwarranted interference. The copy editor should do his rephrasing in material that has palpable errors—incomplete sentences, confusing use of "it" and "this," and other such dreary mistakes. If the author of a manuscript has recently come from some other language area into English, both general editor and copy editor must spend tedious hours testing the prose to be sure that foreignisms have not damaged the reading value of the English. In editing translations the task is even more exacting because translators often have such reverence for the original that they leave bits and pieces of it lying about in the translation, like logs washed upon a beach in a storm. Cleaning up a manuscript is honest work for the copy editor, writing old sentences over again in form or in consonance with the book is invaluable, but useless "improvement" of an author's literary style is futile and wrong. The course that a copy editor should follow is easy to indicate: aid the author, do not judge him.

At the same time certain accepted usages of English writing must be maintained so that a publisher may hold up his head among his fellows and boast of the editing of his books. He employs copy editors to support that pride. Therefore every copy editor should come to his desk for the first time with those usages already firmly in mind. This does not mean that he must know all the rules that schoolteachers in the late nineteenth and early twentieth century attempted to foist upon the language of Shakespeare and Dryden. The most familiar examples of these mistaken ordinances are the prohibitions imposed on split infinitives and sentences ending in prepositions. The revolt against formulations of this sort was severe, but now it seems to have run its course. Today copy editors may edit on the sure principle that certain usages are accepted as standard in English without fear of being castigated as reactionaries because they hold to principles at all. Almost no copy editors today attempt to follow the rigid and now discarded rules of yesterday. But almost all of them do think in terms of standard and substandard English, standard English being the body of usages accepted by educated people today (but not necessarily tomorrow) and substandard English comprising all forms frowned upon by those same educated persons. The line between the two wavers, but any good copy editor knows that standard English is the source of dictionary and style-book formulations, not the product of them. He edits by knowledge of the language, not by rigid rules.

Punctuation. Considering the use of punctuation throughout a manuscript is only a part of the general editing of the text. The mechanical marks for guidance in reading are an intimate and inseparable part of an author's presentation of what he has to say. How intimate a part it can be is shown with blinding clarity in the poetical works of E. E. Cummings. Less astonishing to the ordinary reader than the profuse parentheses and missing periods of Cummings' poems but no less illustrative of the point are the methods of punctuation used by many modern novelists in English, from James Joyce to William Faulkner. Punctuation may be used to set the pace in narrative of the stress in exposition, to push phrases together or to thrust them apart, to slow or to hasten reading, to supply overtones absent from the words themselves. Literary arch-conservatives —among them a few copy editors—who decry such usages as twentieth-century innovations would do well to reread such masterpieces as the eighteenth-century novels of Laurence Sterne and the nineteenth-century works of Lewis Carroll. The employment of punctuation in wry and unusual fashion has a long and honorable tradition. Punctuation is part of the text, not a separate little engine throbbing away at a separate business.

True, for workaday nonfiction intended to inform or entertain the reader, full-blown theories are pretentious and even downright silly. Any copy editor of long experience has come upon authors who punctuate in bland carelessness or ignorance and then defensively claim that the periods, exclamation points, commas, and the rest are intricate parts of a well-laid plan and that it is not mere accident that an appositional phrase has a comma before it and none after it. A favorite explanation is that the punctuation is for the ear or for breathing. To this claim the copy editor is not allowed to answer (a) that if the author takes the book home and reads it aloud there will be in the annals of the book a total of oral readers amounting to one, or (b) that anyone trying to follow the punctuation marks in reading aloud will find himself panting like a dog on a hot day. In extreme cases he may, however, point out the same things in a polite way, saying (a) that since the book is of a type that would be read by most readers with silent attention, perhaps it would be better to punctuate for the eye rather than for the ear, or (b) that readers have the privilege of altering stress to suit their own speaking styles and might find marking according to the author's stress a hindrance rather than a help. In other words, one may question how an author's system of punctuation may work. One should not question his right to choose a system. If he elects close (or tight) punctuation—that is, inserting a comma, a semicolon, a colon, or some other mark at every conceivable pause—it is the copy editor's business to point out spots that have been neglected. If, instead, the author chooses open (or loose) punctuation—that is, having only the minimum of marks necessary to carry the meaning—then the copy editor may suggest removal of punctuation that exceeds that bare minimum. Every copy editor should know, however, that the present tendency is toward open punctuation and that in cases of doubt the simpler forms have more present-day virtue. Further, if the house stylebook was drawn up long ago or concocted by someone with ideas from the long ago, the copy editor must do his best to circumvent the house rules up to the point of actual defiance.

In all editing of punctuation it is well to keep in mind several indisputable facts.

One is that no rules for punctuation were handed down by a stern God from a cloudy heaven. Writing existed before punctuation, and can still serve to communicate ideas with no punctuation as such. Consider ancient Roman inscriptions and such modern signs as this:

DO NOT LITTER THE STREETS
PUT WASTEPAPER IN THE BASKETS PROVIDED
THIS IS YOUR CITY KEEP IT CLEAN

Admittedly the dots marking word breaks in the inscription and the line breaks and spaces in the sign operate like punctuation, but they are hardly punctuation marks. Those marks were invented only to aid more rapid and precise reading, and that is their major function now, though they may be quite legitimately used for other purposes.

A correlative—one might even say a consequent—fact is that punctuation varies from one language to another although they may all use the same alphabet. The Germans put commas before all dependent clauses. The French use *guillemets* to mark off quoted passages. The Spanish warn the reader that a question is coming by putting an upside-down question mark at the start. Though alien to usage in English, these practices have developed according to logic and seem to serve their purposes admirably. They are just as virtue-filled as English usage—but different.

A third fact is that in English punctuation there are fashions, just as there are in women's dress and in popular use of phrases. Certain punctuation practices seem to be fairly stable, for example, the use of capital letters to mark the beginnings of sentences. Some are almost universally accepted by English-speaking readers, for example, identifying a clause as nonrestrictive by introducing it with a comma; these are usually clearer when defined in texts of English composition than when met with in actual manuscripts, where a restrictive clause can approach easily the barrier that keeps it from being nonrestrictive. Some practices are demonstrably obsolete: not too long ago chapter numbers and chapter headings had periods after them; now those periods have the old-fashioned effect of Victorian lamps, beautiful in a proper setting, but ludicrous in a modern décor.

To all these facts a copy editor must be sensitive. The conclusions to be drawn are obvious, but it will do no harm to state them obviously. A copy editor should know that punctuation is inferior to the text in editing, and should avoid becoming a "comma chaser." He should try, within the limitations set by the author, to promote punctuation that will aid the reader today. Period, colon, semicolon, dash, parentheses and brackets, exclamation point, question mark, suspension points, and quotation marks—all are intended to illuminate the text. The copy editor should see that they do illuminate and not obscure.

Copy Editor and Author. Copy editing of a manuscript should fall into several patterns. There are changes that must be made. If an author violates house rules or standard usage—if, for example, he writes *phase* when he means *aspect* or writes *specific* when he means *particular*—the copy editor must make the required alterations in a firm, clear hand. If difficulties arise not from such obvious faults but from ambiguity or possible error, the copy editor should not be so brash; he will note these in the margin of the manuscript or, if there is no room there, on slips of paper attached to the proper page of manuscript. Finally, mere suggestions that the editor thinks may be helpful to the author but in no way essential should certainly not be written on the manuscript itself but only on accompanying slips or sheets of paper, so that they may be removed when the author has settled the question. These distinctions turn out, in practice, to be only rough, but the principle is sound.

In making such changes, queries, and suggestions, the copy editor must keep firmly in mind the truth that he is not a teacher instructing an incompetent student. Any editor who persists in writing notes such as "Awkward" or "Meaning?" or just a contemptuous "?" beside a manuscript passage should be fired. An author, even an incompetent, semiliterate, and pigheaded author, is within his rights in resenting such unhelpful work.

It is in the realm of textual editing that battles between author and copy editor usually occur. Not infrequently copy editors call particular authors "uncooperative," "illiterate," and worse. An author may be plaintive ("My manuscript came back all bleeding") or belligerent ("That editor doesn't know good English when he sees it"). Usually, though not always, such contretemps are the fault of the copy editor. It is his business to see difficulties in advance and to make all adjustments possible, no matter how oversensitive, insensitive, or obtuse an author may be. It is his job, above all, to realize that the book belongs primarily to the author, secondarily to the publisher, and not at all to the copy editor. Even if the author is personally cut off, known only through his manuscript and through letters written to someone else, a copy editor must constantly be aware of him, his abilities and his faults, his crotchets and his genius.

In matters of "apparatus," on the other hand, the copy editor must be to a certain extent the authority above the author. If a copy editor does not know about the form of footnotes, bibliography, and appendixes, it is time for his education. Even if his work at the moment is entirely in juveniles or fiction or how-to-do-it books, in which footnotes are at a minimum, he cannot truly know his craft unless he can place a firm hand upon footnotes and beat them into submission. He may, if necessary, learn by consulting stylebooks, though indoctrination by a skilled copy editor is better. With their subject matter he cannot be concerned. Either the author has done his research properly and in good order, or he has not. If he has not, the copy editor may discover and sadly report that fact. In rare instances, he may be commissioned to check and reshape the notes. Any copy editor should know how to do so. He should at least know that the entries in the bibliography and the citations in footnotes should be coordinated and have some idea how the coordination should be accomplished. Amateur editors do not realize the unity of all the "apparatus"; professional editors should. To achieve the simplest and most workable form of notes, bibliography, appendixes, and subsidiary matter such as tables and charts is specifically the duty of the copy editor. In going through the manuscript he sees whether or not references to notes, tables, and charts match the corresponding notes, tables, and charts. If they do not, he must take measures to restore balance. This can be an onerous business. In one case in my experience the author decided to remove the first three of 159 tables, and all references to the tables had to be altered from beginning to end. The copy editor must in such circumstances plod along, looking at each table whenever a reference occurs. When that job is complete, he turns to editing the tables in series, to insure that the reader is not misled by headings that seem to be similar but are, in fact, different. Notes, tables, charts, bibliography —all these challenge the best efforts of a copy editor, and as sure as there will be some rainy days in a northern autumn there will be some manuscripts with intractable notes, insoluble tables, and unreadable charts.

With illustrations a copy editor may or may not deal, depending upon the practice of the particular publishing house. A usual and wholesome practice makes him responsible for the suitability of the illustrations, responsible for fitting them into the total pattern of the book. Photographs and drawings that neither reflect the text nor supplement what it has to say may be and frequently are used to embellish a book. Yet they gain more value if they are closely related to what is said in words, and this correspondence is the business of the copy editor. In the best of all possible worlds, the copy editor knows enough about reproduction methods to warn the author that material he has submitted for illustrations—a tattered newspaper photograph, for example—will not yield satisfactory results; but his proper business is passing on content rather than form, unless he happens also to be involved in production, which is outside the normal copy-editing scope.

When a book has been thoroughly surveyed, it should be ready to go to the production or manufacturing department and to the printer. In even the least troublesome manuscript, however, there are many problems that must, should, or might be referred to the author for decision. To take full advantage of the services of the copy editor, the publisher should submit the manuscript with all corrections, recommendations, and vagrant suggestions to the author before it is committed to type. To avoid trouble, it is normally wise to send sample editing—say of fifty pages—to the author for his approval before the entire manuscript has been canvassed. Then, further copy editing can be guided by the author's wishes. The author has at least as much proprietary interest as the publisher and will insist upon his rights. If he has at the beginning the opportunity to see some of the copy editing and express his tastes and his distastes, the publisher can gain more benefit from the copy editor's time; it can be an advantage, rather than an annoyance, to the author.

GALLEYS AND PAGE PROOFS

When the manuscript is completed and dispatched, the copy editor is not through with his duties. He must take care of the proofs, and in most houses not only the proofs of the books on which he has done the manuscript editing but also proofs of others. A copy editor must be a proofreader. He may at any moment be called upon to do the actual proofreading and do it professionally. In any case he is compelled to check all corrections made by the author in galley proofs. Such checking would be easy if all authors knew the limits of proof changes. Unfortunately, despite elaborate instructions in style sheets or letters, many authors do not realize that inserting the word *probably* into the first line of an eighteen-line paragraph is not a matter of a one-line change. It is the business of the copy editor, not the author, to know that type is of metal and therefore not elastic. He must be ready to see that an author's correction is about to create trouble for a compositor and suggest substitute changes that will not cause trouble. He must inspect all alterations that are made and adjust those that would not be clear to a typesetter, since all proof changes are intended as instructions to the typesetter. His function as intermediary between manuscript and type becomes clear at the proof stage.

On the proofs the copy editor must also usually give instructions for the beginning of new pages. He must issue instructions so that the page proofs, when they come, will properly reflect the meaning of the book. If he is charged with the "inventory" of the book, he must make sure by a rapid check of the records that everything the book is to include is accounted for, either at hand or expected at a set date—such things as dedication, preface by some eminent person, acknowledgments, and the like. The table of contents and the list of illustrations cannot be prepared finally until page proofs have arrived, but before galley proofs are returned provision must be made for them.

A few niggling tasks also fall to the lot of the copy editor before galley proofs are returned. Word divisions at line ends must normally be checked and made to agree with the dictionary or the style rule approved by the house. Violently uneven spacing must be noted and in extreme cases changed by transposition or rewriting of the text. All headings should be given special proofreading. And if running heads for the chapters have not been made up and listed previously, they must be written out and submitted with the galleys in usable form.

When page proofs are returned, the copy editor must check all the author's new corrections, repeating the procedure used in the galleys. Pages that for one reason or another have been left long or short by the printer must be examined. If facing pages do not match in length, slight changes must be made. The order of page numbers must be checked for that book, and once again headings must be considered. The running heads must be proofread. The copy editor must see that the tables and charts are placed as advantageously as possible in the text (since printers cannot always follow to the letter instructions issued with the galleys). When a book is "dummied up" to show layout of text, illustrations, and headings, the copy editor is usually, though not always, expected to aid the production department in making sure that the material in the dummy does not violate the meaning. When the pages go back to the printer, a good copy editor has already surveyed the whole and has filled out a form either for himself or for the production department, showing placement of all material. The copy editor must in some way assure himself that he has accounted for all content. If something is missing or wrongly placed, he is guilty, and, despite squirming, he must take the responsibility.

INDEXES

Indexes are a weight upon the spirit of the copy editor, though sometimes he is happily delivered of the responsibility when the general editor chooses to edit indexes himself. The copy editor is, however, best acquainted with the copy and normally best equipped, after the author, to perform a clinical inspection of the index manuscript. Some knowledge of indexes and indexing is of value, but if the copy editor does not have it to begin with he will probably gain it in the most laborious and unrewarding way, by experience.

Indexes, unfortunately, are not finished when they are sent out after editing. They return in proof, with author's corrections, and must be handled like regular page proof. In many houses and under many circumstances all page proof is held until the proofs of the table of contents and of the index are ready to be released. It is a good idea, when possible, for the copy editor to see the whole of the page proofs at once and visualize the book as to entire content. Once this last glimpse is allowed, he has no further chance to change his mind or repent his sins. Even if folded and gathered sheets are sent to him later, he can on them do no more than try to discover catastrophes, for anything milder than catastrophic must be left. There comes a time when a book is finished.

TOOLS, TECHNIQUES, AND QUALITIES

The tools of copy editing are simple: a pencil (in some houses pens are prescribed, but since humans err, a pencil is better), an eraser, some bits of paper, some reference works, and a mind. These must suffice.

Chief among the techniques is the ability to mark clearly on copy. Even the beginner at copy editing should know proofreader's marks and especially know how not to use them. A copy editor who makes the mistake of writing corrections in the margin of manuscript rather than in the manuscript itself is being not only unprofessional but thoughtless, for he must know enough of printing to realize that a compositor goes through every word of manuscript and therefore is only impeded if he must look back and forth between copy and margin. He should be able to see also that the contrary holds true with galley and page proofs. In those the compositor is setting only the lines that are to be changed; therefore those lines should be indicated by signals in the margin. The ability to mark manuscript and proof simply, cleanly, and unmistakably is something learned only over the years—and sometimes never.

The capacity to adjust knowledge and principles of copy editing to new conditions has been severely tested in some houses in recent years. Printing techniques depending chiefly on the camera have been developed to make possible the use of new forms of composition. Books are being produced from "cold type." Instead of being set by the now familiar letterpress methods (with typesetting machines that use hot metal) they are being prepared by special office typewriting machines (with various trade names and various ranges) or by direct photocomposition. Setting by typewriter, thus far the more common form, throws old concepts of editing out of line. The copy editor must think, for example, in terms of a final product that in some cases cannot have italics but underlining and cannot have small capitals at all; therefore, the vision of the final product is different, and the copy editor as well as the designer must envision in a different light how much should be underlined and what words should be in full capitals. The copy editor who is accustomed to letterpress printing must learn to view space in terms of the spaces, clicks, and inches of the typewriting machine being used, not in the more comfortable terms of letter and word spacing, ems, picas, and leading. The shift is not easy.

Since these new processes depend upon the camera, the copy editor at some point will usually be faced with material that is not proof in the old letterpress form, but a special "proof" that must be handled with the care given to a photograph intended for reproduction. On this corrections cannot be marked directly; they are usually made on covering tissues or on leafed-in sheets. The restrictions for handling photographic copy prevail; for example, no marks except on the edges and in crayon; no use of clips, staples, or other metal fasteners; no finger marks; no rough handling. These are, however, but samplings from the present day. There may be new requirements tomorrow. It is the business of the copy editor to be ready to adjust to the requirements of the day after tomorrow.

The duties of a good copy editor are exacting. What are the qualities and interests he should have?

First, I should say, he must love books. Books as such, not just their intellectual content. To say that a copy editor should like reading is supererogatory, since no one in his right mind would undertake the job of copy editing if he had no affection for reading. Only readers need apply. But more than this he should like the touch and the smell and the feel of books—possibly even the taste. He should be interested in how books are made, in general and in detail. It is well for him to know a bit of how they are advertised and sold in bookshops and in drugstores, by peddlers and by mail, if he is to take his proper place in the chain of publishing. It is imperative that he know the rudiments of printing processes.

Second, he must respect authors. Primarily he is the servant of the reader, but secondarily he is the servant of the author, and a servant should learn the methods, aims, and whims of even a secondary master. The worst disease that can attack a copy editor is arrogance toward authors.

Third, he must have an eye for detail and a passion for accuracy in dealing with detail: of this the fabric of his working life is made. Yet minute attention must operate within the frame of good judgment. Too much anxiety for detail will cost the publisher money, the author anguish, and perhaps the copy editor his job.

Fourth, he must be truly familiar, even intimate, with the English language and current English usage. Some publishers, many authors, and a majority of English professors would rank this requirement first. It is indeed of prime importance that the copy editor know whereof he speaks on words, grammar, and usage. He should know the old and outmoded usages as well as those that are current, for not all authors have current ideas—some, indeed, seem bent upon perpetuating the most unreasonable regulations that were obsolescent fifty years ago. Yet too great stress upon rules—upon "correctness"—is perilous. If the worst disease in copy editing is arrogance, the second worst is rigidity.

Fifth and finally, a copy editor must be curious, for it is curiosity that spurs him to awareness and to interest in even the dullest manuscript. If he learns a little from each book, he is a little more capable to edit the next. As his curiosity expands, so does his ability.

The ideal copy editor has these qualities and does these things. Could one ask for more? Yes. In special fields, such as science editing, juvenile editing, and reference-book editing, publishers ask for wider qualifications. Such employees are often called copy editors, but here I shall call them special editors and leave them out of account.

The professional copy editor, who sits at his desk with a manuscript planted squarely before him, is not superhuman. He is a humble man in a more or less humble job. Yet upon his shoulders lies the weight of centuries of learning. His calling is honorable, and he stands in line with the Scaligers and the Estiennes. The little marks he puts on paper are for the betterment of mankind.

Edmund L. Epstein

Edmund L. Epstein was born in 1931. He read Candide *at the age of six; it was his first book. He was a Quiz Kid in 1943, went on to the High School of Music and Art, Queens College, Yale, Columbia, Juilliard, Tanglewood and the Vermont School of Modern Critical Studies. He wrote a football marching song for this last institution and is now at work on a doctoral dissertation on James Joyce for Columbia. Mr. Epstein admits freely to having been to Europe and to being an uncontrollable non-smoker. He has been editing Capricorn books since its creation in 1958.*

Mr. Epstein's comments on editing quality paperbacks, written especially for this anthology, capture his drollery, his unorthodox points of view and his unusual and provocative insights. His essay reveals that there is no method (but not much madness, either) in editing quality paperbacks. After all is said and done it is generally an intuition, a personal hunch of the editor that provides the titles for a quality paperback list. Reliance is put on the personal taste, convictions and courage of the paperback editor; the audience, while growing, is indiscriminate and omniverous of all things distinctly worthwhile so it is difficult to know exactly who is buying a quality paperback, or what kind they will buy. My own exposition of Mr. Epstein's findings cannot begin to suggest the humor and wryness of his own development of his point of view. Next to the pleasure of listening to Mr. Epstein speak, reading his candid comments should provide any editor with delight. For with Mr. Epstein, the style is very much the man.

EDITING QUALITY PAPERBACKS

THIS is the newest field in publishing. Oh, I know all about the Haldemann-Julius Little Blue Books and paperback editions of religious tracts and the like, but this is *new*. It's so new we don't know how to sell the books yet, or where.

Quality paperback publishing started ten years ago, when Jason Epstein had a bright idea. (Nobody denies that Jason started the whole business; unfortunately our appreciation of his originality is going to have to stop there, since our budgets won't allow for more material tributes.) I still remember when I got my first quality paperback. It was in the Yale Co-op, and it was a copy of *Essay on Man* by Ernst Cassirer. It was a handsome, sober-looking little book, and the feel of the paper and of the cover told me right away that here was something new, and something that I liked very much. It spoke to me. It informed me that someone outside me knew what was going on inside me. However, in the months that followed it seemed that a hell of a lot of people outside me knew what was going on inside me, and inside of a lot of other people like me: Vintage, Meridian, Evergreen, New Directions: the first-comers, the old settlers.

I worked for Marboro Books for a while, in their main office, and one of my duties (I was First Assistant Hey-You) was to order quality paperbacks for the five Marboro bookstores. Henry Exstein, a man of perspicacity and possessor of a keen eye, soon began to see that putting me in charge of paperbacks was like putting a weasel in charge of egg-candling; I would unpack the paperbacks from their crates and pile them up with my own hands and croon over them. And so when Walter Minton of Putnam's began to discuss the possibility of a joint series of paper and hardback books with Mr. Exstein, my name kept cropping up in the conversation as someone who knew and cared about quality paperbacks, and who might be able to suggest titles for a preliminary list. I gave them twelve untidy pages of likely titles (almost three-quarters of which have appeared in paperback since) and went to work someplace else, at the University of Buffalo teaching English. But Minton and Exstein are both tenacious men, and they did not let the matter drop, so now I am a quality paperback editor.

I usually come to my small, crowded office rather late in the morning, since I'd been up the night before reading through some public-domain monster that might just possibly fit into the series. What crowds my office is books; at least 800 of them, all sizes, shapes and degrees of dullness. On my shelves at the moment (*casual glance*) I can see: the impenetrable masterpiece of a German phenomenologist; the speeches of Franklin Delano Roosevelt; a *Life of David Dubinsky;* a bad translation of *Bouvard and Pécuchet;* a book on nuclear disarmament (which like all books on disarmament that I have read seems to be belaboring, not a dead horse, but a stuffed one); a report, in French, on the proceedings of a historical congress in Europe on the European resistance movements in World War II; a book (with a beautiful cover) on the Tarot deck; a book by a conservative called *Up From Sanity* or something like that; a book on human communication (which is not only dull, but almost impossible to open; something happened to the glue), fourteen color proofs of covers for my fall list; a row of Capricorns from previous seasons; a history of Hungary; a comic novel of 1913; an old saber; and a bottle of bay rum. These last two may be of some use to me.

I have been at Capricorn for almost four years now, and there are still some things I can't figure out. Question number one: who is our audience? Does anybody know? I know we sell in and around colleges, and in some high schools, but that's all. Who goes in and planks down a dollar and a quarter for a collection of documents about the American 19th Century? Instructors recommend some books, I know; they may even buy some themselves. But this is not precise enough information. Is it possible that all quality paperbacks are bought by people who would like to edit quality paperback series? Are they all romantics about learning? A violent drive for education is something which, if we are to believe Jacques Barzun and Dwight Macdonald, should not be occurring in our middle-brow, intellectless, complacent civilization. But quality paperbacks are being bought; and they're being read, too.

Another question is: what sort of books appeal to this nebulous audience? Poetry will not do.* The same curse that attends hard-cover books of poetry attends paperback books of poetry. (The only poetry books that can sell are those of poets who are famous for something else, like Pasternak. Even Wallace Stevens does not do as well as he should. The Harvest Books edition of some of the poems of T. S. Eliot has done pretty well, but it has not been a heavy-weight, as compared to some of the prose works of figures comparable to Eliot in the literary world.) This fact is not particularly widely known among those people who want to edit anthologies of poetry, though, so it's a rare month when someone doesn't come in and suggest a series. I do my best to introduce them to the publishing facts of life, which were engraved on my forehead by the finger-nails of experience, but then they suggest that we do the poetry anyway, not for the sake of the money, but for prestige and to build up the name of the line. How disappointed they are when I inform them that we have all the prestige we can handle at the moment,

* *My criterion for success of a quality paperback would be whether it sells more than 6000 copies a year. Naturally, this would vary for different series.*

and that what we could use is money. (Question: Am I losing my idealism? Answer: Yes.)

Another type of book which it is very difficult to sell successfully in quality paperback is a book on music. Not to do books on music for me is very painful, since I really like music much better than publishing, and even, under some circumstances, rather better than sex. But it cannot be denied that books on music do not do well in quality paperback. The only apparent exception to this rule would be books of opera synopses, but everyone knows that the opera is an impure form.

This situation does not hold for books on art, so it would be difficult to account for it on the basis of a general disdain of aesthetic theory. (As it happens, books of technical aesthetics do rather well.) Some of the best sellers in Capricorn have been books like John Dewey's *Art as Experience,* and Selden Rodman's *Conversations with Artists. Art* by Clive Bell is also selling very nicely. There fore, my guess would be that while people who could not draw a straight line would, nevertheless, buy a rather expensive little book on art, we would not have an analogous audience for books on music. Perhaps people are more honest about their musical deficiencies than about their artistic, or perhaps there is less conversational superiority to be derived from a knowledge of music than from a knowledge of art.

However, while it is possible to vapor away for hours about art and art criticism, *literary* criticism does not do well in paperback. Most quality paperback editors have had some experience with technical literary criticism, most of them as graduate students of one sort or another, and it probably breaks their hearts, as it does mine, that some of our favorite books are passed over like cold-cakes on the racks while their cousins from the art criticism field sell in the thousands. There are a few exceptions to this rule, but they are rare. The same would go for biographies of writers and literary histories. In fact, the whole field of quality paperback novels and works on literature is a quagmire whose sunken paths are not even known to the oldest natives. Who can tell what will succeed? The biggest surprise I have ever had in my publishing career was the success of *Lord of the Flies* by William Golding, which at last report was selling for us at a clip of ten thousand copies a month. Gushers like this are hard to account for. *Lord of the Flies* is an excellent novel, with a thrilling story and powerful symbolic overtones, but so are a lot of books that haven't sold ten thousand copies in ten years.

One sure-fire category for paperbacks seems to be American history. Almost everything in this field will do fairly well, and some books do extremely well. In this category it is certainly college adoptions that carry the load. It will probably be this category that will carry the whole list when and if the "inevitable shake-out" begins, and the quality paperback series begin falling like autumn leaves.

This last cataclysm has often been nervously predicted, but I don't think it will come to pass. America is reading; and it is reading books that it heard about when it was in college. Perhaps after all Johnny learns to read *after* he leaves school, and what he reads for fun is what he should have been reading for credit. If this is so, education is suffering from neglect of a deeply ingrained amateurishness which imbues all enthusiasts for learning. They will not be taught; but they will learn. In the old days, i.e., the thirteenth century, people who went to be educated were hobbyists; that is, long-haired, dirty loonies who fondly imagined that there was something noble in pursuing useless studies instead of going into the wool business like their fathers. "Young Fulk is jabbering about Arabs again with those flea-bitten beatniks from Paris." Well, now young Fulk spends his college years evading work and reads quality paperbacks for fun when he graduates.

Meanwhile I, toiling to satisfy young Fulk, plow through enormous bibliographies in search of titles. I read night and day, in bed and out, on the street and in saloons. I read American history, English history, Spanish history, Afghan history, cute popularizations of revolutionary history by smart liars, German texts on Arabic history where the Germanic transliterations of Islamic names look like barbed wire, memoirs of hacks from all the arts and professions, theoretical works by dead proto-Fascists, machine-lovers, love-haters, word-drunks, intelligent aestheticians, nasty pungent critics of dead political movements, arch accounts of their lives by train-robbers, incomprehensible, interminable military histories which leave out nothing in their search for truth but references to human suffering, minor modern *philosophes* who are very clever on irrelevant topics, and, most of all, documents. Documents are very important in quality paperback; the directed-research projects of the textbook departments have started a trend toward primary sources which have helped quality paperbacks enormously. The most consistently successful quality paperbacks have probably been documentary collections on historical topics, and there are going to be many more. I myself have on my desk at the moment: a selection from the Diaries of William Byrd of 18th century Virginia (a marvelous, earthy fellow); a collection of documents from Cromwell's Commonwealth; a selection of documents on Manifest Destiny, and one on

Imperialism. The textbook editor next door (at the moment he is singing softly a dirty Southern song about Reconstruction) has just finished editing a fat collection of documents on American Government. Yes, I think that from now on we are going to be swimming in primary reality.

The ultimate question that can be asked about any career is, was it fun? Yes, publishing quality paperbacks is a lot of fun, but it would be more thrilling if I really knew what I was doing, which I do now only in a vague, intuitive way. Perhaps intuitive editing is the best editing; it means that you trust to your own personality rather than to abstract parameters of taste. At any rate, I feel sure that I am publishing *to* someone, a lot of someones, even if I don't know exactly who or where they are. I also feel sure that my audience are responsible, intelligent, sensitive people, and are rapidly becoming more so.

How many editors can make that statement?

Donald A. Wollheim

Donald A. Wollheim has been an editor for over twenty years. Since 1946 he has been a mass-market paperback editor. In 1952 he joined Ace Books, Inc. at its founding as its editor-in-chief and has remained in this post to this day.

Mr. Wollheim is one of the leading science-fiction editors working today, and the owner of one of the largest private collections of science-fiction in America. He is also the author of a long string of anthologies and seventeen published novels.

Straightforward, factual and eminently practical, Mr. Wollheim's article on editing the mass-market paperback, written especially for this anthology, provides the newcomer to this growing field with a valuable working guide to the problems, day-to-day realities and pleasures which are a vital part of editing fiction and non-fiction for the non-literary, "escape and entertainment" reader.

EDITING THE MASS-MARKET PAPERBACK

PAPERBACK books are the bastard offspring of an unexpected and unplanned marriage between the hardcover book industry and the now extinct world of the pulp magazine. It is this inevitable (as we can now see with the wisdom of hindsight) merger that makes the particular distinguishing traits of the paperback editor's work.

It would be best to explain this by going back and examining the nation's reading habits prior to 1939, when Robert de Graff perfected the paperback book and began Pocket Books, the first stream of today's mighty torrent. At that time, the only book publishers were the hardcover firms and their books, generally printed in small runs of a few thousand copies (if that many), were sold only in bookstores, whose total probably could be numbered in the hundreds but not in the thousands.

How many pulp magazines were there on sale on any average month in the late thirties? Hard to say, but probably not less than a hundred at any time. Perhaps thirty Western magazines, an equal number of detective magazines, sports magazines, love story magazines, adventures, air, science-fiction, and so forth. These magazines appeared monthly, generally sold at a price of from ten to twenty cents, contained about 70,000 words of short stories, novelettes, and novels, were illustrated, featured bright action-slanted covers, and held their readers tightly. Millions and millions of men and women regularly bought them, regularly toted them back and forth from work to home, and devoured their contents. They were printed on a cheap grade of pulp paper (whence the generic name), edited by hardworking men, written by professional writers who were paid by the word (ranging from a penny a word to several cents a word), and published by a dozen or so companies, each of whom had a string of titles on its list.

That was the pulp magazine world. It no longer exists. But people do not vanish and their tastes do not change overnight. The audience that read the pulps is not extinct. It is right here and it continues to demand and read just what it used to read before.

But now it reads it in paperback books.

How did this change happen? It was the result of several things. For one thing, the advent of the pocket-sized twenty-five cent reprint novel, brought about by Pocket Books and shortly after by Avon Books and Penguin, brought to many pulp readers reprints of good Western novels, detective novels, adventure novels by the best writers of the pulp field: Erle Stanley Gardner, Max Brand, C. S. Forester, Agatha Christie, etc. This lured some pulp readers into supplementing their magazine diet with these available reprints of the "classics" of pulpdom. It also brought to them books of whose existence they had been unconcerned, the better novels hitherto only in hard covers. Many of the pulp readers discovered that these literary works could also satisfy.

Then the war came, paper-rationing, and after the war, a steady rise in the costs of production. The pulps were hard hit. Their paper and printing costs rose until they had to charge 25¢ for their magazines. Now they were on a par with the paperback books. No more could they offer a better bargain, with more copy. And as the two fields leveled in price, the paperback books began to gain. Their shape was more convenient to modern reading than the somewhat awkward-sized pulp magazine. It could slip into a pocket easier, it looked better, it had a somewhat better prestige. And as costs continued to rise, the pulps began to fade away rapidly. With their prices finally forced over 25¢, and economic necessity bringing their pages and page-size down, they lost the battle for existence. Their readers, finding what they liked now in a more economical and handier package, crossed over to paperback books almost en masse. By 1950 the old-style pulp was as dead as a dodo.

So the paperback book caters not to the literary readers of the hardcovers so much as it does to the one-time millions-wide audience of the pulps. And this is what dictates at least fifty per cent of the content of the paperbacks today. Herein lies the essential dichotomy of the paperback editor's problem.

For the paperback book remains as it started—the low-priced publisher of literary classics, the mass producer of works which made their mark as best-selling hardcover novels. Added to which, it has also become the purveyor of fast-action adventure written by the same type of writer who formerly turned out pulp fiction. And this new fiction does not differ by much from that of the old days.

On the one hand, he has got to be alert to the latest best-sellers, on the trends among the literati, on what is doing in the world of good literature. On the other hand, he has got to know just what a Western, detective, adventure reader wants who doesn't care about literature but only wants good, fast, escape reading.

The problems the paperback editor faces are not, therefore, easy. When he sees a hardbound book that he feels will do all right in paperbacks (and he usually can tell this by the reception bookstores report on the book), he will have to get in touch with the hardcover publisher and make a deal with him for reprint rights to the book. This usually means coming to an agreement as to how much advance is to be paid for the book, and this figure is a matter of guesswork between the two.

If the paperback editor thinks he can successfully dispose of 100,000 copies of the book, but not much more, he is likely to offer only $2,000—which is the sum that the paperback reprint might reasonably earn if the book sells for 50¢. If on the other hand, the hardcover publisher feels that his book should sell a million copies in paperback then he is going to hold out for a good many thousands of dollars advance.

It's a gamble and a tricky one. Usually the astute paperback editor can guide himself by the knowledge of what similar books have sold in the past and he can limit his offer to the margin of what was done. The hardcover publisher is more optimistic, but even he knows when he has reached a reasonable limit, beyond which there is going to be hard feelings if the gamble doesn't pay off.

Some books that do well in hard covers and go into several printings may not sell well at all in paperbacks. Some books that did poorly in hard covers may find greater public appreciation in the lower-priced format. It's a tricky question that each paperback editor has to work out for himself on each book he looks over.

When he has bought his hardcover book, he then has to face new problems. For instance, should there be any changes in the sales approach for the newsstand market? Is the title—which may be subtle enough for the bookstore purchaser who has presumably read the reviews and knows a little about the book—too obscure for the hit-and-run readers of the newsstand? If so, should it be changed, and in what way? Then, should the cover be lurid or restrained? Is it best to quote a favorable comment on the cover or devise a short sentence or two which will clarify the nature of the book for the potential purchaser?

Where best-sellers are concerned, books that have sold tens and hundreds of thousands in hardbound editions, the problem of packaging is simple. Keep the title—everybody will remember it. But where the lesser known reprint is concerned, the problem of packaging is a major item in a paperback editor's day.

And that concerns the reprint question and takes care of part of the editor's monthly output requirements. Now he is confronted with the other half of his product—the heritage of the pulps. He has to produce so many Westerns, fast adventures, and made-to-order "category" novels for each month.

So the paperback editor goes to work looking over manuscripts, for he can no longer depend very much on the output of hardcover companies in these fields. It isn't sufficient for the market; it's often too long or too slow or too restrained. He reads, or examines, the reports of his reading staff of novels written directly for the paperback market.

He knows, as the pulp magazine editor knew before him, that there are writers whose talents lie solely in the field of the "category" novels. He has to fill the categories. A Western novel is needed. There are several manuscripts on hand by writers who have done this sort of work, write it well, enjoy writing it. Pick the best for your needs, call up the author or his agent, buy it. Purchase is made the same way as the reprint books: an advance is established which should cover the probable sales based upon royalty earnings. For a category novel, this may run between one and three thousand dollars, more likely in the lesser amounts.

So, before the month is up, the paperback editor may have bought three hardcover reprints, one of which may be a best-seller type for which he paid several thousand dollars; the others for which he may have paid about two or three thousand; about four or five category-type manuscripts which would probably include the fields of the Western, the romance, the historical novel, the mystery novel, the sex-slanted modern novel, the science-fiction novel.

The manuscripts have got to be edited, corrected, made ready for the printer, and for this the paperback editor will have a staff of copy editors and sub-editors. Titles have to be selected and art work considered and ordered.

And while all this is going on, the paperback editor is also called upon to keep track of the months before, that which is in various stages of production and that which, having been already published, may be calling for re-examination or new printings.

I often feel that having started my own career as a pulp magazine editor some twenty years ago that I have an advantage over those who came in later. For I feel that I know perhaps from experience just what the mind of the category reader wants—and that is not something easily learned by the man who comes into the industry by way of the hardcover books. I know what makes a good Western, a good detective novel, a good action novel by having learned it at a pulp magazine desk under experienced pulp magazine editors. I know the readers are basically the same.

The newcomer can only learn these fields by diligently reading the "stock" novels of these categories, by reading them in quantity and determining for himself just what it is in these novels that keeps the reader enthralled. Because this kind of literature is not analyzed and taught in classes; it can only be learned by reading it yourself.

One thing, though, I will admit is different in this market. The sex element. Those who do not know pulps tend to scoff at them. Scoff they might, but the pulps were a very moral type of literature. Detectives did not lust after the lovely damsels they rescued. Cowboys kept their eyes on horses and badmen, not on the honkytonk girls. Historical characters steered clear of the royal boudoirs.

The book format somehow let down the barriers. Books by some mental sleight-of-hand of the censors can be more "adult" in their approach. The paperback original detective not only rescued the damsel, he slipped into bed with her (usually after having previously bedded the female villain). With this as a start, and keeping an eye on the fabulous sales figures chalked up by such literary hardcover classics as *God's Little Acre* and *Sanctuary,* the paperback editors produced a new pulp-quality field, the pseudo-Caldwell, the synthetic Faulkner, the quasi-Farrell. Deciding that many of the readers of such realistic modern novels were only interested in the sexier passages and disregraded all other qualities, editors began to search for writers who do imitations of realism with lurid sex inserted at regular intervals.

There is an old rule that every magazine publisher knows—Sex Sells. And when the paperbacks discovered this, they very nearly undermined their own field. Why publish in other categories, if sex outsold everything? Most of the established companies steered warily around this trap, but others teetered on the lucrative edge, and others went overboard.

At the present time most of the established respected firms in this field are avoiding the too-lurid sex novel, realizing that it has brought a certain bad taste to the newsstands, and antagonized many of their audience. But there still remains a fringe of fly-by-night publishers whose hacked-out bedroom epics perch on other companies' racks, clutter up the less scrupulous newsdealers, and generally create an aroma around the field we would be better off without.

This is one of the pitfalls of the industry, and one that is being avoided at the time by the more responsible houses.

What, therefore, makes a good paperback editor? I would say that it is the ability to be both highbrow and lowbrow simultaneously. To be able to enjoy great literature, fine writing, and good books and also to be able to comprehend and enjoy just plain escape reading with no claim to greatness whatever. It is the ability to say that this type of cover will attract this type of reader and that type of cover will attract that type of reader—and not mistake the two. It is the ability to guess in advance just how many copies of any book are going to sell, and guess close enough not to lose money on the advances and the quantities of books printed. It is also the ability to keep a time span of several months constantly juggling in your mind and not letting a single element slip.

For instance, I am writing this article in the middle of March. In my day's work, I have the following to consider. The books that were published in February—what are the earliest reports on their sales activities? Did I guess right? The March releases are appearing on the stands now. Have the review copies been sent out? Have publicity releases been sent out? Have final payments been made to the authors? The April books are arriving now in advance shipments from the printer. How do they look? Did they come up to expectations? Should we consider any special promotional posters or notices? The May titles are coming down in proofs from the printer. Are they being read by the proofreaders? And when read, has the copy for the opening pages—title page, blurbs, copyrights, etc.—

been prepared and shown to me for correction or approval? The June titles are having their cover artwork completed. Did the artists do right by them? Have the designs the right approach or the wrong approach? Copy must now be written for the back covers and for the few lines of sales material on the front covers. Is there any change to be decided now in the approach, in the number of copies to be printed, in the price of the book? July titles, already selected, are now being copy-edited and sent to the printer. Titles, if they are to be changed, must be changed now. Lengths of manuscripts, if they are to be shortened or lengthened, must be considered now. Are there changes in the story line to be made? The copy editor must make them if the writer has not.

And then there are the August and September titles to be selected. The editor, having worried about all the previous months, must now read and select and buy what he will publish next. This is what is going to occupy most of his time, regardless of what has gone before.

All of which seems like a lot of worry and responsibility—and is. And yet somehow paperback editors seem to be an easy-going lot, ready and able to chat on the phone, talk with authors, drink a leisurely cup of coffee, and sometimes even find time—at home—to read a good book just for the fun of it.

It's nice work. You get to read an awful lot of interesting things. You ride the plains, play cops and robbers, peep on the blondes, get culture too.

And all the while, you're providing reading pleasure for millions of people.

Helen Harter

Helen Harter has been a Social Studies Editor for forty-one years. She is presently the Senior Editor at Rand McNally & Company.

Editing our children's textbooks is no cut-and-dried, humdrum occupation. Miss Harter's panoramic and (almost literally) breathtaking review of the myriad questions and problems confronting the textbook editor conveys with telling force the frenzy for perfection that is vital for the proper fulfillment of the textbook editor's responsibility.

TEXTBOOK EDITING

I HAVE been undecided whether to call this a word-portrait of a textbook editor, quietly and meekly going crazy, or of a textbook editor blowing his top. Judge for yourself. You may or may not be able to pick an idea out of it. If it seems slightly disorganized, distrait, and disjointed, that is part of the true picture of a textbook editor. It should be noted at the outset that one must be very careful in writing about or reading about, or illustrating a textbook editor. No typographical errors.

A textbook editor's thinking must be very concrete and specific. A variety of miscellaneous ideas (generally expressed as "we want this."; "We don't want *this*.") dealing with methods of presentation, specifics of content, language, format into which content must fit, vague generalizations, minute details, taboos, prejudices, and sales gadgets must be brought into some kind of pattern. Everyone who has any contact with the book or any stake in it feels free to express an opinion about what should go into it and how it should go in. Moreover, he expects to see his ideas carried out in the finished product.

Most people who sell or use the book will see its pattern primarily as an organization of factual content, perhaps expressed in an outline or in the headings listed on the contents page. But the pattern the textbook editor must evolve is multidimensional. The outline of factual content is only the surface that shows on the outside of the real pattern. In a great many instances, that surface pattern is really about all even the author is working with. Somehow the textbook editor is supposed to build in all the other factors, and he *should* be able to do it without rewriting any of the author's text.

The textbook editor cannot help thinking about everything everybody else thinks about: trying to harmonize and implement the thoughts that have gone before, and at the same time, anticipate the work that will follow. The textbook editor must see pictures that have not been found or drawn, use maps, diagrams, charts, and artwork that do not yet exist. At the same time, he must be ready to change his approach later, if his original thoughts cannot be carried out. He must provide content that can be put together to make a book, anticipating make-up problems as far as possible. (He must also be able to modify his own work and the author's work later, according to the unforeseen exigencies of make-up.)

A textbook editor cannot keep entirely out of the copy editor's field. He cannot say, "I will go so far and no farther in making the content coherent and grammatically acceptable." He turns the copy over to the copy editor in as good shape as possible, knowing that he has certainly overlooked enough to give the copy editor plenty of work. The textbook editor must also think about format and styling, because that is the framework within which he must operate.

Here are a few other things that flit through a textbook editor's mind from time to time. Will this book please members of a committee that gives it a mere cursory glance? Will it please a committee that really studies it? Will it please people who are using our whole program? Will it please those who want to use it with any other possible combination of books from other publishers?

Will it please teachers at first glance? teachers after they have used it a year? good teachers? poor teachers? teachers who want a textbook as a guide? teachers who want a textbook only as a reference book? teachers who do not know how to use maps and skip the map studies? teachers who talk Progressive Education and teach as they were taught in 1918? teachers who really understand the meaning and purposes of education? committee members who judge a book by how well it deals with their own special interests?

Will it please children, wherever they live, whatever their background, however well they live, however well they read? Will it please all the sales executives? all the salesmen? professional critics of textbooks? people who will point to any selected paragraph and say, "What are you teaching here?" people who want most of the material to be light and teach nothing?

Can any part of the text possibly be twisted to sound like communism, socialism, bias against any minority group, any religious or political group, or any special interest group of any kind except those that it is currently correct to be biased against? How can we concur in currently correct attitudes without being too far out of line when the attitudes change?

Will the content fit in the specified number of pages? Since the general, gross coverage of the content is predetermined, as well as the exact length of the book, how long should this topic be in relation to all the other topics that must be included? If there is too much (there always is) would it be better to take out whole topics (and, if so, which?) or to spread the cutting more evenly?

If this is a geography text, what map activities shall we give children which will utilize earlier map skills, improve those skills, and introduce an entirely new map understanding. Is this the place for it? Are pupils ready for it? What are they going to do with it? Do they need it at this level? Can we go on asking for its use later? Does it go beyond the map-reading skill of many teachers? How much guidance should we give the teacher, while ostensibly making suggestions to pupils? Have any essential steps been omitted?

How far should the map studies go? Should they call mainly for simple recognition of symbols? Or should we sometimes go on to higher levels of map interpretation and the reading of relationship from maps? (The latter is often a good sales argument, but it has many pitfalls.)

Would this be a good place to ask for a special map, or can one of the more general maps be used? How long since we had a map? Are they too far apart? Will they pile up? Are we asking for a possible distribution of illustrations, or will they be impossible to make up?

Is the author talking over the children's heads? (Is he talking over the teacher's head?) Is the idea too difficult, or merely the wording? Do children have the terminology? the necessary background of knowledge? Any specifics to fit the generalizations? If not, is this the place to supply them and develop the idea in whatever way is necessary? Can we avoid the difficulties and still use the idea? Should the whole thing be kept for later? Is it necessary at all? What is to be gained by keeping it? What criticism will it probably bring on? How fond of it is the author?

Shall we let something go that seems to be poorly thought out, poorly expressed, or badly integrated in the context? Are we setting too rigorous standards? Is this grammatically acceptable, even though it may not be considered the very best usage? Should the author be allowed to put his thoughts in this order, even though a different order seems easier to follow? Will pupils get the meaning this way?

What is the author trying to do with this piece of content? Has he done it? Is it clear? If we have trouble following it, teachers and children will probably have more.

Is everything said absolutely accurate? Meticulous accuracy may not be the most important thing in the world, but any slip in this area is almost certain to be caught by someone, and if it is caught, it will be sure to draw scornful comment. What about sources of information? If there is disagreement, who to follow?

What about the organization and structure? Do the headings cover the text under them? Do they make a consistent outline? (More often than not, at least part of the headings must be supplied by the textbook editor.) Do they fit? Are they as dynamic as possible? Do they tell what is in the section without using terminology not yet introduced and without being a mere label of content? Do the headings agree with what the text is teaching? Does the attempt to insert headings reveal irrelevant or out-of-place material in the text itself? (Frequently it does.) Do they come often enough so that there will not be many pages unbroken by headings? Are they spaced widely enough so that the text will not appear too chopped up?

Is there an introductory paragraph after each major heading? What is there to say about the general topic? How can we lead into it, before we begin with the more specific ideas under subordinate headings? Often there is really nothing that needs to be said and no paragraph of the author's that can be lifted to this position; but the styling calls for an introduction so that two levels of heading will not come together (except at the start of a chapter), and an introduction there must be. Moreover, it must be plausible, interesting, and, if possible, useful in helping the understanding of what follows.

Here is something you have been told repeatedly that teachers do not always understand, or you have seen teachers yourself who obviously did not understand this idea. How can you make the text help teachers who do not understand without insulting those who do? Is there anywhere to go between the people who will think the explanation is tedious because there is too much, and those who will think it is not clear because there is not enough?

What about this common misconception which the author and you both want to make sure pupils do not fall into? How shall we explain it so that readers who already have the misconception will not think we are wrong, or that we are not clear because they assume that we are making a poor attempt to say something that we are not saying at all?

What kind of activities can we make for this chapter? Do they supply clear and specific guidance for the teacher who has not had much experience with activities? Do they, at the same time, allow for teacher-pupil planning and flexibility in use? Will they look inviting on the page? Will they be interesting to do? Will they be interesting to read, without working them out?

What about allowing for differences in children's backgrounds, especially in community studies? (Many school people will say they want allowance for individual differences in ability and interests, but we know we cannot do much of that.) Still, if we don't allow for different types of communities, many teachers will say, "There is nothing here that my children can do." If you do allow for them, many teachers will say, "There is too much. My children can't get through with them." The fact that you say over and over, in text and manual, that no class is expected to do them all makes no difference. Finally, as a very minor consideration, but one that will appeal to a few teachers here and there, is the question, "Will the children learn anything by doing them?"

Here is an explanatory sentence between the sentence with the antecedent and the sentence with the pronoun. If you use the antecedent noun again, it will mean repeating the same word too soon. How can you rewrite, without changing anything very much, so that there will be no pronoun separated by a sentence from its antecedent, no repetition of words, and children will still understand it?

Will it cost too much to have this map or that picture? There is no use building any ideas around it if we cannot afford it.

What about transition? Does one idea lead to another? Or is there a mere verbal transition—one word suggesting another idea —or no relation at all?

Does the text go on too long with no chance for pictures? Would a picture, firmly used as part of the teaching material—not a mere illustration—make the idea clearer? What are the chances of getting such a picture? Should you write in the exact thing you would like a picture to show, asking for that exact picture, or should you make the suggestion to the picture editor more general and plan to modify the text according to the best picture that can be secured?

Do the legends reinforce the teaching of the text, or do they lead away from it? Will they fit the design of the book? Will they go into the space allowed for them?

How can you help an inexperienced or unresourceful teacher use this picture or map or idea effectively and easily? How can you suggest methods to teachers who want help without appearing to dictate to teachers who do not want help?

How can you help teachers and pupils relate this learning to their own experience in their own communities? What experiences in the lives of most children *could* be related to this, or is it so far from their experience that we had better not use it here?

What can you suggest that children *do* every now and then, as a relief from mere reading?

Will this appeal to people who know, as educationally and psychologically sound? Will it appeal to teachers who were taught a long time ago? Will it appeal to recent graduates of any and all teachers colleges?

Is it flexible? Can it be used in different types of schools with different philosophies? Can it be adapted to a wide variety in courses of study? Can the methods of adaptation be found easily by our sales people and shown quickly and specifically to committees? (This last is practically impossible, but it is still a headache for the textbook editor.)

Are there facts for those who want to teach facts? Can the facts be made to disappear in a pattern of concepts and understandings for those who do not want to teach facts as such? Are the concepts and understandings comprehensible at this level? (Will most teachers think they are?) Are there too many of them? How many is too many? Can it be shown that the material in this book contributes to the larger goals of the social studies? of education as a whole? Can selected strands be traced all the way through this book and other books in the series?

There are many other problems the textbook editor must think about as work progresses. Some of them he finds himself, but more often they come from other people working on the book. These are examples of the kind of questions he must anwer:

"The text calls for this picture, but there is not enough text here to carry all the illustrations; or they won't all go into the number of pages assigned to the chapter; or it is not possible to get the picture into the same opening with the text relating to it; or it comes too near a major heading. Can we leave the picture out? Can we delete enough copy to make room for the picture, or add enough copy to push the picture over to the next page? If we do leave it out or substitute something, will it change the text just here, or will there have to be other changes, too?"

"This heading is going to fall just three lines above the bottom of the page. It will have to be pushed over or pulled back by adding or cutting."

"This map activity" (it was made to fit an imaginary map, not yet created) "will not work on the real map. It will have to be changed."

"Will it be all right to change the order of the activities? The columns do not break right this way."

"Was any decision ever made about which form of this word we would use?"

"Will it be all right to change the order of the phrases in this sentence to keep from breaking a word that we do not ordinarily break in writing for children, or to keep from having a hyphen at the bottom of a right-hand page?"

"Will it take out anything essential if we crop this picture here and here?"

"Four lines will have to be added between this mark and this mark, and six lines deleted between this mark and this mark, because two headings are going to fall opposite each other on facing pages (or for any one of a dozen possible reasons)."

When you start deleting words to save lines, you often have to weigh the value of your own or the author's punch line in dollars and cents. The cheapest thing is to chop off the end of a paragraph. The next best thing to do is to delete words in the last line or two. But that method may ruin the author's point or make it obscure. Shall we take out innocuous material farther up which will require more resetting?

"This legend (or this text reference) is to something which cannot be seen in the halftone. It will have to be changed." (It was made while looking at the 8 x 10 print, before the cut had been made. Generally you can tell what is likely to be lost, but not always—especially if you do not know how much the picture is to be reduced.)

"Will it change the meaning if we leave this clause out?"

"Which map does this refer to?" (for putting in page numbers after make-up).

"Here is a reference back to something on page 15. There is

nothing about it there." (In most cases it was cut out to make the make-up fit.)

"This paragraph is not clear. I do not know what it means." Or, more often, "*I* know what it means, but it *could* be interpreted this way."

Sometimes a fact is challenged. If it is wrong, it must be corrected. If it is right, the textbook editor must produce sources of information to prove it. If there is a disagreement, he must be able to prove that his sources are more recent, more reliable, or more generally accepted than the one used for a quick check.

The textbook editor is the person who is ultimately to blame for everything; who may be asked five years later why he used this particular word in this particular place; who may also be asked five years later why he didn't make the book conform with another book that had not been written yet; who must never lose his temper; about whom everyone can gripe and be sarcastic, but who must never answer back except in the gentlest and most polite terms; who must offer his ideas humbly, with the preface that they are just his opinion and probably wrong; who must accept without a murmur, having all plans upset by someone who is considering only one or two factors out of a dozen; who is told to use his judgment on how general, vague ideas are to be carried out specifically and how far they are to be carried, but knows he is in for a bad time and implications of obstinacy, uncoöperativeness, traditionalism, if not near imbecility, if his judgment on any detail does not anticipate the judgment of the originator of the idea.

A textbook editor spends considerable time brooding over the injustice of having to accept everybody's whim and snap judgment and incorporate it somehow in a pattern already so complex, so full of details to be remembered and constantly juggled; upon being considered an obstructionist for trying to find out exactly what is meant, or for trying to bring up the repercussions upon a whole pattern of a decision—based upon perhaps five minutes thought on one facet of one angle of one aspect of a problem; upon being expected to produce on order a work of genius that is superior in all respects to all competing texts, while being treated as a semi-nitwit whose ideas must be surrendered instantly in the face of criticism by practically anyone.

The person who made the original prescription can always forget he said it, or say you misunderstood him (which you probably did because he expressed his ideas in general and indefinite terms that have many meanings, and you failed to choose the one he had in mind). He can say you carried his idea too far, or that he didn't mean it to apply in this particular instance. It was to be applied within reason; but if there is any difference of opinion about what is a reasonable application, the textbook editor, of course, is wrong. (If it should turn out later that he was right, he must *never* say, "That was the way I wanted to do it in the first place." At least, he must never say it to the person who wouldn't let him do it.)

Too many cooks may spoil the broth; but the textbook editor must never think that too many people adding ingredients may spoil a book. And if the broth comes out layer cake, it is the textbook editor's fault.

The textbook editor has responsibility without authority. There is no area in which he is free to use his judgment, but his work is an unending series of decisions which cannot be referred to anyone else. He is expected to produce ideas on a moment's notice, but if he tries to think out loud, his first tentative thoughts are taken as his expression of opinion, and he probably never gets to the point of reaching a conclusion. No matter what he does about anything, somebody is going to complain because he didn't do it another way.

An artist is judged by his finished picture. Each interested individual judges the textbook editor's picture by whether his own particular leaves have been hung on the tree just to suit him, or whether his own favorite color has been used in just the right quantity.

Every single thing mentioned in this article, plus a good many more, has actually happened to

Ye editor

Francess Halpenny

Francess Halpenny is the editor of the University of Toronto Press.

In recent years more and more young men and women seeking careers as editors have been attracted to the university press. For the editor with a craftsman's approach, a love for the scholarly book and the meticulously researched work that has a vital contribution to make to learning, the university press offers the perfect milieu.

Miss Halpenny's article provides a concise, informative and reflective review of the special problems, needs and points of view that make up the working day of a university press editor. Her comments are particularly valuable for very little has been written on editing for the university press despite the rapid growth and influence of these presses within the last ten years.

THE EDITORIAL FUNCTION

(Editing for the University Press)

THE editorial function as it is carried out in a university press is one of the most vital and significant aspects of the work of that institution. University press editing may only occasionally provide the high excitements of the commercial field which enliven the reminiscences of its publishers and editors: the sensing of a potential best-seller novel or work of popular history and the final discovery of its desirable shape from which the extraneous and inept have at last been pruned away. Nevertheless, the editorial responsibility in a university press has its own sober rewards and gratifying accomplishments in a succession of titles providing students with dependable and stimulating textbooks, scholars with valuable information and apt discussion in a variety of special subjects, more general readers with descriptive or analytical writing which will further encourage a habit of inquiry.

The editorial contribution begins with the arrival of a large brown-paper parcel on the editor's desk, and each such parcel is opened with ever-hopeful curiosity. The manuscript, once it is acknowledged and accessioned, will usually receive at least a preliminary examination by a member of the editorial staff in whose area of interest it appears to lie. This examination will reveal the particular subject-matter under discussion and something of the kind and competence of the treatment. If the subject-matter and treatment are such as to claim the serious attention of a university press, the manuscript will be taken officially "under consideration." If it does not make a claim on that attention it will very likely be returned to the author without further activity.

A large proportion of the manuscripts submitted to any university press will be the result of years of research in specialized fields of knowledge. Adequate assessment of their content and therefore of their value as published works can only be made by fellow-scholars, although the editorial staff is usually able to make a shrewd guess about the skill with which the information has been marshalled. The assessment by carefully chosen specialist readers is therefore the next step in the process of editorial consideration, and in search of those readers an editor of a university press will often go far beyond the limits of his own campus, although he may consult his academic colleagues about the direction he should take. In the selection of readers, it is always the aim to secure a fair and objective report; at most presses, for instance, it is an unwritten rule that no member of staff of one university will be asked to assess the work of a colleague in the same university. It is always the aim, too, to move through this stage of consideration as quickly as possible, but it inevitably takes time to identify the appropriate readers and to secure their consent to act, and they will often have prior commitments which they must deal with before they can turn to the new assignment. It is a frequent experience at a university press to require readers just when every campus is engulfed in the year-end spate of essays and examinations or when every campus has almost been emptied of scholars traveling in Europe without a forwarding address. It remains, however, the conviction of all press editors that a manuscript which has taken years of devoted labor to prepare deserves the compliment of a report by the person best qualified, and that this person should be given time for reading and reflection; they must therefore do their best to instill patience in authors and at the same time conscientiousness about fulfilling their task in readers.

When favorable readers' reports have been received and the decision has been made to publish, the manuscript has to be prepared for actual production; the key action in this preparation is the careful reading by the member of the editorial staff who will see it through the press. The aim of that reading, which is guided by all the reports prepared while the manuscript was under consideration and by the general editorial rules of the press itself, is the production of "final copy" for the printer. To further that end the author will usually receive the edited manuscript back before it is sent for typesetting, He thus has an opportunity to make any late changes in fact or interpretation and to discuss with the editor the questions that he will have set down in the course of his editorial reading. With all this attention from author and editor at the manuscript stage, the proof can be handled with greater ease and speed, and corrections can be largely confined to those for typographical errors. The saving in cost alone can be considerable.

A more detailed description of the purpose of such copy-editing might well be in order; it is a feature of university press publishing and especially of the North American university presses which arouses a good deal of curiosity, and sometimes even some suspicion. Properly conceived and carried out, this editorial reading can be and should be a genuine service, to author, to reader, to printer. A manuscript is written to *communicate* its author's factual discoveries, speculations, insights; very often that communication will be assisted when the reader is caught up in a measure of the author's own emotional response to his subject. A conscientious editor endeavours to assist this communication. He has in mind as he proceeds that he is working with an arrangement of words not made by himself, an arrangement whose meaning and rhythm must be sought with persistence and sympathy. Ambiguities or obscurities or awkwardnesses may impede the communication of an author, and an editor will endeavor to suggest ways of removing these, at the same time preserving the author's wording whenever possible, or to elaborate on the difficulty in a question so that the author may solve it in new phrases of his own. Thus all editorial suggestions, whether many or few, will attempt to harmonize with the ways of expression of the author. Most authors soon realize that there is a genuine desire to be helpful behind queries which point out to them where over-familiarity with their material or haste or other factors have caused them to fail in the effect desired, and will respond to editorial questions in a matching spirit. Indeed authors who need this help the least are often the most grateful for it.

An editor has the interest of the reader especially at heart when he points out to the author for revision vague phrases, unattached pronouns (*this, that, it*), inaccurate quotations (an unforgivable sin), repetitious comment. He thinks of the reader when on the watch for minor errors of fact, and when trying to secure consistency in spelling and footnote references, for meandering in these matters will only arouse irritation in the reader and a suspicion that sloppiness in technical detail may mean sloppiness of content. "Where are we?" he will ask as he tries, for the reader, to see the structure of a paragraph, to follow the event-by-event outline of the narrative, to return from a digression to the main stream of a chapter. A great deal of attention, too, has to be given to bibliographies or references. The editor tries to see that the information these necessary tools of research contain is correct and as complete as possible within the sphere of the particular bibliography.

An editor is mindful of the requirements of the printer in the final marking-up of a manuscript to indicate the arrangement of type before it goes into production. In this aspect, of course, he is following the work of the Production Department which is responsible for the physical appearance of the book and which will have been preparing layouts and specifications about paper and binding while the book was being copy-edited. Once the book is in production, the editor will serve as an interpreter: to the author about the printing schedule and technicalities of type, and to the printer about the way various questions that arise in connection with galley or page proof are to be handled.

There are certain activities of the Editorial Department at the University of Toronto Press which deserve a special word of description. One is the long association of members of the department with the journals which the Press publishes. Most members of the Department have at least one of these journals to see through the production stage once the articles have been chosen and give a preliminary check for content by the academic editor concerned. The copy-editing of an article is a miniature of that given to a book and the purpose is identical. The associations developed with contributors to our journals have been valuable in many ways (they will often be thought of as readers of manuscripts, for example), and we are especially pleased when they are expanded into collaboration in a book-length manuscript.

The Editorial Department at this Press has also been fortunate in the fact that "the printer" it normally works with is another department of the same organization; it has thus had within easy and cordial reach the technical knowledge of various craftsmen. In turn the editorial staff provides a copy-editing service for certain specialized material from customers, chiefly institutions, who deal with the Printing Department, but whose productions do not appear over the Press's imprint.

Works which bear the imprint of this Press are given a special service by a group of editorial readers who handle proof. The permanent members of this staff develop a familiarity with the specialized and highly technical works we publish, and most of them have a knowledge of at least one language in addition to English.

It is one of the oddities of the editorial function that it is most successful when least observed. It has been well performed when the hovering pencil is least evident in the final result, and the book is clear, valid, and convincing in the procession of its words and sentences. Then author and reader are communicating to the best advantage. This is not an easy function to learn: it takes time to develop the necessary eye for technical matters, the necessary judgment to know when and how much to suggest by way of editing, the necessary skill in presenting queries to authors in order to make clear the reason for them. In a university press, the specialized nature of the list published means that editors must have a university background, often indeed including some graduate or specialist work, and must be alert to what is happening in a general way in academic circles. Despite many manuscripts that remain disappointments whatever care they receive, editors are still hopeful readers of books. As an editor in one university press has phrased it: "We admire the courage it takes to choose, deliberately, to engage in the painful process of putting words together. It is perhaps not too much to say that it is primarily *because* the editor or publisher has such respect for the difficult art of writing that he frets so much about what it is that he is publishing."

Jean Poindexter Colby

Jean Poindexter Colby had served as juvenile editor of the Houghton Mifflin Co. and Farrar, Straus & Young before assuming her present post as juvenile editor for Hastings House. Mrs. Colby has lectured widely before State Library Conferences, Parent-Teachers Associations and at Radcliffe College's Publishing Procedures Course. She is the author of THE CHILDREN'S BOOK FIELD *and* PETER PAINTS THE U.S.A.

Mrs. Colby's remarks on what every juvenile editor should know are presented crisply and with a highly selective eye. Based on her many years of experience, they offer a basic set of criteria valuable to the novice juvenile editor and to the veteran juvenile editor seeking a crystallization of an approach to her craft. The original presentation of the essay was in the form of the first two chapters of Mrs. Colby's book THE CHILDREN'S BOOK FIELD *published by Pellegrini & Cudahy in 1952.*

EDITING CHILDREN'S BOOKS

MANY writers feel that they would have the whole writing game licked if they could see inside the editor's mind. Some believe that the acceptance of their manuscript is a matter of chance or "pull" or whether the editor had a good breakfast that morning.

The question is, what does influence an editor's decision in regard to a manuscript? What does his or her mind look like when examining the latest juvenile jewel? Some authors believe it is full of deep, dark secrets, spells and incantations not unlike those of the goddess of Halloween. Others—and especially those who read the subsequent chapters on production—will know differently. They will realize that the witch's cauldron of an editor is probably a big offset printing tank, and the spells which she spins have more to do with the modern astronomical figures of paper or plate or binding costs than with the spirit world.

Let us trephine the skull of a children's book editor as she is sitting talking to an author. (I say "she" because the majority of children's book editors are women.) We will have to make her an imaginary woman, but with more Colby in her than any other creature because I can speak only for myself.

In this vivisection of an editor we shall work backward on her probable thought processes and those of the author as it is more convenient first to describe such an interview, then work down to the judgment which caused the editor to ask the author to come to her office, and last of all to the manuscript which started the whole series of events.

Let us suppose that it is you sitting there facing her. So let us have a look in *your* mind first.

You have written a book for the 9 to 12 age, which you feel is practically perfect. You think the editor showed only ordinary perspicacity in asking you to come in to discuss it. You can already see your book in a handsome jacket in the middle of a big bookstore window. It is only May, which you believe will give William Jones Company plenty of time to publish your book before Christmas. You visualize yourself standing before a vast Book Fair audience inspiring them with a speech of insight and intelligence. Then the scene changes, and you are being pointed out to certain of your acquaintances, who have never appreciated you, as that new, brilliant author. It is with difficulty that you bring your mind back to the interview and listen to the editor's remarks about production problems and high costs, and the suggestions she would like to make about your manuscript.

Now, what is the *editor* thinking about? Before calling you in for an appointment she has decided—and this passes through her mind at the present moment—that:

The manuscript has possibilities of various kinds.

It has some unusual material which has not appeared previously in children's books.

The manuscript could be printed economically if you would agree to cut it fifty pages.

The art work would have to be limited to keep expenses down.

It probably would be less costly done by the letterpress printing method in the 5½" x 8⅛" size.

It might fit into the company's next year's spring list for that age-group. Otherwise it would have to wait a year because the fall list coming up is already in production.

Then she really looks at you and wonders:

Will you be able to see the need for changing the motivation in the middle of your story, the flat ending, the general wordiness?
Will you be able to produce better manuscripts in the future so that she can build you up as a dependable author of many books?
Will this book be dated in a few years? Will your others be?
Will this one have a bookstore and also a public library sale?
Will the company's educational department be interested in it—sufficiently to promote it along with their publications?
Will it be possible to reprint it at a profit to the company and to you?
Is it too much like the book Smith Brothers put out last year?
Will you be easy to work with over a period of years, or are you a fussy, demanding person who thinks every word from your pen is a pearl of great price, not to be changed or relinquished without a battle?
Are you really serious about writing for children?
What do you know about them?

The editor talks to you and, one way or another, obtains answers to her questions.

You, from your point of view, also have questions, and she answers them somewhat as follows:

No, your book couldn't be published in a couple of months even if the revision were perfect. The fall books are already printed and waiting to be bound. She is now working on next year's books.
No, you do not have to provide the pictures. It is the publisher's job to obtain an artist to illustrate the book. Yes, your artist friend can submit drawings with the revised text, but they must be exceptional to be considered, and they will not help the manuscript to be accepted.
Yes, it would be nice if your friends would buy several thousand copies, but the William Jones Company has found that publishers can't depend on authors' friends, and that a book has to be published for regular bookstore and library sale.
No, sorry, your idea of having a mammoth-sized book is not feasible because of the necessity of keeping expenses down. You see, book-production costs have gone up like everything else, and book retail prices have not increased proportionately. Also, the costs for printing and binding extra-large books are in themselves prohibitive.
No, sorry, the pictures can't be in color because of the expense involved and because the 9 to 12 age-group does not require it.
Yes, the revised manuscript will receive attention as soon as possible, but no definite date can be set for a final decision.

You leave gracefully at that point, lugging your manuscript under one arm, determined (I hope) to do a bang-up revision.

Before *we* leave this mythical meeting with an editor, it might be well to give a little practical advice.

1. Manuscripts should be typewritten, double-spaced, on good white paper of the standard 8" x 11" size. Don't send carbon copies but always have one made or make it yourself.

2. Manuscripts should be mailed or expressed in with a short note giving the author's name and address, and any absolutely necessary details.

3. Don't expect your opus back before two weeks to two months. After that you can telephone or write and inquire about it.

4. Submit the manuscript by mail or express, not in person. The book must stand and fall on its own merits.

5. Make an appointment before coming to a publishing house, if an interview seems absolutely imperative.

6. Don't claim that the manuscript has been read and enjoyed by dozens of children. The editor will not be favorably impressed with this kind of statement. Too many authors of inferior material have made it.

7. Don't think that because you know some one in the firm, or know a friend of the editor, you stand a better chance of getting your book published.

8. Always enclose stamps and a mailing envelope for the return of your manuscript, or request that it be returned express collect.

Of course, the whole business of your manuscript's being accepted or rejected boils down to—what are your particular editor's set standards? I may let myself in for criticism by telling you what mine are. But they won't be exactly like any other editor's and they may be very different. So, if you are trying to sell something to a particular company, why not study what that editor has already published? There you will see concrete instances of what she believes should be published.

For example, it is obvious that one well-known editor of fine children's books puts a great emphasis on literary style. She would be no one to submit a vocabularized reader to, or a book on etiquette or a light, flashy career story. Another editor clearly likes sea stories, and should you have a salty action yarn, she might give it more than fleeting attention. I am especially interested in good stories for the 8-, 9-, and 10-year-old group because I have tramped the streets and "done" the public libraries trying to find them for my two older children, and I know how scarce they are. (One excellent reason why they are not abundant is that they are hard to write!)

If you are particularly impressed with the output of one editor, or one company, write in to their central office and ask for their latest children's book catalog. You can obtain their address from your local bookstore or library, and the catalog will be free. Study it and you will learn a good deal about what kind of book this particular editor wants and takes.

However, to generalize, any editor is interested in well-written, absorbing books on almost any subject, but she is only human and has special interests and also special phobias. She also has many commitments, and is hemmed in by a web of financial restrictions due to the present high costs in the publishing of books.

I feel that the fundamental requirements for children's books are not very different from those for adult books. There are age-group limitations and a certain necessary clean-cutness and lack of digression. But who would claim that the majority of the qualities listed below are not also found in the best adult books?

I believe a book should have the following attributes:

1. *A good central idea.* An accomplished author will not start a book until he is sure that he has something real and worthy of book form. Then when he plans his work, this central theme holds from the first paragraph to the last with everything else subordinate to it. A classic instance of a strong central idea is *Big Susan,* by Elizabeth Orton Jones (Macmillan).

2. *Definite appeal* for the audience at which it is directed. Of course, this is especially important in children's books because no piece of work, no matter how worthy, will be enjoyed or absorbed by youngsters unless it is presented and phrased in an attractive manner.

An excellent example of appeal in a modern juvenile is *Walter, the Lazy Mouse,* by Marjorie Flack (Doubleday).

3. *Originality of idea or individuality of presentation.* A truly original idea makes an editor's eyes sparkle—if it is not too fantastic. Perhaps some of the most outstanding books in this respect have been *Twenty-One Balloons,* by William Pène du Bois (Viking), and the picture books by Dr. Seuss (Random House). Both are distinctive and individual in style as well as in central idea. Oh, that we could have more of these!

4. *Good writing.* The old standards of unity, coherence, and emphasis still hold. Ramshackle organization of material, poor paragraphing, or a halting flow of ideas and words, can damn the most charming material. Probably the difference between the amateur and the professional writer shows up most here. The ability to have a "literary style" is usually born with the author, but this does not grow and flower into effectiveness except with long experience and effort. A feeling for words comes in here, too, and the advantage of a large vocabulary even in children's books. Words do not have to be long and special to be right. For example, read *The*

Tale of the Flopsy Bunnies, by Beatrix Potter (Frederick Warne), or *Bears,* by Ruth Krauss (Harper).

5. *Even, sure plot development,* if it is a story.

Careful, effective handling of material, if it is nonfiction.

Nowadays, a good story book starts the plot practically with the first word, and includes little that does not advance or round it out. Present-day adventure stories exemplify this point, such as the books by Stephen Meader (Harcourt), or those by Margaret Bell (Morrow).

You will see that historical fiction, too, can be just as absorbing as modern mysteries if you will read Enid Meadowcroft's *On Indian Trails with Daniel Boone* (Crowell) and Esther Forbes's *Johnny Tremaine* (Houghton). These books make profitable study for any author who would like to see how historical research can be used to good advantage in children's literature.

Nonfiction can be just as engrossing as fiction if the author cleaves to the line of steady development of events and allows no irrelevant digression. See, for instance, *The Sword and the Compass,* by Margaret Leighton (Houghton), or the classic adult book *The Sea Around Us,* by Rachel Carson (Oxford).

6. *Adequate characterization.* The lack of this is especially evident in books for younger children. Most authors are so concerned with story development that they don't "waste" time building up their characters as people. This is very wrong because—as in adult books—convincing action often stems from personality itself rather than outside forces. Read Elizabeth Enright's *The Saturdays* (Rinehart), and her other books to see expert characterization. The Eleanor Estes books (Harcourt) are also tops in this respect.

7. *Motivation by the central characters.* In children's books this means that the children not only do the majority of the planning of action, but they *carry it through.* There is no place in juveniles for coincidence any more than in adult books. The triumph of the young characters must be of their own doing, or the self-identification of the reader and his final satisfaction in the book will be destroyed. See how effective and essential this motivation is in Warren Garst's *Texas Trail Drive* (Ariel Books, Pellegrini & Cudahy).

8. *An effective and appealing sense of humor.* It is amazing how comparatively few people have a sense of humor in writing. Many authors try to be funny, particularly in juvenile manuscripts, but few succeed.

Authors with a true sense of humor—which is nothing more or less than the capacity to understand and enjoy life, and the equal talent to put this understanding and enjoyment on paper—are rare jewels. They are not made by courses in literature or by discourses such as this; they are born. We Americans have more than our fair share of this precious quality and we should cherish it. That we do recognize and revere a sense of humor is proved by the continued popularity of the books by Mark Twain, *The Adventures of Tom Sawyer,* and others. More modern examples are *Homer Price,* by Robert McCloskey (Viking), the *Babar* stories, by Jean de Brunhoff (Random House), *Ellen Tebbits,* by Beverly Cleary (Morrow), and the *Curious George* books by H. A. Rey (Houghton).

These eight attributes probably would hold for any kind of literature for any age, but in juvenile writing there are further requirements which are exigencies of the trade. These will be amplified in the chapter on children themselves and so will only be mentioned here.

a. The right subject matter, with its development slanted correctly, for each age-group.

b. The art of letting the illustrations tell half the story, if the manuscript is intended for little children.

Some authors need help on several features of their work, while they are proficient and masterful at others. Writing ability varies just as people do. But one thing is certain—that in order to write well for children *you must like them, understand them, and respect them.* Then you will say what you have to say directly and sincerely. Children will enjoy your books because you know what they like and what they understand. You have not forgotten the joys and sorrow of childhood, nor do you now laugh at them or underrate them. You write your best because you know from your own close experience that children are appreciative, sensitive, and wise. You know that they learn easily, that they can be led from one truth to another, and that there is no greater pleasure or reward than in widening their enjoyment and knowledge.

Russell Lynes

Russell Lynes has been managing editor of HARPER'S MAGAZINE *since 1947. He is the author of such witty commentaries on American life and manners as* HIGHBROW, LOWBROW, MIDDLEBROW, SNOBS, GUESTS, THE TASTEMAKERS *and* A SURFEIT OF HONEY.

Many people outside the publishing industry feel that one of the not-so-hidden rewards of being an editor is that it makes everything a snap when he decides to publish a book of his own with his own firm. Well, that bit of folklore is delightfully debunked in Mr. Lynes' pointedly humorous and more than slightly satiric essay on his own perils and pitfalls when faced with that exact situation. And along with the account of his personal predicament, Mr. Lynes has some sharp and pertinent things to say about the condition of publishing today.

CONFESSIONS OF AN AUTHOR-EDITOR*

I AM going to talk about one aspect of the book business that probably very few of you are unfortunate enough to know anything about. I am going to talk about what it is like to be an author who is also an employee of the publisher who publishes his books. I am a man who works both sides of the literary street. I don't know many others who do. I don't ask for your sympathy. If you think it's hard on me, think what it must do to my publisher . . . but let me explain.

I am what is known to a publisher as "a pretty good property." I have written a couple of books that have appeared so fleetingly on best-seller lists that I don't think anybody noticed they were there except me. I had one little book that sold 25,000 copies in seven weeks (it was called *Snobs*) but it only cost a dollar and so the bookshops didn't report it as a best seller; they like to report books

* A talk given at the general staff meeting of The New York Public Library at Hunter College Playhouse October 23, 1957.

that sell at higher retail prices, for obvious reasons. But so far as my publisher (and employer, Harper & Brothers) is concerned, my books make money which I then as an editor spend. In a way I am both an account payable and an account receivable. There must be moments when my publishers wish that I lived in Darien with all the rest of the house authors and like the rest of the house authors wrote them letters about how they advertise books which all start with the sentence: "What is this, anyway—a conspiracy of silence?"

The House has ways of taking care of authors who write letters and occasionally come storming in, but what about the author who is there in the office every day, a prima donna on the payroll? It is true that librarians have to cope with authors every day, and that is, I am sure, enough of a headache, but you are not concerned with where their next meal is coming from, though you unquestionably spoon-feed the brains of many of them. There is a considerable difference between the attitude of an author to his publisher and to a library. (Incidentally, my guess is that the first thing any author does in any library is to look himself up in the card catalogue. If he finds all his books there his day is made; if he finds only one he sulks for hours. If none, he probably tiptoes out and looks for another library.)

But to get back to the author and his publisher. Let me first consider this relationship from the author's point of view. All authors believe that all publishers get rich on the sweat and talents of writers and that they, that is the publishers, are parasites on the artists. All authors also believe that publishers play favorites with books; that they decide in advance which books they will sell and which they will suppress on publication. They also believe that a publisher can make any book sell if he puts his heart and his pocketbook behind it, which, I must confess from my own experience, just isn't true. But there is a belief that goes deeper than any of these; that is the author's belief in his own book, and the conviction that if it doesn't sell it must be the publisher's fault.

Now, I am immune to none of these beliefs emotionally, though it is impossible to hang your hat in a publisher's office for as many years as I have without knowing, reasonably, that publisher's have a little something on their side. When I wrote *Snobs,* and it did so well, I knew that a large part of its success was due to the enthusiasm and friendship of the Harper salesmen, and so I wrote to the head of the sales department a little note asking him to thank his boys for what they had done to make the book a success. He wrote a note on my note and sent it along to Cass Canfield, the chairman of Harper's board. He said: "What hath God wrought? This is the first time in my fifty years at Harper's that an author has ever thanked the sales staff." Then a year or so later I did another little book called *Guests*. The salesmen went at that one with a will, too. Books poured into the bookshops, but then, alas, a few months later books began pouring back into Harper's. I revised some of my ideas about the infallibility of the author and the greed of publishers. Fortunately I had declined to take an advance payment on the book, a quaint publishing custom, so at least if my brow was cloudy, my conscience was clear.

You who deal with hundreds and hundreds of books a day must get rather blasé about them in some ways, and blasé about authors, too. But to an author his book is his child and the excitement of holding in one's hand the first copy to come from the press is a satisfaction that sends a shiver of delight down the spine of even the most prolific author. There it is—his hours of labor turned into an object with some degree of permanence, and usually, until the reviewers get hold of it and sometimes even after, an object he regards as precious. Is it any wonder that he expects the publisher to treat it as something very special, that he should want it coddled and spoiled and made much of? He forgets, of course, like any proud parent, that hundreds of books, like hundreds of babies, are launched on the world every week.

But let's look for a moment at what happens to an author who works for his publisher and not against him. Obviously he knows more about his book than anyone else around the office so why shouldn't he write the jacket copy, known inelegantly in the business as the blurb? So I write the jacket copy, pretending to myself that all those fancy adjectives and those superlatives are not just conceit on my part but what is called "good selling copy." In my heart, of course, I at least half believe them, or want to believe them, so out of false modesty I take some of them out, so that I can later be in a position to watch my editor at Harper's put them back in and perhaps, with luck, he'll think of a few words like "famous" or "penetrating" or "wittiest" that even with my gall I wouldn't have had the face to use. I strike, though, when asked to supply a biographical note for the jacket; I can blow my book's horn, but I'm darned if I am going to blow my own. The truth, of course, is that I don't mind blowing my own horn, not if it will sell books, but I don't like my colleagues to know that I don't. It would seem immodest. Modesty is a very rare quality among authors, very rare indeed, and, of course, I would like to be different. One thing all authors want to be is different. If you are in any doubt about this I suggest you read the biographical notes on book jackets. If the book is a frivolous one the publisher is likely to stress the solemnity of the author's background and his academic prowess. Stephen Potter of Gamesmanship fame is always billed as a professor of English and an authority on the nineteenth century. If it is a serious book the publisher will always manage to dredge up something outlandish out of the author's past that stamps him as a regular fellow. I sometimes think that the most important moment in my background from a literary point of view must be that I worked one summer at the age of eighteen as scullion on a merchant marine ship. This obviously is a primary source of my qualifications to write a history of American taste in the visual arts.

But before the publisher ever gets around to the jacket copy, he likes to have a brief summary of the book to be sent out with bound galleys to book reviewers. Authors think that this is done to save the reviewers the trouble of reading the book, and it is dismally true that a good many reviews turn up in small newspapers which are almost direct quotes of these brief summaries. Usually an editor writes this summary, but I write my own. The way the publisher does this is to get someone in the office to slap one out in a hurry that so misrepresents the book that the author finds it intolerable.

The next problem is the design of the jacket. You would think that the design of a book jacket would be a simple thing. It is. It's the redesigning that is complicated—because no one can seem to agree what kind of jacket any given book should have. The original design for the jacket of *The Tastemakers* was, I thought, very handsome. My editor showed it to the head of the sales staff. "Looks too much like a university press book," he said, so I was asked for suggestions. I made a jacket design which was then taken in hand by an artist and vastly improved. I also laid out the forty pages of pictures for that book and sized the cuts myself; nobody told me that that was the manufacturing department's job. You see, I am a magazine editor, not a book editor, and I am used to menial tasks.

But if I have done a lot of work on the production of my books that normally would have been done by others, I cannot deny that I have enjoyed it. There is only one real drawback. If I don't like the jacket copy or the jacket design or the promotional copy I have no one to blame but myself. When you take away from an author the opportunity of blaming his publisher for everything that goes wrong, you have taken away almost his only defense—the only thing that stands between his vanity and the smallness of his royalty checks. On the other hand, I'm afraid that I have made my publisher pay for this. I said earlier that a publisher who always has an author hanging around the office is in a spot he would like to avoid.

There are many things that can go wrong in the production of a book. Each stage of its manufacture is like a mine field through which (by the time the book is finally between covers and jacketed) the editor and the manufacturing and art departments have picked their cautious way to safety. Mines go off, wounds are inflicted, but authors (since they are not around to witness the pain) are spared the anguish. Every time a mine goes off in the path of one of my books, I can hear the explosion, and I come running to the scene of the accident, not, I'm afraid, to bind up the wounds, but to rub salt in them. Being magazine trained, I am scrupulous about deadlines, and when my publishers give me a deadline I produce the text or the pictures or the layouts or the corrected proofs on time. Then I find that they don't really mean the deadlines. Authors never meet deadlines, I am laughingly told, so they just push them up a few weeks—or even a few months.

When this would happen the explosion in the minefield would be me. All right, I'd say to myself, if publishers don't think that writers are professionals with any sense of time, then they think they are bundles of temperament. If they want temperament, I'll give them temperament—maybe if I don't show temperament they won't think I'm an author. Then I have the pleasure of seeing one of my best friends, who is also my editor, apply his formula for coping with temperamental authors. He's awfully good at it: firm but sympathetic, friendly but a little aloof, just as you librarians have to be when you are coping with authors. I would end by going and straightening out the difficulty with the manufacturing department, where I was viewed as a nuisance who, since I am an author, couldn't quite be told to go lay an egg. The one thing everybody in a publishing house hopes an author won't do is lay an egg. Otherwise what most people in publishing houses hope about authors is that they will please bother somebody else; we're too busy around here trying to get books published to worry about the people who write them. There is a look of patient tolerance that creeps into the eyes of people in manufacturing departments when faced with authors that I have seen elsewhere only in the eyes of teachers of backward children.

I make this sound a great deal worse than it has been, of course. My publishers are the very model of publishers. They have bent over backwards to be considerate to me, and I am fully aware that a publisher having an author in its midst, one who won't just go away and stop making a nuisance of himself, is like having a juvenile delinquent come to live with the family.

Let me conclude on a somewhat serious note. We live in an age of tensions. We are constantly having these tensions impressed on us. Writers write about them, publishers publish about them, libraries get people to read about them. Politicians politic about them and advertising men advertise them. We hear a great deal about peaceful co-existence, about integration, and about bi-partisanship —in other words, we worry about people getting along together.

I would like to contend that if authors and publishers can somehow manage to get along together, anybody can get along together. Possibly more authors than publishers get trampled to death in the process, though the record of American publishing is strewn with the bones of publishers who picked the wrong authors. We have a less good record of the works of genius that never became the printed word. As an editor I like to think that there are very, very few. As a writer I wonder.

George Stevens

George Stevens entered publishing in 1925 in the advertising department of Alfred A. Knopf, Inc. Since 1940 he has been with the J. B. Lippincott Company, where he is First Vice President and Managing Editor.

Tackling the author's manuscript itself is the theme of veteran editor George Stevens' essay on the fine points of editing. Amiably, informatively and with disarming candor, Mr. Stevens discusses the problems of working with a true creative author, what the editor's true function is in this relationship, and, particularly, how to edit "for sense and effect."

EDITING FOR SENSE AND EFFECT*

HIS introducing his own opinions, and even prejudices, under general definitions of words, while at the same time the original meaning of the words is not explained, as his Tory, Whig, Pension, Oats, Excise, and a few more, cannot be fully defended, and must be placed to the account of capricious and humorous indulgence. Talking to me upon this subject when we were at Ashbourne in 1777, he mentioned a still stronger instance of the predominance of his private feelings in the composition of this work, than any now to be found in it. "You know, Sir, Lord Gower forsook the old Jacobite interest. When I came to the Renegado, after telling that it meant 'one who deserts to the enemy, a revolter,' I added, 'Sometimes we say a Gower.' Thus it went to the press: but the printer had more wit than I, and struck it out."

It is rare to find a recorded instance of copy-editing given in such detail as the foregoing; it is almost unique to find an author cheerfully admitting that his editor had improved upon his copy; accordingly, Boswell's report of this conversation with Dr. Johnson regarding certain controversial definitions in the *Dictionary* has

* *Mr. Stevens' article was originally published under the title* Author's Nursemaid.

both a practical and a sentimental interest for the editor of manuscripts today. The point on which the lexicographer accepted his printer's emendation was one involving no mere matter of mechanical correctness and consistency, but taste, relevance, and possibly even libel. Now it is true that without its occasional capricious and humorous indulgence in tendentious definitions, Johnson's *Dictionary* would have possessed far less flavor and literary interest, and it would have been unfortunate if a too literal editorial mind had deleted all of them. However, Johnson was lucky in his printer, who knew when to stop. Indeed, in at least one case he stopped too soon, for, as Boswell reports, Johnson's definition of *excise* was actionable, and the author escaped a lawsuit only by good fortune.

It is pertinent to say that the paragraph quoted at the head of this chapter is from the Modern Library Giant edition of Boswell, page 178; the information about the definition of *excise* appears in a footnote on the same page (inaccurately given the reference number 2 in the text, as it is the only footnote on the page). The relevance of these details may not be apparent. They are, however, useful to my editor. Consider that between the time of my writing and of your reading this chapter, it has been carefully examined by at least one editor for the publishers and one proofreader for the printers. It has been the duty of the editor to check my quotation of Boswell with some standard version of the original; I may have made an error or two in transcribing. Was it Boswell's idiom or my carelessness that produced "the original meaning of the words is not explained" instead of "meanings . . . are . . . ?" Should "Renegado" read "Renegade," and who is responsible for the capital R? Surely Boswell did not omit the *u* from the second syllable of *humorous.* Well, neither did I; presumably it was the Modern Library; and if the editor of the present volume has reinserted the *u,* he has made nonsense of this sentence and the one preceding.

One may say that there are two kinds of editing; editing for correctness and consistency, and editing for sense and effect. The two kinds of editing require two separate abilities, which are sometimes, but by no means always, found in one editor. The first kind requires a careful and methodical mind, capable of sustained attention which must frequently be applied to the dullest sorts of reading matter, and a memory which can recall, when the editor spots the word *maneuver* on page 112 of a manuscript, that the author spelled it *manoeuvre* on page 63, or that *nuance* was italicized on page 46 when *coup d'etat* turns up in roman and with no accents or at most the acute é, on 245.

This kind of talent is both rare and important; I have the greatest admiration for it, for I possess it only in low degree. Like most editors, I have my particular spots of vigilance. I am acutely sensitive to the difference between *infer* and *imply,* and it makes me sad to see the latter word gradually dropping out of the language, owing to mass ignorance and carelessness in which a surprisingly large number of eminent authors participate. (No, not participates.) I am particularly aware of the incorrect handling of words and especially proper names ending with *s*. In fact, it takes an editor whose own name ends in *s* to handle the problems raised by plurals and possessives. Such a simple matter as "We are going to the Joneses'" can and does turn up in any of the following ways:

We are going to the Joneses
We are going to the Jones's
We are going to the Jones'
We are going to the Jones
We are going to the Jone's

Likewise, even "Keeping up with the Joneses" usually emerges as "Keeping up with the Jones'," "Keeping up with the Jones's," or "Keeping up with the Jone's," and "Jones's wife" is more commonly "Jones' wife" or "Jone's wife"; it is a cagey author who calls her Mrs. Jones and avoids all the pitfalls.

I assist in maintaining these outposts of defense, aware that my support is constantly dwindling, but even more aware that the enthusiasm with which I hold these bastions does not compensate for their fewness. Any one who has discovered the inexhaustible pleasure of Fowler's *Modern English Usage*—a pleasure perhaps available only to those with a strong feeling for the English language—will have an eye out for dangling participles, fused participles, "due to," "otherwise" as an adjective (as in "whether this suggestion be practical or otherwise"), "percentage" or "proportion" for "part," "eke out," "protagonist," and all the other subjects to which Fowler leads us, in succession, by an artful series of cross-references that makes his book unique among dictionaries in that one does not merely look things up in it, one eventually reads it through. However, a taste for Fowler, while it is something a good editor ought to have, is not enough; it is what mathematicians call a necessary, but not a sufficient condition. Fowler is not a substitute for a good style-book, and not even the best style-book—that published by the University of Chicago Press or any other—is a substitute for an attentive eye and a retentive memory. The last time I trusted my own styling of a manuscript, I was surprised to see, when the galley proofs came in, that every line of dialogue closed with a period instead of a comma before "he said" or "she said." It had been so in the manuscript, but I had not noticed it. Since the author was an admirer of Ernest Hemingway, and most of the book was in dialogue, a substantial amount of resetting was necessary. I no longer edit manuscripts for style.

I do, however, edit manuscripts for sense and effect, and in this enterprise one is fortunate to be dealing with an author as tractable as Dr. Johnson was in the instance previously referred to. An editor who catches mistakes or inconsistencies in spelling, punctuation, and other usage will seldom get into an argument with his author.

The writer knows that authority is on the side of the editor, and usually the best he can do is to pretend he was looking the other way when the mistake occurred in his manuscript. The other kind of editor has no authority beyond his own opinion, which is sometimes at variance with the writer's opinion.

It might well be argued at this point that in such a case the writer is the final authority. The book is his, the responsibility is his, he knows what he wants to say. No doubt the editor is a frustrated writer making a nuisance of himself and spiking the author's originality. It may even be asked why, beyond mechanical styling, a manuscript should be edited at all. Aren't authors artists, and aren't publishers merely business men? Styling may be grudgingly admitted, a genius is not supposed to keep his mind on trivialities; let a hack watch while Jove nods. But when you come to changing the author's choice of words, to altering the structure of paragraphs, even to cutting out cherished passages, aren't you getting above yourself? After all, the publisher's job is to sell the book; it's up to the author to write it.

The answer to this is that there are many answers, because no two cases of editing are exactly alike. The editor's purpose is not to superimpose his own opinions or tastes on those of the author, but only to be sure that the author is actually saying what he intends to say, that he is achieving the effect he desires. Accordingly there are some manuscripts which require a very small number of editorial suggestions. Most experienced authors do know what they want to say and know how to say it. Most experienced authors, at the same time, because they are experienced, know that is is possible for any one occasionally to convey an effect or a significance quite different from what was intended, and therefore they want to have such passages pointed out while there is still an opportunity to revise. Such authors in the course of time evolve a relationship with their editors in which the minds may meet with little friction. After all, any author would prefer to hear about the weak spots in his manuscript in private from an editor than in public from the book reviewers.

In some technical matters the publisher has the last word. He may insist upon alteration or elimination of any passages which he has reason to believe are actionable; if a definite length is stipulated for the manuscript, the publisher may insist upon expansion or cutting to somewhere near that length—though, except in extreme cases, he is not likely to do so unless he is convinced that the expansion or cutting will actually improve the quality of the book. With such exceptions as these, editorial work on an accepted manuscript must be done on a basis of mutual confidence and good will between author and publisher. Ordinarily this basis is established without difficulty. Editors may sometimes begin their careers as frustrated writers, they do not rise to responsible positions by offending authors with picayune and irritating criticisms; indeed, their early experience in publishing houses usually gives them enough insight into the economic insecurity of authorship so that they end by forgetting, or embracing, their frustration. Thus editors do not want to be writers any more than writers want to be editors, and they end by getting along very peaceably.

This is remarkable when you consider that an editor's function is to make the author work harder and longer than the author originally intended. The editor must tactfully lead, wheedle, and cajole him into rewriting passages that did not quite get across the first time; into cutting other passages on which the author had his heart set—usually because they have a private meaning for the author which depends on associations and is incommunicable to the reader. Sometimes, indeed, the work of rewriting may be longer and more laborious than what was involved in preparing the draft which was submitted to the publisher. This is often the case when a publisher accepts a manuscript subject to the author's agreement to make changes. Here the author is obliged to accept the publisher's suggestions or to take his manuscript elsewhere. This does not mean that he will accept all the publisher's ideas; some of them may be impractical, contrary to the author's conceptions, or beyond his capacities; on these points a compromise will be reached.

Such points are so various that only a few frequently recurring examples may be indicated. In non-fiction, one usually edits for clarity and interest. Often the author will know more about his subject than any one else, or will at least be so steeped in it by the fact that he has been writing a book about it, with the result that details will be included which fascinate the author but bore the reader. (At least the editor assumes that if he is bored, the reader will be also.) The editor suggests cutting, the author contends that it is by virtue of these details that he has written the definitive book on the subject; ultimately a compromise is reached, and the editor piously hopes that perhaps five hundred more people will read the book than would have otherwise, and stamps upon that gnawing doubt whether he may, after all, have taken any edge off the book's scholarly importance. Another matter which often arises in non-fiction, particularly in journalistic history and biography, is to make sure that there are distinctions drawn between fact and probability, and between probability and conjecture. The editor may call upon the author for his sources, much to the author's annoyance; but it pays dividends in the end, for reviewers are skeptical and can be mollified only if authors provide their own grains of salt. And, above all, the editor must be constantly on the alert to see that the author is saying what he means in terms that can be understood by the audience at which he is aiming. This question of the audience is one on which wide differences of opinion are possible. The editor naturally wishes the book to reach a wide audience, and may have suggestions for clarity which the author feels would result in stultifying vulgarization—only to complain, after the book is published, that it has not sold more copies. On the other hand, the editor should restrain his zeal for popularization short of the point where the book suffers from anemia and undernourishment, and is treated by the reviewers as an ephemeral triviality.

In fiction, the editor's eye is again on clarity and interest. Clarity of style, however, is not usually much of a problem at present; the influence of Proust, Joyce, and Virginia Woolf has declined; the problems of clarity are those of making convincing the action and the motives of the characters. The problem of style is one of interest rather than of clarity. The most tantalizing kind of manuscripts is the novel which ought to be interesting because of its material, but is not because the author does not know how to write with flavor or interest or life. Every publisher turns down dozens of these in any period of time you care to name; occasionally one of them, which has made the rounds of the publishing houses, will several years later turn up and do very well for the one publisher who was stubborn enough to make the author rewrite and rewrite until she (it is usually she) managed, by the incubator process, to infuse life into a manuscript that had seemed stillborn.

That kind of nursing sometimes repays the effort, but often it does not. Ordinarily what the editor of fiction does is to call the author's attention to all the points which are open to criticism or suggestion; minor inconsistencies; possible anachronisms; actions of characters whose motives seem obscure; passages too lush in style; passages too barren in style; dramatic scenes that do not quite come off as effectively as they should; dull spots; promising episodes left offstage which the editor thinks should be developed. All the editor's suggestions may go into a single-page letter to the author; on the other hand he may pile up a correspondence with the author that rivals the length of the manuscript itself. It all depends. Some experienced authors like to show their editors first drafts in sections, hot from the typewriter; others wait until they have revised several times on their own initiative.

Naturally editors try to make their suggestions as tactfully as possible consistent with whatever degree of firmness the situation calls for. The degree may be high if the author is riding a hobby-horse or off on some tangential enthusiasm. Ordinarily, however, with experienced authors, editorial suggestions are not taken personally. With inexperienced authors who have not reached the professional stage, sometimes a considerable amount of diplomacy is necessary. Often a first novel is publishable for its promise and freshness and sense of life, but needs to have its amateurish passages rewritten. Such passages may be—indeed customarily are—thinly veiled episodes of autobiography, detectable at a glance by any trained editor. It is not always easy to inform a sensitive author that the hero or heroine, in such and such a passage, is not altogether winning the reader's admiration, but is, on the contrary, behaving with conceit and immaturity. The message has to be conveyed with skill and delicacy.

The autobiographical novel is a special case. Another is the detective story. This takes more detailed editing, page for page, than any other kind of novel, simply because, in detective stories, all details have to be right. There must be no inconsistencies, no red herrings, no moments of carelessness. An editor who queries point after point in the manuscript of a detective novel may easily be accused by an exasperated author of being picayunish and insupportably irritating. The author will frequently add, with feeling, that detective novels do not sell well enough to justify so much effort. The editor can only reply that the detective novels which do sell well are those that have been written with the most careful attention to detail—granted the other indispensable qualities of plot, style, characterization, and atmosphere which it is the author's business, not the editor's to supply.

Enough has been said to indicate that it is nearly always with inexperienced authors that editors have their difficulties—and that is, set down in brief, a proposition so self-evident as to have obviated the need for this chapter. It is consoling to an editor, in any event, to realize that inexperienced authors in the end become experienced authors. That is indeed something, in a world in which most writers will go to their dying day saying *infer* when they mean *imply*.

Harry E. Maule

Harry E. Maule has, for many years, been one of the illustrious names in American editing and publishing. Prior to his joining Random House in 1939, Mr. Maule was with Doubleday, Page & Co. During his career, Mr. Maule has worked with such authors as Sinclair Lewis, Edna Ferber, Henry Treece, Don Marquis and many others. A Westerner, Mr. Maule has always had a great interest in Western Americana and has been responsible for notable books in that field.

In the following essay, written especially for this anthology, Mr. Maule treats of the special problems involved in editing today's "far-out" writers—writers of the avant-garde.

Editing such writers, many of whom are stylistically unorthodox and thematically obscurantist, demands of the editor the exercise and application of his finest sensibilities, taste and critical detachment. To these writers' subjective, intensely personal visions of the world as expressed in their novels and short stories, the editor must—keeping the reader always in mind—maintain the "objective view."

THE OBJECTIVE VIEW

IN ONE of his recent syndicated columns (*New York Herald Tribune,* December 15, 1961) entitled "Chimps and Rembrandt," John Crosby paid his respects to the trend of far-outness in the arts—painting, music, the theater, architecture. He mentioned the fact that a lady viewer at the Museum of Modern Art had discovered a Matisse hung upside down. He cited a chimpanzee named Beauty, who had been finger-painting for six months. She had her first exhibition recently, and eighty paintings were sold for twenty-five to ninety-five dollars each. He further saluted *The Caretaker,* which drama he said "is as far out as a playwright can go and still stay inside the confines of language."

He did not get around to the far-outness of many books today. Years ago we had a phrase for it—*avant garde*—but now the movement is so split up, so divided into cliques and schools, that no one term will cover it. What can we call it? Symbolism, obscurantism, or (in some cases) just plain lack of writing disciplines. There is the fading beatnik school, which is easy to pin down. There are those who are writing novels so heavily laden with symbolism that it is frequently difficult to know who's who or what's what. Some scramble past, present and future. Some write in a deliberately difficult style. Is this a reflection of the chaotic times we live in? Or is it a rebellion against the old rules? Or a combination of the two?

Some of these authors show remarkable talent and should be encouraged. Some of their books will make respectable sales, others emerge into best-sellerdom; but every one of them will benefit by close and expert editorial scrutiny. Sometimes—not often—it is stipulated in a book's contract that the publisher shall have a free hand in the editing. More frequently, the contract provides that no changes shall be made without the author's approval. That means that any editing, other than the normal process of house-styling, must be done in consultation with the author. This may take long days and nights of discussion, weighing each point, scene or sequence which the editor singles out for cutting, expansion, clarification or rearrangement.

Any work of creative writing is done by the author in solitary agony. During this time his whole being is absorbed in his characters and events to the extent that they seem more real to him than his normal life. Family and friends are only irritating interruptions of the problem of how best to present the people and action of his story.

Obviously the author gets so close to his book that it becomes *his* life, rather than a work of imagination. In such a mood he may see everything clearly himself but does not always succeed in getting down on paper what is in his mind. The function of the editor is to bring a sensitive understanding to the work and, with it, the objective view that the author may have lost in the writing process. If he can do so, the chances are good that he will be of service to the book and will enhance its artistic effect without impairing the author's basic conception or aim. In such happy circumstances the improvement will likely be reflected in reviews and in sales.

The old bromide that editors are frustrated authors is nonsense, of course. With few exceptions, editors have no desire to be collaborators. They have other concerns; many authors to deal with. If an editor does become imbued with the desire to write, he will insist that his book be his own conception—in theme, subject matter, characters and style.

Naturally the problems of editing "modern" books are more subtle and delicate than those of the "straight" novel, biography or other work. The far-out writers have thrown overboard most of the accepted standards of storytelling and have adopted in their place far more complicated methods. Having contracted for a book, the editor must accept the author's style, and usually his structure, no matter how strange they may be. To clarify such writing, one must approach it with the greatest caution. The old rules of syntax do not necessarily prevail, and the author's use and arrangement of words should only be questioned where they actually defeat his own purpose. What then is there left for the editor to do? Naturally it all depends on the author and how nearly he has attained his artistic goal. What some inexperienced writers fail to realize is that far-out writing, to be successful, places even greater obligations of control upon them than the more conventional type. Free-wheeling manuscripts often defeat themselves by basic obscurities, needless imposition of chaos, or a failure of their authors to understand their own objectives.

Editors see many degrees of excellence in modern writing. The scripts they consider bad or hopeless they simply reject. Their immediate concern is with the ones they take. Even here, the line between acceptance or rejection has shifted to a new set of standards. For one thing, literacy is no longer an absolute criterion. There have been several best-sellers in the past few years which, as published, approached illiteracy. I cannot guess what they may have looked like as raw, unedited manuscripts. Usually such books have a crude power, a rapport with our times, that evokes a favorable response from critics or public.

I am not bemoaning the trend toward far-outness. When successful, modern treatment can achieve a social or psychological significance that many books following conventional techniques do not. It is part of the editor's role to determine whether such work will be accepted by a wide public on its own terms.

At this point I should try to define the relationship of author and editor. Some authors would like to think of the editor as a fiscal agent and as a liaison between him and the printer; in other words, to get him his money quickly and rush his book to the printer. Nothing could be further from present practice or more detrimental to the author's interests. The author-editor relationship is many-sided. The editor is "guide, philosopher and friend," but with qualifications. He is, and must be, by his faith in the author's book, the author's advocate; he must also be a loyal member of the publisher's staff. If he cannot maintain this nice balance between advocacy of the author and sound business management, his usefulness ends.

Sinclair Lewis was one who understood this subtle relationship. (I was his editor at Doubleday, and later at Random House, until his death in 1951.) Contrary to general belief, Lewis sought the advice of his editor and acted upon it when such criticism seemed, to him, sound. I have seen him cut or rewrite many scenes or sequences as the result of editorial discussion. He planned and wrote his books in seclusion but once they were finished, he was ready to talk about them with his editor and to listen to constructive suggestions. He had many friends but discussed his books with few of them.

The editor's first obligation, then, is understanding and appreciation of the author's aim. With that, he can be the author's advocate in the counsels of his firm and, if he is sufficiently convinced about the book, he often can transmit his enthusiasm throughout the organization. Of course, the editor may pick the wrong horse. In that event, any one of several things can happen. He may be outvoted and the book rejected. He may persuade his colleagues and the book fail. He may yield to their doubts, turn the book down and see another publisher make a success of it. No one can be sure of the response of a fickle public.

Once he has taken the book, the next step is editing. The author will frequently make revisions suggested by the editor. If his degree of confidence is particularly high, he will sometimes agree to give the editor a free hand, even though this may be unspecified by contract. In no event does this give the editor the right to put words into the author's mouth, to alter his characters, or to change the essential aim of the book.

Today the problem of editing is more complex than ever before because of the increasing number of far-out books, in which meaning and intent are obscured by layers of symbolism, flashback and flash-forward are mingled, time sequences shift unaccountably, motives change from page to page, and even characters shed their personalities.

Obviously, being an editor myself, I am slanted in his favor, but I hope not blindly so. In America editors do a great deal more editing than they do in England. I could expand various reasons for this, not the least of which is economic. The Englishman's case is put forth succinctly: "It is the author's book; we take it or we don't." Other factors prevail in this country, and the decision isn't that easy or simple. A large number of books are edited here which could never be published without such attention. The extreme example is *Look Homeward, Angel*—not a far-out book, by the way. I do not think I will be contradicted when I say that this novel could not have been published without the Herculean efforts of Maxwell Perkins, his editor at Scribner's, who sat with Tom Wolfe for endless hours, cutting and reducing that cluttered mass of manuscript into a cohesive whole. To invest so much time on one book implies supreme confidence in the ultimate result. (I dread to think of the extra hours Max Perkins had to put in to catch up on the affairs of other authors he was handling at the time—Hemingway, for example.)

Not only does immersion in his manuscript cause an author to lose perspective, as already mentioned, but also the ardors of inventing people, creating backgrounds, and maintaining a style may cause him to overlook inconsistencies, lapses in time sequence, contradiction of fact. Small wonder if some scenes are overdeveloped and others understated. I remember reading a piece by Lawrence Durrell, perhaps an introduction to a new edition of his Alexandria Quartet, in which he ruefully admitted that while reading a script for revision he found such lapses as a woman entering a room in a white dress, leaving it in a black one; and time sequences that failed to jibe. Of course, such flaws should have been caught by the editor in the first instance.

The job of the editor, then, is to bring to the manuscript the objective view, to understand what the author is driving at, and, in consultation, to help him to achieve as nearly perfect a work of art as he can.

An editor is sensitive to reviews by responsible critics, as well as to sales figures. If, as sometimes happens, a leading review deplores something that should have been changed in the editing, he takes it to heart, especially so when it is something the editor has vainly pleaded with the author. Harry Hansen said in a recent article in his Chicago *Tribune* column: "From my point of view many novels published today would be much improved if cut down by one-half, and some would read better if all the dirty words were shaken out."

More specifically, Herbert Mitgang in the New York *Times* made this comment on an ultramodern novel: "——is not so long as it seems. The double-takes—for obscure literary citations—and the double meanings . . . only make it seem so." Another grievous comment from a critic: "The author and his editor have not helped much to make it readable." No one has the means of knowing exactly what happened at the manuscript stage of such a book, between editor and author—what pleas for clarification were made, debated and rejected. There are some books which a publisher accepts for their factual content rather than literary style, knowing full well that no amount of editing can make it an accomplished piece of prose.

One must bear in mind that the editor, while a purveyor of his own enthusiasms, is also the mouthpiece of his firm. If the author's book has progressed to the point of acceptance, he should bear in mind that it has now been read by several competent judges—other editors, sales people, members of the firm. The position that the editor subsequently presents is the result of a house judgment. Whatever the merits of a single brilliant opinion, and whatever the drawbacks of the committee-type decision, the book at least has had the benefit of scrutiny by several experienced readers who are all eager to develop a best-seller on the list.

Another basic point should be borne in mind by the author when exposed for the first time to the bewildering processes of getting a book ready for publication. After the round of conferences with the editor, after the revision or cutting, the manuscript advances to the next stage, known as copy editing or styling—final preparation for the printer. The copy editor or stylist is an editor in his own right. He constructively checks the whole, without regard to what has been done already, and questions anything that seems to him to be wrong, either in a literary sense or factually. The stylist checks spelling, punctuation, capitalization, the use of italics, etc., for consistency and for conformity with the publisher's house style. He also checks the spelling of proper names, classical or historical references, and quotations. Like that of the book's editor, the success of the stylist's job depends upon his understanding of the author's aim and his selfless desire to turn out a book which, as nearly as possible, reflects the author's vision of it.

The final stage is not to be confused with the functions of either editor or stylist. This is the proofreading. Few authors are good proofreaders of their own books. They are preoccupied with style, reading quality, the effectiveness of a single passage, the rounded presentation of character. The proofreader is meticulous by training and temperament and takes nothing for granted. His work is the final check upon author, editor and stylist, and many is the woeful blunder prevented by a proofreader who caught a blind spot undetected by the others. The beginning author should welcome the ministrations of these people, whose sole motive is to turn out as fine a book as human fallability will allow.

No article on editing and the new writing would be complete without some attention to the change in recent years in the treatment of sex and the use of words which, up to a short time ago, were never printed in books for general circulation. The problem of obscenity did not bother publishers and editors very much prior to World War II. The free use of four-letter words in books was generally frowned upon. With few exceptions, the reluctance of publishers to fly in the face of custom—dictated perhaps by their ideas of good taste—and backed up by legal advice—caused them to edit out words and situations which violated the laws of obscenity.

Times changed. After the war, the reproduction of G.I. talk and G.I. conduct seemed right, from the literary point of view. Certain publishers, despite the headshaking of their lawyers, let the four-letter words and shocking situations stand. A profound social change was taking place. Were books leading the way in this freedom of expression or where their authors merely reflecting the social scene? One book that got by led to another—especially in the paperback field—until many good people, and many stupid ones, became alarmed. This finally led to the censorship actions of 1959-61 and the series of court rulings that the books under attack were not obscene according to law. The famous decision of Judge Woolsey in the case against James Joyce's *Ulysses,* handed down in 1933, provided a forceful precedent in favor of freedom of language. According to that ruling, the intent of a book as a whole should be the determining factor, rather than isolated words or passages.

By mid-1961 the lid was off. If the censorship cases had not been so ill-considered and so stupidly pressed, the results might have been different. I submit that there are books which are vulnerable but not if they are attacked without regard to common sense or the Bill of Rights. I believe that all forms of censorship are bad and self-defeating, but one hopes that the literary resources of authors might be equal to the task of achieving their effects without the excessive use of scatology and overly explicit sex scenes. An ironic fact is that many far-out authors, who reject the old realism as "square," today defend scatology on the grounds of realism—"That is the way the characters talked."

Some editors and publishers have deplored the postwar tendency on the grounds of good taste. But today what *is* good taste? If an editor follows the canons of good taste as defined ten years ago, he is laughed down. Words which were taboo in mixed company a few years back are common usage. An editor must live in his own times. Where the true balance lies, rests within the conscience of the individual, but in the long run the public will get what it wants. Authors and publishers will see to that, and the courts, always sensitive to public demand, will uphold its desires.

BOOKS

Part Two: *Editor-to-Author Correspondence*

Maxwell E. Perkins

Maxwell E. Perkins joined Charles Scribner's Sons, the distinguished American publishing house, at the age of thirty in the year 1914. He remained with that house until his death in 1947.

Maxwell E. Perkins, perhaps the best-known, most revered (and envied) trade publishing editor of our time was the editor of Hemingway, Fitzgerald, Wolfe, Lardner, James Jones and many other of the leading literary lights of the Twenties, Thirties and early Forties.

Not a man given to satiric thrusts of humor, overflowings of emotion or deep personal involvement with his authors (except, of course, in the very special relationship with Thomas Wolfe), Perkins' power and greatness came from his superb taste, which was exquisite without in any way being effete; his unwavering belief in his author; and his rigorously adhered to standards for integrity, craftsmanship and artistry.

Without taking one whit of praise away from him, let us not forget that Perkins' greatness was augmented by the unusual stable of wild talents he commanded. His "list" was the dream and the envy of all his contemporaries.

In this selection from John Hall Wheelock's EDITOR-TO-AUTHOR: THE LETTERS OF MAXWELL E. PERKINS, *published by Scribner's in 1950, Perkins is revealed in several of his editorial roles: soliciting new material, direct editing and revision, bucking up the spirits of momentarily dispirited authors, praising new successes, and propounding his beliefs in freedom of expression.*

TO F. SCOTT FITZGERALD

Dec. 12, 1921

DEAR FITZGERALD:

Don't ever *defer* to my judgment. You won't on any vital point, I know, and I should be ashamed, if it were possible to have made you; for a writer of any account must speak solely for himself. I should hate to play (assuming V.W.B.'s[1] position to be sound) the W. D. Howells to your Mark Twain.

It is not to the *substance* of this passage[2] that I object. Everyone of any account, anyone who could conceivably read this book, under forty, agrees with the substance of it. If they did not, there would be less objection to it in one way—it would then startle them as a revelation of a new point of view which, by giving a more solid kind of value, would lessen the objection on account of flippancy. (I hate the word. I hate to be put in the position of using such words as "respect" and "flippancy," which have so often enraged me, but there is some meaning in them.) The Old Testament ought not to be treated in a way which suggests a failure to realize its tremendous significance in the recent history of man, as if it could simply be puffed away with a breath of contempt, it is so trivial. That is the effect of the passage at present. It is partly so because Maury is talking and is talking in character; and that is the way men do talk too, so far as ability enables them, even when they fully appreciate every side of the matter. It is here that the question of the public comes in. They will not make allowance for the fact that a character is talking extemporaneously. They will think F.S.F. is writing deliberately. Tolstoi did that even, and to Shakespeare. Now, you are, through Maury, expressing your views, of course; but you would do so differently if you were deliberately stating them as your views. You speak of Galileo: he and Bruno showed themselves to have a genuine sense of the religious significance of the theories they broke down. They were not in a state of mind to treat the erroneous beliefs of men with a light contempt. France[3] does not so treat Christ in that story of Pilate in his old age. And "Whited Sepulchre" is an expression of a high contempt, although applied to an object which had no such quality of significance as the Bible.

My point is that you impair the effectiveness of the passage—of the very purpose you use it for—by giving it that quality of contempt, and I wish you would try so to revise it as not to antagonize even the very people who agree with the substance of it. You would go a long way toward this if you cut out "God Almighty" and put "Deity." In fact, if you will change it on the line indicated, by

1 Van Wyck Brooks, American critic, author of *The Ordeal of Mark Twain,* Dutton, 1920. In this book, the influence of Howells on Mark Twain is revealed as, on the whole, a restrictive and injurious one.

2 In *The Beautiful and Damned* (Scribners, 1922), in which Maury makes light of the Old Testament.

3 Anatole France.

that change you will have excised the element to which I object.

I do agree that it belongs in Maury's speech; that it does bring it to a focus. But you could so revise it that it would do this without at the same time doing the thing to which we object.

I hope this gets over to you. If I saw you for ten minutes I know you would understand and would agree with me.

As ever,

TO F. SCOTT FITZGERALD

Dec. 31, 1921

DEAR FITZGERALD:

The letter from Reynolds[1] which you sent and which I return is rather pathetic, but so far as it concerns your writing, I think it represents a temporary condition. The time ought to come when whatever you write will go through and where its irony and satire will be understood. They will know what you stand for in writing, and they do not really know yet. It is in recognition of this that I want very much to have this book[2] so announced in our lists, and so on, that it will be regarded as "important" as well as the other things.

There is, especially in this country, a rootless class of society into which Gloria and Anthony drifted, a large class and one which has an important effect on society in general. It is certainly worth presenting in a novel. I know that you did not deliberately undertake to do this but I think "The Beautiful and Damned" has, in effect, done this; and that this makes it a valuable as well as brilliant commentary upon American society. Perhaps you have never even formulated the idea that it does do this thing, but don't you think it is true? The book is not written according to the usual conventions of the novel, and its greatest interest is not that of the usual novel. Its satire will not of itself be understood by the great, simple-minded public without a little help. For instance, in talking to one man about the book, I received the comment that Anthony was unscathed; that he came through with his millions, and thinking well of himself. This man completely missed the extraordinarily effective irony of the last few paragraphs.

As ever,

1 Paul Reynolds, literary agent.

2 *The Beautiful and Damned,* Scribners, 1922.

TO RING W. LARDNER

July 2, 1923

DEAR MR. LARDNER:

I read your story, "The Golden Wedding,"[1] with huge enjoyment. Scott Fitzgerald recommended it to me and he also suggested that you might have other material of the same sort which, with this, could form a volume. I am therefore writing to tell you how very much interested we should be to consider this possibility, if you could put the material before us. I would hardly have ventured to do this if Scott had not spoken of the possibility, because your position in the literary world is such that you must be besieged by publishers, and to people in that situation their letters of interest are rather a nuisance. I am certainly mighty glad to have the chance of expressing our interest though, if, as Scott thought, you would not feel that we were merely bothering you. Would you be willing to send on any material that might go with "The Golden Wedding" to form a volume, or to tell me where I might come at it in periodicals?

Very truly yours,

TO F. SCOTT FITZGERALD

November 20, 1924

DEAR SCOTT:

I think you have every kind of right to be proud of this book.[2] It is an extraordinary book, suggestive of all sorts of thoughts and moods. You adopted exactly the right method of telling it, that of employing a narrator who is more of a spectator than an actor: this puts the reader upon a point of observation on a higher level than that on which the characters stand and at a distance that gives perspective. In no other way could your irony have been so immensely effective, nor the reader have been enabled so strongly to feel at times the strangeness of human circumstance in a vast heedless universe. In the eyes of Dr. Eckleberg various readers will see different significances; but their presence gives a superb touch to the whole thing: great unblinking eyes, expressionless, looking down upon the human scene. It's magnificent!

I could go on praising the book and speculating on its various elements, and means, but points of criticism are more important

[1] Published by Scribners, with other stories by Ring Lardner, under the title *How to Write Short Stories*, 1924.

[2] *The Great Gatsby*, Scribners, 1925.

now. I think you are right in feeling a certain slight sagging in chapters six and seven, and I don't know how to suggest a remedy. I hardly doubt that you will find one and I am only writing to say that I think it does need something to hold up here to the pace set, and ensuing. I have only two actual criticisms:

One is that among a set of characters marvelously palpable and vital—I would know Tom Buchanan if I met him on the street and would avoid him—Gatsby is somewhat vague. The reader's eyes can never quite focus upon him, his outlines are dim. Now everything about Gatsby is more or less a mystery, i.e. more or less vague, and this may be somewhat of an artistic intention, but I think it is mistaken. Couldn't *he* be physically described as distinctly as the others, and couldn't you add one or two characteristics like the use of that phrase "old sport"—not verbal, but physical ones, perhaps. I think that for some reason or other a reader—this was true of Mr. Scribner[1] and of Louise[2]—gets an idea that Gatsby is a much older man than he is, although you have the writer say that he is little older than himself. But this would be avoided if on his first appearance he was seen as vividly as Daisy and Tom are, for instance—and I do not think your scheme would be impaired if you made him so.

The other point is also about Gatsby: his career must remain mysterious, of course. But in the end you make it pretty clear that his wealth came through his connection with Wolfsheim. You also suggest this much earlier. Now almost all readers numerically are going to be puzzled by his having all this wealth and are going to feel entitled to an explanation. To give a distinct and definite one would be, of course, utterly absurd. It did occur to me, though, that you might here and there interpolate some phrases, and possibly incidents, little touches of various kinds, that would suggest that he was in some active way mysteriously engaged. You do have him called on the telephone, but couldn't he be seen once or twice consulting at his parties with people of some sort of mysterious significance, from the political, the gambling, the sporting world, or whatever it may be. I know I am floundering, but that fact may help you to see what I mean. The *total* lack of an explanation through so large a part of the story does seem to me a defect—or not of an explanation, but of the suggestion of an explanation. I wish you were here so I could talk about it to you, for then I know I could at least make you understand what I mean. What Gatsby did ought never to be definitely imparted, even if it could be. Whether he was an innocent tool in the hands of somebody else, or to what degree

1 Charles Scribner, Senior (1854-1930), president of Charles Scribner's Sons.
2 Mrs. Maxwell E. Perkins.

he was this, ought not to be explained. But if some sort of business activity of his were simply adumbrated, it would lend further probability to that part of the story.

There is one other point: in giving deliberately Gatsby's biography, when he gives it to the narrator, you do depart from the method of the narrative in some degree, for otherwise almost everything is told, and beautifully told, in the regular flow of it, in the succession of events or in accompaniment with them. But you can't avoid the biography altogether. I thought you might find ways to let the truth of some of his claims like "Oxford" and his army career come out, bit by bit, in the course of actual narrative. I mention the point anyway, for consideration in this interval before I send the proofs.

The general brilliant quality of the book makes me ashamed to make even these criticisms. The amount of meaning you get into a sentence, the dimensions and intensity of the impression you make a paragraph carry, are most extraordinary. The manuscript is full of phrases which make a scene blaze with life. If one enjoyed a rapid railroad journey I would compare the number and vividness of pictures your living words suggest, to the living scenes disclosed in that way. It seems, in reading, a much shorter book than it is, but it carries the mind through a series of experiences that one would think would require a book of three times its length.

The presentation of Tom, his place, Daisy and Jordan, and the unfolding of their characters is unequaled so far as I know. The description of the valley of ashes adjacent to the lovely country, the conversation and the action in Myrtle's apartment, the marvelous catalogue of those who came to Gatsby's house—these are such things as make a man famous. And all these things, the whole pathetic episode, you have given a place in time and space, for with the help of T. J. Eckleberg and by an occasional glance at the sky, or the sea, or the city, you have imparted a sort of sense of eternity. You once told me you were not a *natural* writer—my God! You have plainly mastered the craft, of course; but you needed far more than craftsmanship for this.

As ever,

Nov. 27, 1929

DEAR SIR:

We have received your letter with regard to——. We are sorry that you feel as you do about the book—it is far from pleasant to us to have given offense to anybody, and in particular to those who belong to your faith, which we respect. At the same time, you seem not to understand the function of a publisher, nor to attach any importance to one of the greatest principles in the whole world—that which upholds free speech for the sake of the freedom of the intellect. According to this principle any serious and careful book upon any person of importance and significance to the general public should find a publisher; and any publisher who refrained from publication, even if he did not agree with the author's conclusions, because of fear of some particular sect, would be untrue to his profession, and indeed to the cause of intellectual freedom.

You assume that this book is manifestly unfair and irresponsible, but not one single reviewer has thought this. The very opposite has been the opinion of all the leading publications which review books, including the greatest newspapers and magazines of the United States.

It is a part of the American philosophy as expressed in the Constitution—that, except in the most extreme cases, people should be allowed to express their opinions, and that the result of this is to stir up thought and controversy, out of which will emerge the Truth. It is only what is false that is killed by discussion, not what is true.

Ever truly yours,

TO ALLEN TATE

June 27, 1931

DEAR MR. TATE:

I am taking your poems home to read, but I know a number of them already, well, and of course anybody would be proud to publish them. I shall write you more definitely next week, and everything would be very simple indeed if it were not for these detestable practical questions that cannot be eliminated. I am not referring to the mere matter of a contract, for that too would not be difficult, but there is also the serious question of an author dividing his work between two publishers.[1] I think your letter shows that you have considered that, and you would not intend that it should always be divided. And I only raise the question because you should. Our policy has always been definitely to publish for an author rather than to publish individual works, and it has also always been opposed to taking steps to detach an author from another publisher. I am not asking you to discuss these questions with me, but I

1 Putnam and Scribners. Putnam had published Tate.

thought I ought to explain our position, although I do not wish to do that even, in any way that will be embarrassing to you, and I need hardly say that—like any publisher—we should value your name on our list.

I shall write you again next week. It was a pleasure to hear from you, and to receive a manuscript of yours.

Ever sincerely yours,

P.S. I have been trying hard to get proofs of your wife's book.[1] I am pressing the printer for them, and should very soon begin to have them, and then they will go to her rapidly.

TO THOMAS WOLFE

Jan. 21, 1935

DEAR TOM:

I'm committed to Key West now, however impossible it seems to go, and since, when I return, "Of Time and the River" will be a book; I'm taking this last moment to say what I've long been on the point of saying:

Nothing could give me greater pleasure or greater pride as an editor than that the book of the writer whom I have most greatly admired should be dedicated to me if it were sincerely done. But you cannot, and should not, try to change your conviction that I have deformed your book, or at least prevented it from coming to perfection. It is therefore impossible for you sincerely to dedicate it to me, and it ought not to be done. I know we are truly friends and have gone through much in company, and this matter, for my part, can have nothing to do with that, or ever shall. But this is another matter. I would have said this sooner but for some fear that you would misinterpret me. But the plain truth is that working on your writings, however it has turned out, for good or bad, has been the greatest pleasure, for all its pain, and the most interesting episode of my editorial life. The way in which we are presenting this book must prove our (and my) belief in it. But what I have done has destroyed *your* belief in it and you must not act inconsistently with that fact.

As for your preface, there is this obstacle to it at the start: a reader is meant to enter into a novel as if it were reality, and so to feel it, and a preface tends to break down that illusion and to make him look at it in a literary way. But perhaps that is, in some degree,

[1] *Penhally,* by Caroline Gordon, Scribners, 1931.

a literary objection to a preface and when yours began so finely I thought you might be right to have it. But when I read more of it today, it seemed to me you did the very things you meant to avoid doing in the novel: you made the book seem personal and autobiographical, and by showing resentment against those who objected to the apparent reality (as the preface implied) of the characters in the "Angel" [1] you opened yourself to the same charge against *this* book and notified the whole public that it might rightly be brought. And of the whole public not a handful can understand the artist's point of view or the writer's conscience. In these, and other ways, I thought, you bared yourself to all the enemies you have and I told you so because I am your friend——

P.S. I thought that woman looked dangerous!

In his answer to Wolfe's twenty-eight-page letter, Perkins had written, on January 13, that he had as yet only had time to glance through it, and so could not answer it properly. He referred to it again, briefly, in his letter of January 14th. The letter that follows was written after he had read and pondered this long and important document in the Wolfe-Perkins correspondence.

TO THOMAS WOLFE

Saturday, January 16, 1937

DEAR TOM:

In the first place, I completely subscribe to what you say a writer should do, and always have believed it. If it were not true that you, for instance, should write as you see, feel, and think, then a writer would be of no importance, and books merely things for amusement. And since I have always thought that there could be nothing so important as a book can be, and some are, I could not help but think as you do. But there are limitations of time, of space, and of human laws which cannot be treated as if they did not exist. I think that a writer should, of course, be the one to make his book what he wants it to be, and that if, because of the laws of space, it must be cut, he should be the one to cut it; and, especially with you, I think the labour and discipline that would come from doing that without help or interference would further the pretty terrible task of mastering the material. But my impression was that you asked my help, that you wanted it. And it is my impression too that changes were not forced on you (you're not very forceable, Tom, nor I very force-

[1] *Look Homeward, Angel,* Scribners, 1929.

ful), but were argued over, often for hours. But I agree with you about this too, fully, and unless you want help it will certainly not be thrust upon you. It would be better if you could fight it out alone—better for your work, in the end, certainly; and, what's more, I believe you are now in a position to publish with less regard to any conventions of bookmaking, say a certain number of pages almost, whether or not it had what in a novel is regarded as an ending, or anything else that is commonly expected in a novel. I believe the writer, anyway, should always be the final judge, and I meant you to be so. I have always held to that position and have sometimes seen books hurt thereby, but at least as often helped. "The book belongs to the author."

I certainly do not care—nor does this House—how revolutionary your books are. I did try to keep you from injecting radical, or Marxian, beliefs into "Time and the River," because they were your beliefs in 1934 and 1935, and not those of Eugene in the time of the book. So it did not seem that they could rightly belong in the book. If they could have, then the times could not be rightly pictured, I thought. It must be so. Still, you were then and always conscious of social wrong and that is plainly in the book as you then saw it. There was the Astor story. What was told was not heard by Eugene. It was second-hand, and second-hand material—something told, not heard and seen—is inferior to first-hand. If cutting had to be done, ought that not to be cut? I know your memory is a miracle, but it seems as if you must have forgotten how we worked and argued. You were never overruled. Do you think you are clay to be moulded! I never saw anyone less malleable. And as for publishing what you like, or being prevented from it, apart from the limitations of space, you have not been, intentionally. Are you thinking of "K 19"? [1] We would have published it if you had said to do it. At the time, I said to Jack:[2] "Maybe it's the way Tom is. Maybe we should just publish him as he comes and in the end it will all be right." But if we had, and the results had been bad at the moment, would you not have blamed me? Certainly I should have bitterly blamed myself. I do not want the passage of time to make you cautious or conservative, but I do want it to give you a full control—as it has done in the case of great writers in the past—over your great talent. And if you can stand the struggle, it will. But you must

[1] Section of manuscript removed from *Of Time and the River* but never separately published. "K 19" was the number of an overnight Pullman car between New York and Asheville. This material was later used in *You Can't Go Home Again,* Harpers, 1940.

[2] John Hall Wheelock, an editor at Scribners.

struggle too, and perhaps even more than in the writing, in the shaping and revising. That might be the hardest thing of all, to your nature. You have so much in you, that the need with you is to get it uttered. Then to go back and polish and perfect seems petty, and goes against your nature, I guess.

Tom, you ought not to say some of the things you do—that I find your sufferings amusing and don't take them seriously. I know something of them. I do try to turn your mind from them and to arouse your humor, because to spend dreadful hours brooding over them, and in denunciation and abuse on account of them, seems to be only to aggravate them. It does no good. You have to suffer to write as you do, and the slings and arrows that strike you from outside madden you the more because you instinctively know that all that matters is your work and so why can't you be left to do it. I understand that. Have you seen me amused by other people's sufferings? You know that was unjust.

Then comes the question of your writing about the people here. I don't want to discuss it, because I agree that you have the same right to make use of them as of anyone else in the same way, and if there is an argument on it the whole thing may be bedevilled. . . . But when I spoke of resigning after we published—and the moment I inadvertently said it I told Miss Nowell[1] she must not repeat it, and she said she would not—I did not mean I would be asked or wanted to resign. That would never happen on any such ground. But it isn't the way you think, and it's up to you to write as you think you should. Your plan as outlined seems to me a splendid one too. I hope you will get on with it now.

There remains the question of whether we are in fundamental agreement. But it is no question if you feel it is not so. I have always instinctively felt that it was so, and no one I ever knew has said more of the things that I believed than you. It was so from the moment that I began to read your first book. Nothing else, I would say, could have kept such different people together through such trials. But I believe in democracy and not in dictators; and in government by principles and not by men; and in less government if possible, rather than more; and that power always means injustice and so should be as little concentrated as is compatible with the good of the majority; and that violence breeds more evils than it kills; and that it's better to sizzle in the frying-pan until you're sure your jump won't take you into the fire; and that Erasmus, who begged his friend Luther not to destroy the *good* in the Church because of the bad in it, which he thought could be forced out with

1 Elizabeth Nowell, literary agent.

the spread of education, was right, though not heroic, and the heroic Luther wrong—and that Europe is the worse for his impetuosity today. I don't believe that things can't improve. I believe that the only thing that can prevent improvement is the ruin of violence, or of reckless finance which will end in violence. That is why Roosevelt needs an opposition, and it is the only serious defect in him. I believe that change really comes from great deep causes too complex for contemporary men, or any others perhaps, fully to understand, and that when even great men like Lenin try to make over a whole society suddenly the end is almost sure to be bad, and that the right end, the natural one, will come from the efforts of innumerable people trying to do right, and to understand it, because they are a part of the natural forces that are set at work by changed conditions. It is the effort of man to adjust himself to change, and it has to be led, but the misfortune of man is that strong will almost always beats down intelligence, and the passionate, the reasonable. I believe that such as you can help one change, but that it ought to be by your writings, not by violent acts. I believe that wealth is bad but that it should not be confiscated, but reduced by law, and in accordance with a principle, not arbitrarily and in passion; and if it is done in passion and violence the result will be a new privileged class made up of delegates of the man or the oligarchy that has seized the power. But it may be that the great underlying changes will dictate Communism as the best society for most people. Then we ought to have it; but if we can evolve into it gradually how much better (though I know many on both sides say that is impossible) than if we go in by revolution and civil war. At least let us try the way of evolution first. It seems to me that our Civil War and many of the great convulsions were caused by extremists on both sides, by those too hot-headed to wait for natural forces to disclose their direction, when the inevitable outcome could no longer be resisted. I do not believe the world can ever be perfect, of course, though it might in a sense approximate a political and economic perfection if conditions ceased from changing so that a long enough time was given to deal with known and permanent factors. But this is getting to be too much of a philosophy of history or something, and I don't think it has anything to do with fundamental agreement. I had always felt it existed—and I don't feel, because you differ with me, however violently, on such things as I've said above, that it does not, necessarily. It is more that I like and admire the same things and despise many of the same things, and the same people too, and think the same things important and unimportant—at least this is the way it has seemed to me.

Anyhow, I don't see why you should have hesitated to write me as you did, or rather to send the letter. There was mighty little of it that I did not wholly accept, and what I did not, I perfectly well understood. There were places in it that made me angry, but it was a fine letter, a fine writer's statement of his beliefs, as fine as any I ever saw, and though I have vanities enough, as many as most, it gave me great pleasure too—that which comes from hearing brave and sincere beliefs uttered with sincerity and nobility.

Always yours,

TO NANCY HALE

June 18, 1937

DEAR MRS. WERTENBAKER:[1]

I got your address from Miss Nowell.[2] I had been asking her about you because I cannot help being impatient to see the novel done, or even to read some more of it, and yet I do not want to keep bothering you and perhaps worrying you about it. But she thought it would be all right if I wrote you, and she told me you were working well. I am delighted to know this. Writing a novel is a very hard thing to do because it covers so long a space of time, and if you get discouraged it is not a bad sign, but a good one. If you think you are not doing it well, you are thinking the way real novelists do. I never knew one who did not feel greatly discouraged at times, and some get desperate, and I have always found that to be a good symptom. Anyhow, I have seen enough of the novel to have no anxieties about the outcome, but rather the very greatest hopes. I hope you will be able to go on steadily until you get to the end.

I hope when you go through here, in the Fall, on the way back to Virginia, you will give me a chance to see you. Maybe by then you will have the manuscript complete.

Ever sincerely yours,

TO ERNEST HEMINGWAY

Jan. 19, 1940

DEAR ERNEST:

I cabled you the morning after I read what you sent of the ms.[3] The impressions made by it are even stronger after the lapse of time. The scenes are more vivid and real than in the reading. This

1 Nancy Hale, the novelist.
2 Elizabeth Nowell, literary agent.
3 *For Whom The Bell Tolls,* Scribners, 1940.

has always happened to me after reading your novels, and it is true of mighty few writers. That Chapter Eight is terrific, and as one gets further away from it the characters of those different men when they came out to be killed, and the way they took it, seem as if one had seen it all, and had known them. It is truly wonderful, the way the temper of the people changed as things went on and they got drunk with killing, and with liquor too. The first chapter, or the first eight pages, had the old magic. Last night, I had to talk about forthcoming books to the people in the bookstore,[1] and I ended by saying what a simple thing it was to be a real writer, the easiest thing in the world, and I was going to give them an example to show it, how anybody could do it, and then I read them, without saying who had written it, the first three pages, through the point where Jordan gets his glasses adjusted, and sees the mill and the waterfall and all. Having him do that makes the whole scene jump out at you as real as real. I said, "Why couldn't any of us do that? It's perfectly simple." But of course nobody can do it. Then I did tell them that they were the first pages of a novel by you, but I told them nothing else about it. You could see how even that little bit impressed them all. Well, of course, I am mighty impatient to see more.

I did not put in about depositing the check for $250 for the sake of keeping the cable short—Yankee frugality.

I had lunch with Waldo[2] yesterday, and he was in fine form, and talked awfully well, and so we were much longer at it than we should have been. But as we went out, we met a man who looked exactly like he ought to, which does not often happen. That was Sweeny,[3] the soldier, who said he had had a letter from you, and took it out of his pocket, but didn't read it to us. I was mighty glad to see Sweeny, and to see what he looked like.

Anyhow, I think this book will be magnificent.

Always yours,

The letter of June 17, 1943, which follows, was written after Perkins had received, and read, a book on writing and publishing which, in the course of an attack on editors and publishers in general, alleged that Thomas Wolfe had been the helpless victim of his editors, who had cut and mangled his work in such a way as to do him, and it, serious injury. Perkins resented these allegations, not

1 The Scribner Bookstore.

2 Waldo Peirce, the painter, a friend of Hemingway and of Perkins.

3 Colonel Charles Sweeny, soldier and writer, author of *Moment of Truth*, Scribners, 1943.

only as regarding himself—for he had been Wolfe's principal editor and had sacrificed time and health in an effort to help him—but as regarding editors in general. As Perkins points out, Wolfe's own letters give the lie to these allegations.

June 17, 1943

DEAR——:

I got a copy of your "——" because I heard it contained a furious attack upon me. It does, and one that is plainly libellous, as Thomas Wolfe's own letters alone will show. But I found the book such good reading, upon the whole, that I suppose I now shall read it through. And I'll enjoy it, for the most part. But I am the slowest reader in the world, and so hardly ever get to read anything but what we are publishing. Which is a very bad thing in an editor.

But then I found your chapter called, "——," and I thought you should hear a few facts which are at complete variance with what you say. One thing you say is that if a manuscript of a novel "did not come in through one of the big agents" it is condemned "to cursory and dilatory reading." When we take on a new novelist we advise him to get an agent for the sake of magazine, dramatic, radio and movie rights. These he owns, and they must be skillfully handled. But here are a few of the authors that came to us on their own and got thorough, deeply interested, and immediate readings:

Struthers Burt
Scott Fitzgerald
S. S. Van Dine
Robert Briffault
Ernest Hemingway
Marjorie Rawlings
Marcia Davenport
Christine Weston
Nancy Hale
Arthur Train
John Thomason
Will James
Taylor Caldwell

Most of them still have no agents in connection with book publication, but only for these other rights.

Then you come to tell how ninety percent of the novels published bear "bruises and slashes" from editors. I should say that ninety percent of them are barely touched, and then only in view of such matters as libel and other legal points. The publisher has to take some care in those regards, of course. Even so, I should say that ninety percent of our novels were very slightly changed, and that if they were changed it was because the author asked for help, even demanded it, even thought he or she was neglected if it were not given. When it is given, it is given very reluctantly and fearfully because, as you say, the book can only come out of the man. Editors know that mighty well, at least those I am acquainted with.

As for the greater part of Thomas Wolfe's manuscripts being torn out and thrown into the waste-basket, it is not true. Not a page was thrown into the waste-basket. A good deal of what was in "The Angel" [1] was removed, and a great deal of that was used in "Of Time and the River." [2] A great deal was removed from "Of Time and the River" and was used in the two later novels[3] which Harpers published. Almost nothing of what Tom wrote failed to appear in print except much that was so unfinished, as he himself thought, that it could not be published. But that too would have been revised by Tom and would have appeared, if Tom had lived.

As for Tom not being in a position to resist sabotage, why not? He had a contract. We were bound to publish everything he wrote except what was libellous and obscene—what would have endangered him with the law. The truth is that nothing was ever taken from Tom's writings without his full consent. When he could go no further with "Of Time and the River," he brought it to me and asked me to help him, and I did it with very great reluctance and anxiety. Tom *demanded* help. He *had* to have it. No one who did not know him could possibly understand it, but he would get into a state of such desperation that one realized that if he were not enabled to complete his book soon, something very serious would happen to him. He intended to proceed in the same way with Harpers. He called his book, which they made into two books,[4] "finished," when it was not at all. And he knew that, and he expected to work with Edward Aswell [5] as he had with me. What's more, I know Aswell's feeling about the matter, one of great anxiety for fear he would do damage. You seem to know only one kind of editor, and it is not the kind that I know. Certain authors absolutely demand help, and if it is not given them they will go to another publisher to get it. But most real writers do not. Most of them know what they want to do, and do it. Nobody ever edited Hemingway, beyond excising a line or two for fear of libel or other legal dangers.

Then you speak of fun being poked at Tom because of the hugeness of his manuscripts—because he delivered a packingcase from a truck. In fact, it was a taxicab. You say he was ridiculed. To my

1 *Look Homeward, Angel,* Scribners, 1929.

2 Scribners, 1935.

3 *The Web and the Rock,* Harpers, 1939; *You Can't Go Home Again,* Harpers, 1940.

4 *The Web and the Rock* and *You Can't Go Home Again.*

5 The editor at Harper and Bros. who was in charge of the publication of Thomas Wolfe's books after he had left Scribners.

knowledge, he was not. He was admired. This peculiarity of his genius was interesting and was told about for that reason, just as such peculiarities as that of De Quincey, in working in a room until it was so full of papers and books, etc., that there was no room for him and so he locked it up and got another, were told about. It was not ridicule. It was affectionate admiring surprise. When Tom's book[1] came here, it was instantly recognized as a work of genius, and we were all excited about it, and it was read in sections by three of us at once. It was too long, and there was one big cut[2] of about 70 pages at the beginning, concerned with events which did not seem to come within the scope of Eugene's story, for they related to things before Eugene's birth, and remote from Altamont. Tom fully agreed that this cut should be made. I have a wonderful letter he wrote to his old teacher,[3] telling how he came here, and when we mentioned certain passages that were pretty rough he said he would take them out, and we said, by God he wouldn't, that they were among the best things in the book. You don't know what you are talking about. Even a good deal of that first part got into the later books in improved form. It is a long and complicated story. It may not interest you, but you have absolutely misrepresented the situation.

As for Henry Miller, I haven't read enough of him perhaps to be a qualified judge, but from what I have read, I should fully agree with you and Bunny Wilson.[4] But I suspect that the reason he cannot get published is that he does not sell. Publishers do have to think about that. It is like a law of nature. They would have to do it even under communism.

Anyhow, from what I have read of the rest of your book, which is a good deal, you have said many right and true things that have not been said before. Editors aren't much, and can't be. They can only help a writer realize himself, and they can ruin him if he's pliable, as Tom was not. That is why the editors I know shrink from tampering with a manuscript and do it only when it is required of them by the author, as it was by Tom. When an editor gets to think differently from that, to think he knows more about a writer's book than the writer—and some do—he is dead, done for, and dangerous. When he thinks he is a discoverer because he

1 *Look Homeward, Angel,* Scribners, 1929.

2 There were many other deletions of material used elsewhere in later books. This one cut may, in parts, have been lost to print—but not the best of it.

3 Margaret Roberts (Mrs. J. M. Roberts) of Asheville, N. C. Excerpts from Wolfe's letters to her were published in the *Atlantic Monthly* during 1946-1947.

4 Edmund Wilson had expressed admiration for the writing of Henry Miller.

doesn't fail to recognize talent—was a jeweler ever praised because he knew a diamond from a lump of glass?—he is a stuffed shirt, and through. But I've known it to happen.

As to libel, I shall look up the law. But I think suit can be brought until one year after the sale of a book has ceased. But my suit would ask no more compensation than would meet the expense, since the purpose would be only to show that what you said was grossly untrue, ignorant, and injurious. On the other hand, from what else I've read of your book—such as that refutation of those silly so-called laws or rules of fiction, since genius can break any law and indeed always does—I think you spoke from misinformation and irresponsibility, and so I should prefer to let the matter lie until—if there is a chance of that—you come to New York and will give me an interview. I don't like quarrels, and I hate the law, but I can't by silence seem to acquiesce in what you have written, for if you now think it is the truth, you will then have grounds to assume that it is.

Ever truly yours,

Excerpt from a letter to
an unidentified author

I have read a good deal of your novel about the editor. You obviously regard me with contempt for approving the publication of such books as "The Women on the Porch," [1] although it seems to me that, if one wants to look at it from a moral point of view, it is of value to show what frustration and futility our present civilization produces. But if I were what you had supposed, if I remained the helpless employee of an organization in which I disbelieved, and which I thought was what you think it is, I should be utterly despicable in my own eyes too. That would be the lowest thing possible.

Then, in the end, you have your editor go out for himself as a publisher, on the basis of certain resolutions. One of these is, to my mind, a complete betrayal of his profession—that he will only publish books which will coincide with his own views. If he is that kind of man, let him speak for himself and be a writer. But the function of a publisher in society is to furnish a means by which anyone of a certain level of intelligence and abilities can express his views. A publisher should not be, as such, a partisan, however strongly partisan he may be as an individual. If he allows his partisanship to govern him in his choice of books, he is a traitor to the public. He

[1] A novel by Caroline Gordon, Scribners, 1944.

is supposed to furnish a forum for the free play of the intellect, in so far as he possibly can. That is the whole American theory—that opinions can be given a means of full expression, and that the public, hearing all of them and considering them, will eventually approximate a right conclusion. Every profession has its own particular code of ethics, its own morality, that its members must adhere to or they betray it. And a primary element in the morality of the publisher is that he shall not let his own personal views obstruct the way for the expression of counter-views. I should say that no individual in this House, for instance, is a believer in communism. But when we got so fine a book as "Soviet Communism: A New Civilization," by Beatrice and Sidney Webb, who have been lifelong students of social questions, we felt that it was our obligation to publish it. Then the ways of the Russian system would be ably set forth, and the arguments for it, and the American citizen could, from that source and others, form his own opinion. The American idea is that public opinion rules, and the American publisher's idea is that it is his duty to get individual opinions bearing upon issues before the public in order that it may be given the materials from which public opinion may competently crystallize.

Ever sincerely yours,

May 31, 1944

DEAR——:

Your novel has been read by several of us, and we are very sorry that we have had to conclude that we cannot make an offer of publication. It is quite readable and has vitality, but, in general, it is our impression that you have not yet sufficiently mastered the technique which is necessary to present its thesis impressively and logically. Apart from this general consideration, your conception of publishing houses and their function in society is quite contrary to the reality—at least, you have not established its validity. It is clear that publishing houses, even as churches and hospitals, etc., can function only on a stable financial basis. The ideal of publishing would be a forum where all sections of humanity could have their say, whether their object was to instruct, entertain, horrify, etc. Nevertheless, there are certain rules of quality and relevance, which can only be determined by some sort of selection and this the publisher, representing humanity at large, attempts—with many mistakes—to make. Or, to put it differently, artists, saints, and the other more sentient representatives of the human race are, as it were, on the frontiers of time—pioneers and guides to the future.

And the publisher, in the capacity mentioned, must make some sort of estimate of the importance and validity of their reports, and there is nothing he can base this on but the abilities to judge that God has given him.

I realize that our correspondence is futile and had better be ended, but I should like to say, if you'll let me, that I knew from your face that you were an utterly sincere and good person.

We are returning the manuscript to you under separate cover.

Ever sincerely yours,

Oct. 3, 1944

DEAR——:

It is very hard for me to express a certain uneasiness I feel about——, because it is really instinctive, though backed by experience. It is, first, that books written in anticipation of events and developments often lose a great deal of the relevance they are intended to have because things develop quite, or somewhat, differently.

Another consideration is that a writer does best what comes entirely from himself, and not so well in carrying out the ideas of others. This I know, considerably, from having myself suggested books to writers who had nothing at the moment and wanted to write. Such books were always below their best, though sometimes successful.

A third reason is that the best fiction does not arise out of an idea at all, but the idea, or argument, arises out of the human elements and characters as they naturally develop. And this seems to apply particularly to——, because her nature is to begin a book without knowing the conclusion, or even the steps of development, so that the development and conclusions come from the situation and the people.

Your idea I think is a good one except for the reasons given above, and they *may* not apply. I cannot tell about it. Apart from an uneasy feeling that comes from these considerations, I should be all for the plan. Anyhow, if——wants to do it, as I think she does very much, we could be sure that the outcome would be what we should regard with great favor—even though it fell below her best work. We are for whatever she may do. Anyhow, she has at present to complete "——," and I thought we might be able to see more clearly what the probabilities for "——" would be by the time that was done.

Ever sincerely yours,

TO G. P. BRETT, JR.

Sept. 27, 1946

DEAR MR. BRETT:[1]

I am afraid I cannot coöperate with you as fully as I should wish in this matter because I did not read "Forever Amber." [2] I did look it over, to see what it was like, and my impression was that it was an honest piece of work and that, in respect to the great events of the Restoration and the character of the King and his brother, it was historically good—particularly the plague and the fire. I thought, too, that the ending was quite admirable. From what I saw of those doings that might result in what might be legally called obscenity, I should not suppose that there was anything in the book that could rightly be so described. The events were rather referred to as happening, than described. There was no attempt, that I could see, at salaciousness.

That is all I can say about the book because, as you know, a man becomes an editor because he loves books and then finds that he cannot possibly get time to read the books of any other publisher than the one he works for. That is too bad.

As to censorship of literature, while I must agree that there are sometimes books which are deliberately contrived to appeal to vicious instincts, I believe that freedom of speech is the very basis of this nation, and that what damage, if any, may come from such books should be risked because of the much greater damage that would come if the principles of censorship were introduced and progressed. Nobody knows who is qualified to exercise censorship. I have read the opinions of various people of high repute, in the *Journal American* "Crusade" against salacious or obscene books, and most of them seem to me to have no understanding of literature at all. They constantly assert that writers introduced an element of salaciousness, as they called it, into books to make them sell. A true writer never wants to introduce that element. He does it because his book is a revelation of life—and life should be revealed as it is—and he generally hates it just as much as any genteel reader or censor, and generally much more, for he is bound to be a sensitive person if he is a true writer.

Ever sincerely yours,

The Scribner files reveal many instances in which Perkins made similar detailed suggestions, to a great variety of writers, but the

[1] President of the Macmillan Company.

[2] A novel by Kathleen Winsor, Macmillan, 1944.

following, like one or two other letters of the same sort in this collection, has been selected as representative.

TO MARCIA DAVENPORT

April 28, 1947

DEAR MARCIA:

I think you have written a notable book[1] in a first draught but that it needs, as any book, to be revised. The revision should be almost only a matter of emphasis, for the scheme is right. Having borne the heat of the battle, you must not fail it now. It is a book about a person, Jessie, but it is also about New York, and that must never be forgotten. Jessie is a New Yorker who came out of the East Side and the West Side. In one week many things occur, quite naturally, which change her life and herself. In telling of these you should always keep the reader aware of New York, as you mostly do: when Jessie recalls the past, she should still be aware of the present, in motors, cabs, or walking, or in bed, or in a bath—as people always are. New York is a foremost character in the novel. Jessie is in a crisis of her own life, in New York, but in all her reflections, here and there, she is in the place she came out of, New York, and is aware of it. So you give New York, top to bottom, and that alone is a great thing to do. Make Jessie more aware, as she goes about in cars, cabs and afoot, of the way New York is, of how Fifth Avenue looks in the haze of afternoon, or whatever, even when she is lost in the past. This means that you should emphasize what you have already done. A person, like Jessie, walks or drives along a street in deep reflection, but is still aware of how it looks, and of its *quality*. So get that in more, by a touch here and there, to make this book realize one of its great motives, to give New York as only an East Side, West Side New Yorker knows it. You have done this, really, but emphasize it—and the fact that these Park Avenuers, etc., don't belong to it, don't really like it, but that the children of immigrants who never got out of it, even Jessie and Mark and others, do belong and love it and couldn't for long be anywhere else. So make the book say that, by blending Jessie's present with the past as she recalls it. The reader must be aware of time and place, as it is and as she remembers it. That is what you intended, and means only an occasional reference to give a sense—by sight or smell or whatever—of a spot of New York. In truth, I only know this from what you have said and written, so you have done it. But strengthen it. For instance, you tell of her in a taxicab as being *oblivious* to the ugliness

[1] *East Side, West Side,* Scribners, 1947.

of the street. I think she should be *aware*. People are oblivious only momentarily. And in this book that gives New York through Jessie, you must not have her oblivious unless she has to be—which would be briefly. I ought not to be telling you, because you told me: maybe the biggest thing this book can do is to give a realization of this unique place, New York.

But the book is also about Jessie, who is an indigenous New Yorker, as her mother, the child of immigrants, was. Her character and talent brought her into wealth, and into the society of the upper East Side, but never even blurred her sense of reality, her sense of values. Jessie, her daughter, would have inherited and learned that sense of things, and so, as you have it, she would, as she did, have worked. (I think you should have had her work on the *World,* and not on a literary-sounding review.) She gave up working when she married—this should be made plain—which was even more natural for her when the depression made those who had money, or some, feel ashamed to keep a job from someone who needed it. But in the week of the book, and early in it, I think you should show that it was on Jessie's conscience that she was not pulling her weight, as it would be. And at the end of the book you should show, perhaps even in only a paragraph, that she was through with that, that this week of crisis had changed her, and restored her sense of values—those of her mother and, I hope we could say, of all true New Yorkers. Anyhow, New Yorkers are not fooled by any pomps and vanities or by the sinful lusts of the flesh. They know them for what they are, and may like them, but they reverence nothing. Jessie is real and not unhuman, but she is too much always in the right and Brandon too much in the wrong. About that I don't know what you can do, except by having Jessie realize that in some ways she had been exasperating, and by the use of two more outside scenes. You have the one where the two women who knew her recall Rosa Landan. One could say this violated the scheme of your book—that all should be presented through Jessie's senses. That scene is essential, I think. But it would be less obtrusive if you added *two* others, and one of them could be where people commented on Jessie, and more or less unfavorably. But the great thing is to have Jessie come out of this book as a woman different from when she went in. That you must do. She's been through too much to be the same. It was a week of culmination. It must end, must indicate a changed life for Jessie. Must be conclusive.

So much for generalizations—forgive me for telling you what I know you know and most of which you told me—and now to come to particulars. Perhaps for that I should have kept the manuscript by me. But I did make notations on the margin, up to the last hundred or hundred and fifty pages. There was nothing to be said against them, I thought, except that some of the speeches were too long to be natural, though great novelists have made them so and perhaps rightly. Writing, like drawing, is an art, and whatever conveys the *meaning* is justified. But I think, as we are today, that when Mark talks so long among his people, without interruption and a fresh start, or even Jerome Block (who is grand), the effect is reduced, because it seems unnatural. Just consider this a little. If I'm right, a few trifling interpolations, here and there, will make amends.

You say you will have to rewrite the first chapter in the light of the last, and that is right in principle, but I have no fault to find with it. But work it in there that she has worked and thinks she should. And I think there should be more about Matthew Kernan.

I put a note on page 30, which said: "Generalizations are no use —give one specific thing and let the action say it." Can't recall the instance, but it's true. By the way, don't they still have an orchestra on the Staten Island boats—they do on others—and would you be phony to have one play for Jessie and Mark, some old-time song? They could ask for it. Even if not true, I think it would be fair. They have music on the ferry to Blauvelt.

I should have kept the manuscript, but look at notes on pages. When you have people talking, you have a scene. You must interrupt with explanatory paragraphs, but shorten them as much as you can. Dialogue is *action*. You can't take the reader's attention from it much without impairing its effect. Think of watching a duel, with someone explaining the *why* of it. I think this was about Millicent, that there you do too much explaining. The action and dialogue, which is action, should do it. They can't do it altogether, but you don't trust them enough. You must interpolate and explain, but you tend to overdo it.

The truth is you're right, you can't see a book before the end. It must be revised in the light of the end. Now there are two weak scenes in this book, where you were "planting" things that have to be there. They are weak only at the start, where you tell, expositionally, of the various people present. Ideally, you should let them come in and *reveal* themselves in talk and action. You can't, but I think you should trust more to the talk and action. One scene is the committee meeting and the other is the Stillman dinner. (Let me put this in as I think of it: You must make people talk, as they do, in elision. Not, "You will," but "You'll" etc., all through.)

On page 55, or thereabouts, I have made a note that your exposition stops the action for too long, that too much is explained that comes out anyhow.

Lorraine and the dog are very good, and might even be somewhat enlarged upon. She is a real type, all over New York's East Side.

A little thereafter, Jessie is preparing dinner, shelling peas. And she remembers about Brandon and how he had acted. In this, while she is remembering, you should still have Jessie aware of New York.

Wherever you bring in the sounds of the East River, and the scene, you always do wonders, and I don't think you could overdo it.

Chapter 6, page 111. The Stillmans' dinner party. I have commented on this. It just needs to be pulled together and organized. More should be said by the action and the talk. It gets to be all right when Mark turns up, but I think you might make more of Stillman's telephonitis, and if you could explain the characters by what they did and said, in the early part of the chapter, it would be better. Then they go home. Just emphasize New York. Couldn't you make more of their drive up, I think, Fifth Avenue in the dark, in brief description, which you do excellently well. But about Mark and herself, I think you explain what the reader gets by inference. What they say and do tells all. You tend to explain too much. You must explain, but your tendency is to distrust your own narrative and dialogue.

I may be getting out of order, not having the manuscript, but when they have that dinner before the play, you explain too much. Once they get to talking, everything is right.

Now we come to Thursday. My notes say, "Cut down Anna and Sarah somewhat." The cat, Putzl, is good and he, or she, should be brought in several times, later in the story, and not just here.

Now we come to the committee meeting. Make the people come out through talk and act, just as far as you possibly can. Avoid all possible exposition. You introduce characters, such as Althea Crowe, who reveal themselves in what they say and do. But then you stop the narrative to explain what should come out in the movement of the story.

When Mark comes to dine with Jessie, you have the chance to bring out all about her work—the work she did on the *World*—and why she isn't doing it now. She could just simply say it. She could tell why she stopped.

Wednesday. This is where she remembers the agonizing time when, because Brandon wanted it, she was pregnant. Helen Lee comes and, after Helen Lee goes, she remembers. But even here, along with her remembrance, you should keep her aware of the present. It is Jessie *now,* remembering her mother's death.

I think the brief chapter which breaks into the scheme of the book, where Serena and her friend, waiting for Serena's car, talk of Jessie, is admirable. But since you have to have this chapter, I think it would be well, as I have said, to have two other chapters, and in one of them you could have people talk about Jessie in a way to show that she was fallible herself.

Iris's call is good, very effective in showing the aspect of New York life that she represents. If anything, it might be enlarged upon.

Then, when Jessie is in her bath she remembers. This is a good example of what I mean. She would be absorbed in her memories, but still she would be aware of her bath, and of the sound of the river, and of New York. She should realize at the same time, through interpolations of the present, both the past and the present.

Again, after they realize the deadly character of Rosa's illness and go there to dinner, which is good, Brandon wants her to have a child. She agrees to it. This is told in memory and somehow, during those memories, the reader should be aware of what was going on in the present. I forget exactly where she was, but at one time her memories come while she is walking. There, too, I think you ought to break in upon her abstractions with things she notices, so that the reader will be conscious of the present, as she would be, even while the concentration is upon the past. Always the present and New York should be kept in.

I did think that perhaps you overdo Brandon's brutality during the period when she was in all those agonies of pregnancy. I have a note, "Around page 319: too obstetrical and should be cut, and compressed."

Then, we come to her going to market, and that is very good. And then, later, to the theater. There is the dinner party at the night club, before it, and there you begin again with too much generalization. Try to make the people stand out through the dialogue and action. I think they almost would do it alone, but you do not put enough confidence into your dialogue and action.

Then you come to the play. Everything is right with this, excepting that it would be better if you could give some running account of the action of the play. I know what play it was, I suppose, and I realize that you do not want to put that failure before the reader, for the sake of the author. But couldn't you just give snatches of some imaginary play, so as to make the whole thing more actual? Couldn't you invent a play, of which you would only have to give trifles, that was somewhat parallel to the real one?

The Elizabeth Betts incident of the party is extremely good. The rest, I think, might stand compression.

You really know all about this book yourself. It is true that Althea's loyalty—though one knows right away what kind of person she was and that she would be loyal—should be based upon something more than the reader is given. I do think you should account for this, for her strong feeling for Jessie, through Jessie's memory.

I do have some fear that the murder runs too far toward melodrama, but not so much in what quite plausibly happens. But, in revision, I would think of that danger. When Serena Lowdon tells them off, she does it wonderfully. Even so, I would try to compress what she says, because I think she too speaks at greater length than people actually do speak at unless they have been prepared in advance, which she was not. She was speaking out of her emotions and her character, without forethought. I have argued to that effect about Mark's talk to his people, which is very good, as they are, and about Bloch. Mark begins to speak on page 530, I think. I would try to have more questions thrown in while he is speaking.

I have referred to it before. It is on page 593, where you have Jessie oblivious. The story is told through Jessie's senses almost wholly, and she must not be oblivious. You might be, for a block or so, but when you were stopped by a traffic light it would bring you back to awareness of the present.

I have referred to the Staten Island ferry. I hope you can find it rightful to have music on it, and that maybe they could ask for some old New York song. I think you could do it, even if they do not any longer have three-piece orchestras there.

If this book can give the quality of New York and show the wonderful people, mostly the descendants of immigrants, as the real New Yorkers, and also at the same time show the corruption among people of wealth and supposedly of culture, who just live here without belonging, it will be a very great achievement in that alone. It could be simply the story of Jessie, a woman whose life comes to a week of crisis in which she must come to conclusions with all the most important things in her life. That would be enough in itself. But if you can only get all this meaning into it—and it is in it, in fact—about New York, and also the situation the world is in, which comes out when she goes with Mark to visit his Czech relatives, you will have done wonders. To accomplish this, you need only to intensify throughout what actually is there—and I think you would naturally do this in the revision, anyhow. It is largely a matter of compression, and not so much of that, really. It is, as you said, that you can't know a book until you come to the end of it, and then all the rest must be modified to fit that.

Always yours,

June 4, 1947

DEAR ——:

This is in answer to your letter of May 29[1] with regard to certain passages in the tale of Aladdin in "The Arabian Nights." We deeply sympathize, as individuals, with the development of better understanding among all groups, but we do not think that in this country there should be any groups, as was the intention of its Founders, and we deplore, as individuals, the development of group consciousness. While we are, therefore, wholly in favor of the intentions of your League,[2] it does not seem to us as publishers that it would be proper for us to edit a classic of some centuries' standing. Only the author would have the right to do that, it seems to us, and if we did it, we should in some degree betray an obligation to our profession.

Nowadays, publishers are under pressure from all sorts of groups. What if they should trim their books to suit every point of view and every element of religious and racial pride? What, then, would remain of that one relatively free realm left, the republic of letters?

Ever sincerely yours,

1 A letter requesting the removal, in future editions, of certain passages involving Jewish characters.
2 The Anti-Defamation League.

John Farrar

In this diverse selection from his recent editor-to-author correspondence, John Farrar's integrity, idealism, generosity, wry humor and technical virtuosity as an editor are displayed—to use one of Mr. Farrar's own favorite words (in speaking of pet authors)—"brilliantly."

Both the novice and veteran editor will find much to learn from and admire in Mr. Farrar's various approaches to authors and their problems. He can be gentle, cautionary, folksy as a fox, stern and delighted —it all depends on what the author needs at that moment in his relationship with Mr. Farrar. Whatever his tone is, however, Mr. Farrar, one of the last of the still-practicing editor-publishers of "the old school," maintains the traditions of that great age in American publishing when a firm's list, in the main, represented the personal taste, high standards and convictions of the editor-publisher and not the characterless compromises of today's many board-and-broker-run houses.

Most of my letters to authors have been lost through the years, buried in the files of other publishing houses or strayed otherwhere. It occurred to me, however, that some of the letters I have written to authors this year might give a picture of how one man, and, to a certain degree, one publishing house, feel about the disarrayed state of current publishing and its effect on the author. It's to be understood that the letters reflect my personal opinions and not necessarily those of my partners and associates, though I might add that we are fortunate in our many agreements.

John Farrar

A question which has interested me for years. I am happy to say that Mr. Richard M. Baker agreed to let us be explicit in our description of his situation.

DEAR DICK:

Your letter of November 15th is one of the finest letters I have ever received, and it made me proud of you—prouder than ever.

So far as my own health is concerned, it is all right, except for a bout with laryngitis. You can really rest easy about it; my doctors have always been honest with me, and there is no reason for supposing that they are not, in this case. Naturally, one cannot expect to live forever, but apparently this particular episode has reached a happy conclusion.

For many years I have firmly believed that to keep facts under cover that have a direct bearing on an author's work is unwise from all kinds of points of view. Not to come out right at the start and say that you have multiple sclerosis would mean that, sooner or later, if the book makes the effect I believe it will, or even if it doesn't, many questions will be brought up which will have to be answered.

I suppose there will be some people who will think, as they did with our Dr. Thomas Dooley, that we are, you are, exploiting illness. This cannot be helped. Your own life and ideals are the things that made your book, since it deals so poignantly and in such great detail with experiences and, oddly enough with experiences that you didn't have. It is bound to excite curiosity, and there is really no possible way to make of you a mystery, since you and your family have so many friends; and, after all, you are not completely isolated from the world. Why people are always trying to pull down the good men of the world, I don't know. Tom Dooley was dedicated. And how much more important a national symbol he was than, say, Frank Sinatra! I also suspect that he was a saint. Saints were always thorny characters.

I find the same difficulty confronting me with a well-known woman who has written an extraordinary first novel and for some reason doesn't want anyone to know that she has written it. She may indeed put a pseudonym on the book, but it never helps. Sooner or later, particularly in these days of highly personal reporting, it is bound to be discovered. In fact, many years ago, when Lady Jones wrote *Serena Blandish,* anonymously, there was a document as I remember it, in our safe saying that we were bound not to disclose who had written it. It was not too long, in spite of everything we could do, before it was discovered. Her other writing name is, you'll remember, Enid Bagnold.

The most successful secret of this kind was long, long before and I was not involved in it. Basil King wrote *The Wild Olive* and other great best sellers under a woman's name.

The various Patrick Dennis pseudonyms and games also didn't work for long.

Forgive me if I seem to be writing you an essay on the subject, but I hope you will bear with me, for I took the matter into my own hands, and have put on the back of the jacket the following:

"Richard M. Baker, Jr. was born in Worcester, Massachusetts in 1924, was graduated from Bowdoin College, and now lives with his wife and five children in South Portland, Maine. He started as a public accountant. However, in 1957 he decided to make writing his career, 'to gamble on writing and leave tax accounting behind.' He is a victim of multiple sclerosis, severely handicapped, and likely to be more so in the future. He does not mind talking of this, partly to encourage other handicapped people, partly because his handicap lay behind the impulse that led him to writing. Mr. Baker has never been to Japan, volunteered for the Army but was only in it briefly. Everything in this strong and compelling book is the result of years of research and of the reconstruction of events and the creation of characters by his powerful imagination."

In this respect, another interesting parallel is that of R. C. Hutchinson whose first book was about Africa, the next about Germany, and the next about Russia. There were all creations of his imagination, and he had never been to any of these places.

You must, of course, expect the reviewers may spend some time talking about this, but to repeat myself, I do believe that putting the facts right on the line is the best thing to do.

In the last part of the book (with your permission for cuts), I have toned down the episodes with the Negro girl, and some of the explicit material in the final scenes with Michiyo. It seemed to me and to some other readers here to give the effect of coyness on her part, and almost a feeling of vulgarity. Not that I don't presume that she would have acted in this way, but by this time you are telling a real love story and that is the note, I believe, on which the book should end. I do not think that you will find that it detracts from the power of the story. Of course, I have added nothing.

I would love to have a copy of the photograph, and please do sign it.

All my very best,

DEAR MRS. ——:

Thank you for your kind and appreciative letter. Of course I meant it when I said you could call on me for future suggestions.

You say: "It would help me immensely if you could find time to mention a couple of publishing houses which in your opinion might be interested to see my novel. The agent I tried had not time to handle my work. I do not plan to approach another literary agent, for I have concluded that most agents are concerned only with the Established Name or the Genius. If I had an independent income I would like to found an agency which did not need to concern itself with profit, but could afford to offer guidance and marketing services to writers of promise as yet unpublished. Lacking such an agency I shall send my novel out myself, and would be immensely grateful for any suggestions you might have. I realize that to some extent the book falls into the "old-fashioned" and "romantic" categories, and so would find a place on selected publishing lists only. My difficulty; which lists?"

I remember that you told me certain publishers have already seen your novel. Forgive me if I do not dig back into our pleasant, lengthy correspondence to check. Here is a list of eight publishing firms I think might well be interested.

Perhaps it is best in your case to send out the novel yourself. However, I ought to point out that while agents, too, must make a living, most of them do take an interest in writers of promise. I'm doubtful that a subsidized agency would prove practical or effective from any point of view, any more than would a subsidized publishing house, with the exception of special interest publishing houses such as the university presses. It is true that these days some of the agencies are forced to husband their time because of the high overhead. When they have refused to take you on, I suspect it is honestly because they feel that for one reason or another they could not place your work.

As I pointed out in earlier letters, it is my opinion that what is wrong with your novel in its present form is not that it is "old-fashioned" or "romantic" but that it is, first, too long for its purpose, and that the purpose itself is not clear. You have definite ideas you wish to impose on your readers, and you also wish to write a good story in the Romantic tradition. There is no reason why you should not accomplish this, but, somehow you haven't, or so I believe. There would undoubtedly be several ways to triumph over this difficulty. Any editor wishing to help or suggest a remedy would, I fear, find you both puzzled and argumentative. This has been true in the past, hasn't it? I can sympathize with your own belief that the book, if published in the form you desire, would find readers. Yet, you have now had a number of professional opinions to the contrary. There is, of course, the possibility that they have been mistaken. Nonetheless, you must face the world of writing and publishing as it is.

From your various letters I do conclude that you are loath to change the novel, or at any rate that your arguments in support of your own point of view incline to be long and complex. This, in itself, can be frightening to an editor or agent.

My hope is that if you do find an editor who is enthusiastic about the possibilities of the novel, you keep an open mind about his suggestions and do not overwhelm him in lengthy rebuttal. Your reply to this will undoubtedly be that it is your book and that you wish it to remain so. I'd be the last person to maintain that books have not been harmed by insensitive and mistaken editing. The dilemma exists and each author must finally decide whether honestly offered criticism can be accepted and made a part of his own thinking and re-writing.

With my best regards,

To a young writer, at work on his first novel:

DEAR ALEX:

Now that I have finished reading the re-written parts of your novel I must tell you how strongly I admire the way in which you have acquired technical skills you did not show in earlier drafts. You and I always knew how well you could write, and how far you can go, but to find that your powerful drive and nervous energy can summon up such disciplined patience, is even more exciting than when I first read your work.

One of the things I like first about you, Alex, and about working with you, is that you don't ask for answers but accept hints, run away with them and manage to come up with your own answers.

I have gone over the first chapters carefully again, looking for the big words, the clichés, the repetitions, the usual faults of a re-write done for overall effect rather than detail. This section is, as you know, the most difficult part of the book. (By the way, if you like, it might make sense to call this Part One. There is a real break when Quentin goes back to the South.)

What I like most now in this first part is that you have prepared for all that follows, and yet kept your preparation subtle and almost concealed. You are dealing here with material which is, I suppose in a sense sensational, and you face it honestly but with good taste and sensitivity. There is a great (here's a word I have cautioned *you* not to use too much) difference between the suggestion and the ability to suggest. Your complicated hero has become understandable now. You do not mean him to be sympathetic, nor can he be, until the last part of the book. Even then, he must remain somewhat of an enigma, a product of the time, but, by

Heaven, Alex, you, the author (this seems to be full of exclamation marks, another bad habit I deplore in others. And I don't much care for parentheses either, you'll remember.) never pule nor whine! Bless you, for that!

You are giving us fresh material. I don't know of any book like it. You could have written it with ugliness and crudity. Instead, you have chosen to give us the effect without the deliberate coarseness. And there is nothing prissy about your book. When you need a strong word, you use it. Your dialogue is excellent, often brilliant. When you tackle a strong scene, whether it is in the barracks room or the bedroom, it is alive; but always, these scenes, whether they detail the normal or the perverse, are a part of the fabric, belong to the book.

The most important thing left for you to consider now, is the texture of your style. In characterization, in the big scenes, in the dialogue, you are yourself and you are damn good. But in connecttions, in the troublesome "say words," in various other necessary utilitarian paraphernalia of the novel you stumble. This is easily fixed in consultation. But, of course, you want it also to become part of yourself. That is why I sent you a copy of *Pride and Prejudice* and a copy of Ted Morrison's new book and suggest you read them. You should also read C. P. Snow. There seems to be a singular devil abroad in the schools and colleges these days that suggests a kind of tasteless jargon in the underpinnings of style. This will not ever get you where *you* wish to go and where you shall go!

I look forward to Saturday. We'll tackle Part One to an accompaniment of Beethoven. Happy New Year. May it see the publication of the novel. By the way, everyone except me, is satisfied with the tentative title. For some reason, it suggests Sloan Wilson to me, and while I respect his abilities, the echo isn't good enough for you.

Ever,

A letter I include for several rather special reasons. For one, the "young writer" is working on his beautiful first novel at the age of seventy-one.

MY DEAR FATHER ——:

It is, I'm afraid, presumptuous of me to write what follows. When you realize how enthusiastic I am about the book, you will perhaps absolve me. There is every chance that I may be wrong about a number of my suggestions. As the book progresses, it becomes the story of a remarkable human being, and that is assuredly one kind of novel. Most of my notes are intended to make the reader, laymen in particular, more aware of Fr. Martin and more concerned over him at an earlier point.

The most remarkable fact to me is that you could, in your first draft, and in your first novel, succeed so well.

I am sorry that I cannot get to the monastery before Christmas, and I realize that since you do not have the manuscript, some of these points may not be clear. Since it is a unique manuscript we must not trust it to the mails, and, besides, as I promised to do, I have made check marks and minor points on the manuscript itself which might be baffling to you. We must have our conversation? Conference? Meditation?

The notes follow. One of my chief difficulties in writing them was one we share; trying not to use the words *fine, beautiful, inspiring,* over and over again.

Hoping that I shall be seeing you before too long,

Faithfully,

Notes on the author's novel:

On p. 2, before Fr. Martin visits the communities, it would help if you were to give us a flashback to some childhood episode, some look at his earlier life so that the general reader, the less-informed layman, perhaps could form a human and simple picture of our hero, so to say.

Also it would be good, perhaps to visualize the Aunt before she tells him of her vision and to expand this episode by a paragraph or two. It seems to me you throw it away, while with some extension and some use of sounds and possibly colors it would more strongly affect the reader. After all, you and I may have been privileged to see angels and converse with them, but it's not precisely an ordinary occurrence! And "Pillar of Light" is the theme of the book.

The meditation before his "second conversion" could well be expanded. Here, also, some relation of a former episode in his life that had made his "anti-everything" would help.

Chapter II ends somewhat abruptly.

After "This lecture made a great impression on Father Martin's mind," I feel we need to have a meditation or another episode related to outside life. My own preference here would be one of your fine and inspiring meditations.

I have no suggestions for the Requiem chapter. It has dignity, tenderness and depth.

On p. 39 in the lovely Advent and Christmas chapter—and it *is* lovely—at the bottom of p. 39 things would again be strengthened and pulled together if we had a flashback (and I am not at any time suggesting long additions) which would let us see him at another time when he perhaps did not realize that Christmas was "a feast of light as well as joy."

Chapter V. Here again we have a chapter trailing off. I have no specific suggestion. Possibly, again a personal meditation by Fr. Martin. Possibly a feeling of inadequacy as he thinks of conducting his own first retreat. Possibly wondering if his prayer life is wrong. I'm sure you'll solve this but I'd cut that last sentence. It sounds as though you wrote it because you couldn't quite figure out what else to do.

By p. 66 when the Devil again appears, had Fr. Martin conducted retreats so that he knew how popular he was or does this go back to his former parish work? This should be made clear. If he has had retreats, I believe we should be shown one. Also, to describe which one of the "works" the bishop suggested appealed to him and why?

When he goes home to make his final decision about his vocation, why not a line or two about what sort of friend it was with whom he goes mountain climbing. Did they perhaps pray together?

I have no suggestions on "Profession." It is serene and filled with a sense of devotion. The sermon on "Holy Hope" is strong and, of course, applicable to all Christian living as well as monastic living.

The entire "Jubilee" chapter holds the interest and seems most helpful.

The conference on Plainsong is informative, absorbing and clear. The conference on "Baroque" is, as you know, controversial, but bold and convincing. There are many who will say that the most beautiful of the "modern" churches follow somewhat similar principals and are not like factories. Did you happen to see Kidder Smith's article on church architecture in the new edition of the Encyclopedia Britannica?

The conference on penance is excellent and so is the one describing "Corpus Christi."

Some of the material in the first four pages of "The Guestmaster" is an exact repetition of material used earlier. This is easily remedied by referring to the earlier material, saying that Father Martin used it here, then giving only such points as are new or freshly said.

The meditation on "The Way of the Cross" is striking. But again, the end of the chapter is probably too swift; a paragraph or two more about his possible inner struggles would help.

"Holy Week" is graphic, has color and sound. (Forgive a personal note here. It was my good fortune to attend my first retreat at Holy Cross on the Palm Sunday week-end. Your description brings back the wonder and the awe.)

"Problem" is human and revealing. The story of Stephen shows this type of modern rebellion clearly and your appreciation of objective psychiatry most helpful. I could wish you would add a few more words on analysis and psychiatry. So much fun is made of it these days that I hope it will be made clearer and clearer how freeing (at its best) it can be to clear the mind for the reception of the Lord. The sermon on Cowboys and Indians is certainly refreshing!

The "Failure" chapter is poignant. Nothing more needed here!

In "Night" you have succeeded in conveying this terrifying period, so difficult to describe and so difficult to survive. Perhaps you do not need the last sentence.

There is nothing I dare say about "Light", If you are as honest as I believe you are, in spite of your humility, you know that it is truly beautiful.

This young man is gifted and will probably one day write a good book. He did not answer this letter. He had said in his letter to me that a couple of other publishers had seen the novel and, from their letters to him, had obviously not read it. He felt he "deserved" a reaction. Well, I bless him. I hope he lets me see his next book.

DEAR ——:

I'm sorry to have been so long writing you about your novel. It arrived at the Club while I was in the hospital. My recovery has been good but the convalescence has been slow, and concentrating on reading was one of the things that was difficult.

I did promise to read your book, I remember, and to write you about it. However, one of the reasons editors don't write authors about their books is not that the editors don't read them but that it is really unfair to write an author what must necessarily be a surface reaction. Unless one is going to work with an author and takes time to study a book, it is impossible to help materially.

The notes on your novel which follow were made *as I read.* You have attempted a most difficult technique in using the first person.

You do have talent, and, at times, a vitality in your writing which is impressive. However, many editors would immediately be put off by your inability to spell, your curious use of words which don't exist, and your lapses into ungrammatical writing. Many young people today have these faults, but it is safer to find someone you trust to correct them for you before you approach publishers.

I'm sorry to say that, in my opinion, this novel is unpublishable. My honest advice is not to try to re-write it but to put it aside and to start on a new one. As you read my notes, you'll discover that I had no idea what you were driving at as I read, and that the denouement was a surprise. Unfortunately I never believed in the girl from first to last.

I'm sending you a copy of Bernard Malamud's *A New Life* which we are publishing on October 4. Malamud, as you may already know, is a writer with original methods and a highly individual style. I am not offering this novel as a model, but you will see that he had some of your problems, and, indeed, some of your ideas.

Sincerely yours,

Notes on the author's novel:

The Prologue a mistake . . . somewhat out of key.

Every now and then you make a curious slip in grammar, such as your use of "graduated" on pages 17 and 19; "like" on page 20. Curious use of "prowess" on page 27. *Like* for *as* on page 55.

There's a somewhat patronizing attitude . . . use of middle-class too often? Chip on the shoulder about the middle-west? All right, if it is illuminated by character of narrator, but I don't feel that it is.

You should watch over-use of "a bit." Probably never should use it. Also, a pet horror of mine, although it's being used by many good writers these days: "remain", "enter". Why not "stay" and "go in" and "put" instead of "placed"? After all, you're writing what is supposed to be colloquial style. "Rose" for "got up," p. 62. "Remove" for "took out"; "glanced slowly"? Why not "looked"? you use "glance" too much.

Also, you use curious words, slips for the right word: "obstensively" on page 62, Anyhow, what's an "obstensively pensive mood"? "Plaintiff" for "plaintive" on page 87; and there are many others.

Your editorial parentheses are usually unnecessary, sometimes seem naive and, in general, your editorializing isn't good. (This might be acceptable if it were not in the first person and we could get some light on this strange young man from other points of view.)

A point about construction: school matters are left out too long. In a couple of the S—— episodes, the book seems lacking in focus. Exactly what are you writing about?

"Demurity," "patulous," (102) "connatation" (109).

Some of your descriptions are good, both of people and of nature. I liked the hunting party. But, frankly, some of them are dreadful! The description of Mrs. —— at top of page 113 is so overwritten that I'm afraid it becomes comic.

What in blazes do you mean by "sensually-tenor"? Whatever you mean, it's mannered and bad writing!

This whole scene is silly. It might well be a burlesque of a Victorian novel.

You see, by this time, your book is beginning to irritate me. Sorry.

Wouldn't such pretentious people have had at least one servant, even in this day and age?

Mrs. —— is completely unreal. *Nobody* ever talked like that. As for ——, you haven't made me believe her either. If you're trying to re-do Dante's Beatrice you haven't succeeded.

Amusing touch at bottom of page 128, but most of this story is, believe me, silly, unreal, miles away from what you do best.

Which is—the wild young people. The surprise in chapter XII is good and seems real, and when you get into a scene like this, you do it well. It is as if you knew these people and didn't actually know the others.

Page 139—here is one of your worst parentheses.

Page 142—an example of what I mean by editorializing. "When the soul becomes *accustomed* to a certain vitality," etc.

There is no real preparation for the Lesbianism. It doesn't ring true, and the finish becomes melodrama and again, is overwritten.

To Dr. Theodor Reik concerning a new book:

DEAR THEODOR:

Here it is, almost twenty-five years since Florence Powdermaker introduced us! Your continuing friendship and loyalty through those years, in spite of (or I like to think because of) the fact that I have been associated with the publishing of your books have meant much to me. I thank you.

Everyone here at the office applauds your outline of the new book, and Roger Straus and I are heartened by the news that you plan to spend more time on it and make it, a firm unified work rather than a related series of essays and anecdotes. *The Need to Be Loved* is a fine title. A subtitle would be superfluous. The theme is important, universal in its appeal, and your development of it in the outline shows vigor and the results of your latest psychological thinkings and the extension of your own insights, your work with Dr. Salzberger, and your willingness to stay young. You are always loyal to Maestro Freud, but here, it seems to me, there will be much that is freshly conceived and worth the labor you are expending in doing it.

(I was amused the other day to read that one of the new master race of publishers sent a memo to his office staff forbidding them to use the word "doing" as in "doing a book." Heavens to Betsy, is this not pretentious and pompous? Doesn't a book take a deal of *doing*? Doesn't *writing* take a deal of doing?)

So I'm happy that you're doing this new book. You ask me if I have any suggestions. As always, you will take my reactions to your ideas as amateur. We have often argued over psychiatric and psychoanalytical matters, but never quarreled.

From personal contacts and the confidences of a number of our young friends, it has seemed to me that the shift in parent roles in the last ten years has affected the children, often making them violent, and indeed producing violence in the fathers toward the children. Many young fathers are now sharing in duties which in our youth were considered maternal. The wife plays a more and more dominant role. In the cases we know, the husbands are disturbed, cannot understand what's happening to them, and in some cases, where they can afford it, seeking psychiatric help. There is also the growing importance of the baby-sitter on the domestic front. A psychiatrist friend of mine who specializes in work with children tells me my thinking in this matter is muddy. Probably so, but, nonetheless, if you are not planning to discuss these variations and changes, it might be interesting for you to do so, and you must have much data on the subject. I presume Margaret Mead would find that we are simply changing our tribal customs, or that the change in the apparel of men and women has something to do with it all. Maybe so.

The other point has to do with your discussion of "moral status." Where you first used this in *Listening With the Third Ear*, I thought it brilliant. I believe you were the first to use the term. That men have a limit to their abilities to live according to certain ideals and principles is, of course, true. In many cases, also, it is apparent that requiring themselves to meet standards too high for them could be dangerous to their health and sanity. However, in many cases, I suspect this is a religious problem. In religion, you and I have never thought alike, but respected our differing points of view. Fundamentally this seeking for "moral status" is the sin of pride. In my belief it can be brought to the confessional box as well as the analyst's couch. Moreover, I have known men whom the Lord has helped to reach higher in escaping compromise with sin than, perhaps, their nature allows. You will say that often, certain religious rigors produce the neurotic and the psychotic. I'd point out that Satan also plays his part here. This is complicated, involved and my theology is weak. All I mean to suggest is that you might find it in your heart and conscience to say there are those who believe that unsuspected triumphs of this nature apparently have and can be achieved by the grace of God.

Always with affection,

To an honest and indefatigable literary agent, whom I trust as a friend and admire as an operator.

DEAR ——:

I wrote you as follows on September 21.

"We had a very favorable report on ——, but my own point of view is that if everybody else is as sick as I am of this kind of thing, it isn't going to have much of a sale from here on in. I may be wrong. There is undoubtedly a reprint sale here, although I do not think it would be a very large guarantee. Also, it just isn't written well enough. The writing is smooth but completely lacks distinction, and I rather think the ear for dialogue isn't good. Now, here I am, breaking my own rule about giving my opinion in a rejection letter.

Thank you for thinking of us."

Sincerely,

Now you send me back this novel I had previously rejected, along with two others by the same writer. You say that both you and the writer are determined that we should be his publishers. I accept your praise of us and your bow to my own abilities for the care and feeding of authors, as sincere and not as flattery.

However, we must say, "no." Since in this case we are obviously rejecting a writer of exceptional talent, and one who will certainly make a pile of money for some other publisher, I think it behooves me to explain myself. You'll be sending us other manuscripts by other writers and I trust, as in the past, we shall be publishing them.

This man, as you point out, has had much success in his acceptance and publication by a number of the great popular magazines. He is adept, facile, and able to produce a smooth product in a variety of themes and moods. Since I have never met him, it is easier for me to say that I dislike his manuscripts and don't want to work with him. He doesn't belong on our list.

As you well know, I have worked with many authors, and still do, who are considered "popular" rather than "distinguished." In many cases, I disagree with the tags tied to them. In our shop, however, I am perhaps the only editor who addresses himself to this particular problem in publishing, and in order to perform sucessfully I must have a genuine enthusiasm for the work.

You'll be able to find a good home for this writer in one of the huge houses where cubicles are filled with editors eagerly listening to their account-minded business departments and finding satisfaction in the success of the "no-books," the "non-books", or whatever you choose to call them.

I am still actively engaged at the job I like best, which is working with authors and promoting them. But, at this time in my life I have made it a rule to cosset myself by refusing to spend my time on things I plain straight don't like. Our list is a distinguished one. We have managed to keep free of the current phenomenon of big-business publishing; the book stores and our own salesmen expect us to give them books we believe in.

The trouble with this writer is, I believe, that he doesn't feel deeply anything he writes. He is the slickest of the slick. Every great popular writer I have ever known has been emotionally *engaged* in his stories. I do not recognize this here. I may be wrong, but if I am, it is still my privilege to reject this determined suitor.

Forgive me, my dear lady, if this seems to be a rude letter. Perhaps it is. But I'm sure that you, as friend, would not wish me to spend my time on a project that gives me no joy. Let's leave this to the eager youngsters. Someone should be able to set the cash registers jingling with the results of this gentleman's speeding typewriter. But not I, please, not I.

Thank you just the same, for your confidence, your compliments, and your always admired enthusiasm.

My best also to the author in question. He certainly knows his craft, but you may tell him, if you think it wise, that from my point of view he's too crafty.

All best,

To a lady who had read "Letter to An Unpublished Writer" and wrote asking if I would read some of her stories. Part of her letter which came with the manuscript follows, along with my reply.

"Enclosed you will find six of my completed stories which you were kind enough to agree to look at. I decided it would be far better to let you judge half of the work, now, so that you may decide whether or not you are interested in the rest of the collection.

This will save you the bother of wading through manuscripts you have lost interest in and spare me the ultimate suspense as to whether or not I am going beyond my hopes in thinking that I have something to say to an audience.

Of course, as you well know, it would be folly for me to say, casually, that a rejection will not bother me. I have worked long, hard hours on these, through a serious illness, childbirth, financial difficulties, through crying children, visiting relatives, friendly neighbors and calls from organizations who want help. All in all, I have taken over a year to write just these six. I have tried to give you different samplings of my style and to be as critical of the final works as any author can attempt to be.

I have changed, re-written, written again, thrown out, agonized over a comma, an expression, wondered if I could write at all, decided that I was shooting too high above my limitations, cursed even the people I am writing about and have become so involved in their lives that my own seems almost unreal to me. I feel that the stories are finished, but, I am reluctant to let them go, for fear that they will return.

I have faced the fact that my work may prove unsuitable for your purposes, that my letter may have misled you as to my ability and that you may expect more than I am actually capable of producing. I do know, however, that these are not for magazines: they must have the format of a book to have any impact at all. I have probably made all the errors every eager amateur makes and for this I apologize to you."

DEAR ——:

Let me say at once that I found your stories original and much more than promising. I hope you'll send me the others. Meanwhile I'll hold on to these, if I may. I'm afraid I missed the possibility of seeing you by being caught by troublesome minor ailments. If you are coming down again, please let me know and we'll arrange to have a talk.

Meanwhile, I do have some thoughts about your problem. That your stories would make a book, even with the others, I doubt, quite apart from questions of marketability. While they do show your own personality and style, they differ enough so that I cannot feel them as an effective whole. I am certainly not convinced that some of the magazines would find them unpublishable. I may, indeed, be wrong, but I do think it imperative that you recover from fear of rejection. Forgive me, but that *is* the sin of pride, and you must avoid that particular manifestation of the sin if you are to reach the goal of writing achievement you hope for.

In your case, I hope you'll consent to allow me to ask a good agent's opinion, to ask him whether or not he'd like to undertake to send out some or all of these stories and the others, too, when you send them on.

I wish you could free yourself to write faster, in spite of all the day to day duties to which you, and, indeed, most of us are committed. Perhaps confidence is all you need for that. Your humor is excellent, your conception of life's realities and hopes, fine. I have no specific suggestions for re-working the stories. I like them as they are. Occasionally sentiment shifts toward the sentimental, but this honestly does not worry me.

Do let me hear from you soon.

Sincerely,

To one of the best unpublished writers in the U.S., perhaps the best:

DEAR CHRIS:

It was kind of you to send me the statement of how you feel at this time in your writing career. As with everything you write it has sense and sincerity:

"The first thing an unpublished author should remember is that no one asked him to write in the first place. With this firmly in mind, he has no right to become discouraged just because other people are being published. He must also remember that only by the grace of the typewriter and the printing press are so many people writing and being published today. If most authors writing today had to write a ms. in long hand, there would be fewer mss. to reject.

"Therefore, having been fired by some Muse to dedicate a life in this pursuit . . . much guts will be needed. Guts may also be termed artistic conceit, which is necessary to anyone writing these days. In addition to artistic conceit, if the author be lucky, he will have outside confirmation from people who count and this can be a strong source of encouragement. Often it is the only source of encouragement. He must also be prepared to be buried with his unpublished mss. as a shroud if nothing else happens.

"An unpublished author must also know and learn how to evaluate criticism. He must also not be prepared to re-write for every Tom, Dick and Harry. This can often ruin his original ms. Besides, the art of re-writing has to be learned.

"Of course, like water finding its own level, if the author be serious and sincere in his intent, he is bound to find an outlet for meeting his public. From time to time there will be crumbs of publication thrown his way, and he must know how to accept them, how to feed upon them and how to treasure them.

All this comes from one who has dedicated more than fifteen years of his life to writing as he must, and from one who is prepared to spend another fifteen years in the same way if it must be. There is no key to publishing and success. Each author carries the question and the answer within himself . . . and of course the key."

You have, of course, had many confirmations in your own belief in yourself: the production of plays in the hinterlands, of television scripts, the enthusiasm of one of the best literary agents.

However, your plays have always escaped (narrowly at times) being produced in New York City, and your novels do not get published.

I once thought that you use such difficult themes because unconsciously you did not want to be published. I've observed this happen in other cases. Many an author dodges finishing his work because he shrinks from the possible disillusionment of publication. I've performed a couple of Caesarians myself. It is not a legend that I locked Hervey in a room at the Yale Club before we could succeed in extracting *Anthony Adverse* from the womb. What a gigantic baby that turned out to be!

You know from ——'s recent letters that had he remained editor-in-chief of —— at least one of your novels would have been published. Under different circumstances, I might have sponsored one of them myself, and I think it probable that in its re-written form the one about which I was most enthusiastic will find an imprint either with us or elsewhere.

One thing I have admired greatly over all these years is that you have insisted on writing on your own terms. I'm sure that you are aware that with your imagination and your facility you could have made a good deal of cash by collaboration, by ghost writing, by all the tricks of the trade. You could make the life of Zuzie Swickett or anyone else as interesting as *Little Me*. You haven't done so. If you weren't eating regularly or if you had a family to support I might feel differently. But under the circumstances I applaud you loudly.

As I look forward to the New Year I find myself more and more distressed about the changes in publishing. They are bound to have an effect on authors. Fortunately there are still some publishers who are privately owned and have every intention of remaining so. I thought the Viking Press manifesto of faith after Harold Guinzburg's death was magnificent. What a man he was! And how gravely he deplored the changes in the publishing world. You must know what an inspiration and comfort it is to me that my partners and associates agree, and intend to make every effort to preserve our corporate set-up.

When one reads *Publishers' Weekly* with its report on stock-market activities in publishing stocks; when one hears of the shifts of editors and executives from firm to firm; when one sees more and more evidence of the account-minded upsurge in publishing, it is discouraging. People say it is good to have the public know more about the book business. Maybe so. I find dinner parties too often cruel affairs these days when I am exposed to questions about prices and shenanigans and the solidity of this or that house. I don't want to know much about it and I just tell them it's not my kind of shop, that I think it all can't last anyhow.

They talk about new shining merchandise ideas. I can't see that anyone has come up with an actually helpful one in years. They say the type of book published will not be affected by the changes. Nonsense! I've seen publishing house after publishing house succumb to dry rot as the business men got control. Only in rare exceptions can they help transferring to the creative side of the business. Prestige was first affected. Then, inevitably, profits.

There is one comforting thought for authors. In spite of all, the genius will thrive, though he may have a more difficult time of it. Much good honest talent will suffer, both among authors and, indeed, editors. Sooner or later, the business men will wake up and find out that you can't appeal to the imagination in men, without imagination. It is as simple as that.

So, keep on in your own special way.

All best,

Henry W. Simon

Henry W. Simon, Vice President of Simon and Schuster, has since 1944 been senior editor of the firm founded by his brother and Max Schuster twenty years earlier. He also served as an editor with the firm in 1924 and 1927. For ten years he was an Assistant Professor of English at Columbia University and for four years the music critic for the newspaper PM. He is the author of over a dozen books in the fields of literature, education and music.

The editor's function does not stop at selecting and revising a manuscript. He works with the manuscript through every publishing operation: copy editing, promotion, publicity, "packaging," etc.

How to best present an author to his public is the theme of this trenchant, humorous and revealing exchange of letters between Henry W. Simon and the novelist Niven Busch. The give-and-take, the admixture of the personal and the professional, the emotion and the business flair—they are all part of the editor-author relationship and they are all present in the Simon-Busch letters.

October 5, 1961

Mr. Henry Simon
Simon & Schuster
Rockefeller Center
New York, New York

DEAR HENRY:

I've forgotten whether it was you or Jack Goodman who once said to me "Niven, cast modesty to the winds, and write a blurb for yourself in the manner you would write in a dream, if you could command John Hutchins or Clifton Fadiman to do it for you . . ." Could it have been you? I hope so, because I've taken the liberty to run over THE PUBLISHER'S PREVIEW you sent along. I think it's a damn fine blurb for the purpose for which it's intended, but it might not serve equally well on the dust-jacket (though you will note I have used a good deal of it . . .)

The blurb problem for me, as I see it, has always been to present a book of mine in a way which will induce critics to accept it as a serious piece of work rather than a purely popular or commercial one. Not that I want to diminish the popular appeal. I'm counting on it for sales, just as you are, and I design my books to appeal to a reasonably large audience. Maybe the trouble with them is that they're better written than the material calls for—or so I flatter myself—but even where sales, and nothing but sales, are the author's and publisher's concern, there is no sales implement as productive as snob appeal, and if we can't get some critical accolades we lose a large segment of the audience, which buys a book for no other reason than that it is recommended as a status symbol.

In the tentative material I have knocked out (and you realize I don't hold any strong brief for any part of it—only for the general point of reference) I have tried to combine two elements which are conventionally, but I feel unnecessarily, separated in many dust-jackets: the bit about the author and the bit about the book. There are many advantages in splicing these two lines of sales appeal into one chunk; I am sure you realize better than I what they may be. Maybe you have some special reason for wanting to separate them, but if you haven't, I would suggest for the back of the book or in place of any portion of the jacket you intend to use the author-crap, you simply insert a candid camera shot of my ugly puss. This will scare off a certain segment of the public, probably the most desirable segment. However, I think that the basic appeal of the author write-up is simply to find out, to some extent, what the guy is like. Maybe reader curiosity demands this. If your experience confirms my theory, curiosity should be settled, probably ended forever, by a picture. I've never had a really expert one taken for a book, since most of the stills I've sent over have been last-minute jobs by the corner photographer. I thought the ones for *California Street* exceptionally fag-like, and those for *The Actor* strictly rural. Maybe we can hit a happy medium . . . Anyway I'm willing to try.

Another thought for general layout:

Do you think it would be a good idea to give the book a general resemblance to *California Street,* especially in view of the fact that it is a sort of vague successor to that volume, in general technique and theme? At least *California Street* was successful, and people often like to put two related books on a bookshelf, and if they have one, to buy another that looks like the first . . . Also, if we ever write a third and want to box the three, for any purpose, the idea might serve a useful function. Not that I mean this resemblance to be close enough for any confusion, but simply to apply to size, type of binding, and colors used in the dust-jacket and title lettering . . .

Needless to say, I'm most happy about the first printing and the advertising budget. Many a best-seller has been launched for less—and this has got to be a best-seller or I will take off for Tasmania and live out my days in a bomb-shelter there. In fact, I may do this anyway.

Cheeta and I just got back from L.A. We found a new and really terrific hotel—The Bel Air Sands—it's really two hotels on separate levels: the upper level is quiet and has its own pool and patio. We had a lanai and balcony and a kitchen so big that we put Jerry's rollaway in it, all for $23 a day. There is also food, yet, down in the main hotel, but we didn't bother with this much—not with Cheeta able to lift a saucepan. I worked hard getting my deal with Joe Levine* straightened out, and see a flicker of hope that he may come through with the contract. I hope so, since I'll be running out of money before long.

All the best,

October 10, 1961

Mr. Niven Busch
1421 Thomas Road
Hollister, California

DEAR NIVEN:

Thanks for the prompt answer to my questions about the PUBLISHER'S PREVIEW, the blurb, and the jacket.

The distinction you make between a "commercial" book and a "literary" book is constantly being made in this office, in the reviews, in fact wherever people get together to talk about novels.

* Joseph E. Levine of Embassy pictures contracted with Niven Busch to write an original screenplay based on the San Francisco earthquake of 1906, tentatively titled *The City That Lived.*

And every time it gets me mad. For (I may have said this to you before; Lord knows, I have said it to plenty of others), there *is* no legitimate distinction between the two. Or at least, most of the literary novels have and always have been commercial. Dickens, Balzac, Austen—even Joyce and Proust—have been commercial in the sense that sooner or later (and mostly sooner) they were best-sellers and made money for both the author and the publisher. We have always published you exactly the way we would publish Dickens if he were writing *David Copperfield* or *Our Mutual Friend* for us. And if he were doing that, we would be saying in effect on the jacket, "Look, folks, what a marvelous new story we've got from that prince of storytellers who has moved you to laughter with *Pickwick Papers* and to tears with *Oliver Twist!*" And we would leave it to the pundits to discover that even if the book was at the top of the best-seller list for six months, it was nevertheless Literature.

Furthermore (and I have just discussed this point with Phyllis on the phone, and she agrees with me), I always think it is a very bad idea to tell very much of the story on the jacket. British publishers often do it, and even some of my benighted colleagues at S&S do it when they can't think of anything better to say.

And so I shall take full advantage of your extremely well-written but (I think) not well-considered copy, lift phrases, maybe whole paragraphs from it, and come up with something that we will both like. At least I hope so. Anyway, as soon as I get it done, I will send you a copy to see how you like it.

I say "as soon as I get it done" because today is my 60th birthday, and I feel very depressed partly for that reason and partly because there are so goddamn many unanswered letters on my desk, and so many unread manuscripts next to them that I don't know when I will begin to catch up with myself. But soon.

As for the jacket, while I was reading your letter this morning, our art director came in with a rough sketch which at least in one way fits in exactly with what you asked for; that is, it looks like a companion volume to *California Street*. The background suggests San Francisco (cable car on one side, for instance) and there are figures in the foreground of Laura and Galvin with a big, misty head of Charlie between them. Some aspects of the coloring stink and the author's name, as a result, is not sufficiently prominent. Back it goes to the artist, and I will be sending either the artwork or a photostat to you when I am completely satisfied.

Tourjours à toi, mon ami,

October 17, 1961

Mr. Niven Busch
1421 Thomas Road
Hollister, California

DEAR NIVEN:

O.K., so here it is, still not in final shape. The modifications still to be made are:

1. Name of the author is to be larger.
2. Underneath his name will be the legend "Author of *California Street*."
3. The top of the big head will be more clearly delineated from the bank building behind it.
4. There will be a little more space between "San" and "Franciscans."
5. There will be lettering on the spine.

I think it is an excellent selling jacket and hope that you do too. It doesn't have a literary flavor, but I don't think it should. The best-selling novels of "literary" authors like Robert Penn Warren are also published with frankly commercial—even double-breasted—jackets, and I think the publishers are right to do this. I hope you will agree too.

I am enclosing with this package an envelope so that you can airmail it back as soon as you have had a good look. Our art department is anxious to get at the revisions and make the plates just as soon as possible.

All the best to both of you,

October 20, 1961

DEAR HENRY:

The jacket design arrived, and I can't say I felt it was quite right. To come clean, old buddy, I thougght—and I mean with two gs—it was horrible. The lettering and colors were fine. That's as far as I liked it. But the figures—God. Personally, I've always felt people like to form their own images of characters in a book. It's okay of course to have the jacket convey the idea that there are characters, and that the characters are interesting: but they shouldn't be "defined." The young guy looks like a clothing ad., the dame like a twenty dollar call girl, and the big head in the middle like a retired ad executive. Please don't get mad. I just mean to sell this book we ought to invoke a city—the most fascinating city in the USA and maybe in the world—in its beauty, evil, wonder, excitement and complexity. With people. Sure with characters, but not cutouts. Not a pattern. This kind of jacket is for newsstands, not for book stores. It's the wrong kind of selling. Customers paying five bucks for a book want to feel they're paying for something of worth. Sexy cheapness they can get in paperbacks . . .

Couldn't we go to a design—arresting, new and highstyled: maybe the whole jacket, front and back, an impressionistic drawing of a sombre, big old S.F. house, clearly from the turn of the century—with a white Jaguar, today's model, at the door, very small and clear like a New Yorker cover. Or a portiere (this is a different jacket) made of red velvet, as if for a four-poster bed or a ballroom, with a man's arm pulling it back, and the diametrics of the city visible behind through a window. . . .

Just wild notions, on the spur of the moment. But let's for the sweet Jesus sake have class. That is what sells. I'm convinced of it. Please Henry, as you value our friendship, get a new artist and a new jacket. Make it seem original and make it suggest a fine book, not a bum piece of merchandise. I beg you most urgently to do this . . .

I was about to write you some philosophy with regard to your achieving (in damn good shape, I may add) the age of sixty . . . but will save this till next time, in the hope that after all this we can remain on speaking terms.

But I'm sure you see what I mean!

Always yours,

GZS PD FAX ESSANDESS 10/24/61

NIVEN BUSCH
1421 THOMAS ROAD
HOLLISTER CALIF

NEW JACKET IN WORKS. BEST

HENRY SIMON

Anonymous

Intense, intimate in their revelations of the spiritual and creative relationship between editor and author, this fragment of correspondence from the files of one of the most distinguished of today's women editors is perhaps the frankest exchange of correspondence in this section of EDITORS ON EDITING.

Less restrained and detached than Maxwell E. Perkins' style as an editor; possessed of much of the warmth, engaging humor of John Farrar's ways of working with authors, this editor's approach is preëminently her own. She is giving everything of herself to her author so as to insure the author's giving everything of himself to his novel. Whether responding to him with sternness, enthusiasm or careful questioning, she is at any given moment exactly what that particular author needs in the way of editorial guidance.

The editor saw ninety pages of a projected novel. In this, the hero, Jerry, is found having drinks in the local bar with Evvie. He showed signs of difficulties with his rich wife, Leona, with his sixteen-year-old daughter, Marianne, and, of a special emotional tie, with his six-year-old daughter, Joanna. In this brief section also, we meet Paula, a woman to whom he is strongly attracted. The correspondence follows:

From editor:

"Damn it all, this is one novel which doesn't reveal enough in 90 pages, which is what I meant by 'mixed reactions' in my telegram.

"There are beautiful lyric sections in the book, and there are some that need some toning down if only for the sake of contrast. The major problem, however, is that I am not yet snatched up by any of the characters to the degree that one should feel involved in any work of fiction. Obviously, I will know much better how to get myself involved—through you—if I know where you are going.

"Outlines are murder, of course, but how about a short letter to your dear friend and editor saying, I'm writing a book about a father's involvement with his daughters or with his daughters' sweethearts or whatever."

From editor:

"All your ideas on where you are going seem excellent to me. Therefore, it becomes increasingly important that Jerry should have enormous stature and reader sympathy from the start. We meet him first in a rather ambivalent scene with a very unimportant character. Just what is his relationship to Evvie? It's dangerous to give an impression here that he is a habitual drunk. On page 5, for example, when he asks himself what's wrong with himself, I think you might play around with the idea that kids at the dance have made him feel non-existent. Teenagers have a capacity when they are in groups of teenagers to make grown-ups feel simply not there. It isn't a question of being unwanted, but rather a question of not existing. It might be best to start him just before the dance, to see him being pushed aside by his rich wife, by his 16 year-old daughter, etc. etc. Incidentally, you can accomplish a great deal right at the start by introducing the hearty lover who shows up later at the swimming pool. Leona, let us say, has already had an affair because Jerry, who is a complete romantic, could never satisfy her. She is essentially a lost lady, a romantic sensualist, which in our society only women can truly be. The money for her is as much a matter of texture and sensation as it is comfort and power. Women like mink, let's face it, as much for the way it feels as for its status symbol. It's men who love money as power. Rich widows are always rightfully depicted as being frustrated and miserable. Rich bachelors or widowers are very desirable types. At any rate, Jerry knows and has forgiven or overlooked or taken in stride Leona's affair with a texture man. Certainly, it would be the fist in the teeth if he found out this character was coming to the dance. Then, his daughter simply doesn't notice him, etc. etc. If you can do this without self-pity, you have a fine beginning.

"Above all, your male hero must never really be inept or powerless. He can fail in a tragic sense—as Gatsby did—but that is only because he is a god living in the world of men. He can be an enormous villain, but only for the right reasons. He wants more than people are capable of giving him and he has more to give them than they are capable of accepting.

"You have done this instinctively already, or perhaps knowingly. His relationship with Joanna is superb. He is at his best with innocence. His relationship with Elvira is superb. He is totally needed and he totally gives.

"What went wrong between him and Leona originally? Did he mind about the money? What did he want from her that she couldn't give him? The dance is a symbol. What's so bad about this dance? To most readers, it could seem like a fine type dance. Why do you think it's wrong? The kids are having fun, aren't they? Did Jerry originally want a different kind of 16th birthday affair? If so, what kind? If he doesn't really know what's wrong on his terms, he loses some sympathy.

"I have made notes throughout of very minor things, but I have tried to cut to the heart of what you are doing here with these suggestions and questions. If you are deeply involved with writing forward, don't necessarily answer at once, but perhaps answering me will help you as well as me. In any case, write me soon if only to send love."

From author:

"As an editor, you are plain genius and I know two beautiful stars fell and touched each other on the days you and I were born. I also think you wear a bandanna and hoop earrings, for forecasting so completely what I have been trying to say in the book. You are also a witch, pick your own spelling, for making me work so damn hard. Worst of all, I think you are a third grade schoolteacher, because when I think I can sneak by with something because I haven't quite understood it myself, you grab me by the seat of my pants and make me go back to my desk and open my answer book. It wouldn't surprise me in the least if you practised face-lifting without a license. I love you.

"Honestly, your letter was brilliant. In almost every instance you mention, I know where I've gone wrong. After a few days of thought there will be lots of questions I'll ask you in return, just to be sure I understand what you mean. In the meantime, will you answer something posthaste? My agent wrote me a few weeks ago that you, and she also, felt *Leona* was the central character. Maybe *that's* what sent me to the hospital. But the moment I read it I knew you were right—and curiously (the marvels of the creative mind!) I realized subconsciously I had already begun to understand this myself, though I'd not yet recognized it. Originally in my plans Leona was just going to fade out around now—the story was to be all Jerry's and Paula's. And yet in my notes I found myself outlining more and more scenes about Leona toward the end of the book—when J asks her for a divorce (which is what starts

Paula on her big binge when she learns about it, because now *she* must make the decision about love, which she can't) and also L's complete moral lostness when her bread factory burns down (the symbol of her money and power and the substitute for her forgotten dream)—oh, it's all going to work out fine, I know. But can you just try to explain a little more to me just *how* you feel Leona as the central character? After all, you're a woman. I ain't.

"One more thing to clarify my aching brain: you suggest introducing the 'hearty lover' at the beginning of the book. At first I thought you were speaking of Paula. Now I trust I'm right in thinking you meant Mike Balding?

"I think I may revise these first 90 pages before going on further, though I have already written about 50 pages ahead—but I feel if I can get this beginning perfect (and I won't settle for less, sorry) and absolutely firm in my mind, then I can zoom ahead.

"Don't you DARE think about, correspond with, or have RELATIONSHIPS with any other writer!"

From editor:

"As you must have known it would, your letter made me insufferable for days. It came in while I was away, but my angel secretary had sense enough to forward it to me. I was dying to read the first paragraph aloud to everybody, but with admirable restraint, I settled for the last two sentences, which are really a triumph of witty flattery. As for the salutation, nobody will ever again be Perkins, just as nobody will ever again be Fitzgerald or Wolfe or Hemingway. But let us all praise heaven for the fact that the true professionals don't try. The truest line that ever was said or written is that good editors are made by good writers.

"Certainly, my feeling that Leona was the central character (which, incidentally, was not the way I put it—what I said was that she was the catalytic character) came entirely from what you had written and outlined as the balance of the book. I am like an echo chamber or a camera eye in that I can record and see and feel only what you yourself have put on paper. If we are to understand Jerry and his sense of being lost in a world he once thought he possessed, then we must know all about Leona and why they have so left each other stranded.

"A great deal of nonsense, both pro and con, has been written about the superiority of women over men, and most of it stems from the fact that people forget to use the word natural as the motivating and clarifying adjective. There is a superior endurance and survival rate built into women for the most obvious biological reasons. This is not only physical (men can lift a heavier load off the ground, but women can carry it longer), but also psychological and spiritual. Leona survives from the start by accepting the lost dream, and seeks momentary comfort from other men, other sensations. Jerry, before the opening of your book, has found his satisfactions, which are romantic only and not sensual at all, in his daughters. At her 16-year-old dance, Marianne, in effect, shows up the hollow nature of this transference. She has a perfectly healthy love for her father, which means that she will transfer all of her passionate love to another suitable male. What is Jerry to do then? Even his relationship with Joanna is seriously disturbed. The handwriting is on the wall. Indeed, you have him plead with her in his own mind not to come downstairs. Stay young enough to be my love, to be my romance.

"Do you remember *Philadelphia Story?* The movie, I mean. There's a wonderful scene in it along these lines between the father and the heroine where he tells her that a man of a certain age must have a strong romantic attachment with a young woman. Ideally, it's a loving young daughter. At worst, it's a predatory young chorus girl.

"In effect, therefore, Jerry is almost thrust into the affair with Pamela, where he displays a hero's sense of judgment. He picks a woman he need not be ashamed of and who needs him instead of wanting to exploit him. At the end, of course, she betrays him in the sense that she used him as a father. Thus, you have the perfect circle. His daughters use him properly as a father and this is not enough because his wife has used him only as a lover, as, in fact, a gigolo would be used. Even in this relationship, he has been inadequate for her needs because *he is not a gigolo*. This goes much deeper than the conventional husband who won't use his wife's money. I think at the beginning Jerry didn't give a damn about the money. (You make a point of how much he admired her father and his eccentricities and after all, it was her father's money.) It was Leona who felt that she had bought him and not Jerry who felt that he had been bought. This may be the very reason for the opening wedge of hostility between them.

"Yes, of course, I meant Balding when I spoke of the 'hearty lover.' Paula is conceivably lusty, but the major impression I got from Balding was of flexing muscles and clapping people on the back. Leona would characteristically choose him as her first lover because he is so directly the opposite of Jerry. Restlessly, undoubtedly, she moves on from him because this type is rarely the great lover. And just as restlessly, she is playing with the idea of trying him again. This is her way of flexing her muscles and refusing to accept growing old.

Does all this help? I hope so, and it's been fun to write."

From author:

"About your letters—they most certainly do reach me and affect and clarify things for me greatly. Some points I resist at first, and suddenly a week later I wake up and it's all resolved and I know you've done it again—clarified my own feelings and pointed the way for them to go. If I don't answer much about your letters, it's because by the time I'm ready to answer they've already made things clear to me and they are firm in my brain. Like introducing Balding earlier, for instance—that bothered me for weeks. Then just this *morning* it was all clear, without my knowing I had been brooding about it subconsciously at all. Of course he is important now, and Leona's affair before the book opens, *very* important. Because Balding is Jerry's opposite—the sexual vs. the innocent, believing romantic. But Balding's way of lust is not necessarily WRONG, yet it will strengthen J's RIGHTNESS in his final stubbornness in continuing to believe, and will *forever,* that fidelity (or maybe I mean human *quality*) is a handmaiden of nobility.

. . . "You make me feel I can at last be the great writer I always was determined to be, knew I could be though I've never yet made it except in fragmentary, lyrical passages, which is not much. But now I know I'm on the way to something adult, sustained, and I hope deeply moving. God help YOU if I fail! I've already planted a hemlock tree for you, in case of need, so I need speak no more."

From editor:

"Your letters do for me in a sense of clarifying the growing book what mine do for you, which simply confirms my absolute conviction that editors can only affect and never direct. For example, J's relief that 'fidelity is a handmaiden of nobility' is no more necessarily right than Balding's way at last is necessarily wrong. It is essentially a Puritan concept and, of course, the great romanticists are the Puritans, which is one reason why they were capable of so much valor and so much cruelty. J and B are, of course, opposites, but there's at least a third way, which is the philosopher's way. So marvelously done in *Major Barbara* in the scene between the father and son. If one does not know what truth is, how does one know what right is? The way that causes the least inner conflict, of course, is the arrogant way of fidelity essentially to oneself. I don't think Leona thinks along these lines at all because, in fact, she never really thinks . . . any more than Daisy did in *Gatsby,* and look what hell she created for good men. Sometimes I wish I could be like her for a day, and then I know that 10 minutes of it would be enough—like Las Vegas."

From editor:

. . . "don't brood too much about the beginning. If it doesn't come right for you to have anything happen before the book opens, don't do it. It simply struck me when I read the original draft that our hero must have a strong personal reason to dread his daughter's party and to avoid it as he does. A hint is really all you need for the reader of an affair or affairs if you put in some sense that it is at large brawls that Leona is indiscreet and Jerry has to watch her being enticing with other men. Don't fret, you'll think of something."

Harold Strauss

Harold Strauss was born in New York City in 1907, attended the Horace Mann School for Boys, and was granted a B.S. magna cum laude from Harvard, 1928. The following year he began his long career in book publishing as editor for Alfred H. King, 1929-32. He then went to Covici-Friede as production director, 1932-4; editor in chief, 1934-8. In 1938-9, Mr. Strauss served as director of the New York City Federal Writers' Project and editor of the New York City Guide. He became associate editor at Alfred A. Knopf, Inc. in 1939, and editor-in-chief in 1942, which post he has held since. Among the writers with whom he has worked at Knopf are C. W. Ceram, John Hersey, Ruth Moore, John Steinbeck, and Nicholas Monsarrat. Mr. Strauss is a member of the executive board of P.E.N., and has contributed book reviews, articles, and stories to the New York TIMES BOOK REVIEW, THE NEW YORKER, THE ATLANTIC, *and* THE REPORTER, *among other publications.*

Taut, tart, perfectionist, with a rich vein of glittering humor, these selections from the editor-to-author correspondence of Harold Strauss display his meticulous taste, wide range of knowledge, and vigorously applied high standards for intelligibility and readability in a manuscript. These are qualities, of course, one would expect to find in so distinguished an editor; they serve, too, as a set of criteria any *editor might find invaluable.*

A FEW NOTES ON POPULARIZING SCIENTIFIC OR MEDICAL DISCOVERIES:

Excerpt from a letter to a writer we subsequently published.

ONE of the most important distinctions between good and bad popularizations is the direct relevance of human interest detail *to the discovery*.

Bad popularizations stress irrelevant detail, such as the discoverer's hobbies or his father's religious beliefs. Good popularizations rest on good sensory reporting, if that is possible; if not, on good research. What did the place in which the discovery was made look like at the climactic moment? Who was there at the time? What irritating distractions were there? What was the weather like, and did it have anything to do with what the scientist was doing that day? What about the physical equipment? Something missing? Some failure? Improvised substitutes? Anything of this kind is useful. It is much better than saying abstractly, for instance, that controlled tests took two years to complete.

Biographical information is of course useful and desirable. In a book, however, it must be handled quite differently than in, say, *Time Magazine*. Here the principle is motive impulse. What made Schliemann stop being a merchant and start digging? What made Darwin decide to ship aboard the *Beagle?* Generally speaking, the question of motivation has two aspects: first, why did the particular individual become a scientist in the first place? Second, what put him on the track of his greatest discovery? Was it planned? If so how and why? Was it accidental? Was it planned in one direction, but ended in a slightly different one?

Admittedly, this could lead to heavy-handed metaphysical questions, or to overly sensational "iffy" ones. But these tendencies, too evident in German popularizations, can easily be controlled.

Both of the above points are subordinate to narrative. Usually a scientific discovery is a process which moves through time, thus lending itself naturally to narrative treatment. A general format for a particular chapter (subject to pleasing variations, of course) might go something like this:

1. A quick, broad sketch of the prevailing state of knowledge at the time, pointing to the crucial unsolved problem.
2. Abortive attempts of others to solve it.
3. Then Mr. X comes on the scene. Why? I.e., what motivated him to become a scientist in the first place, and to embark on a particular course in the second place.
4. The events or steps leading to the discovery, told in as dramatic a narrative *order* as possible, but without excessive verbal embellishments, such as superlatives. In other words, the color and human interest must be drawn from the events, not varnished on by means of the author's comments.
5. The significance of the discovery. *Here* is the place for metaphysics, if you like; for speculations and editorial comment.

Finally, beware of jargon. The common language is much better and more communicative, not only because it does not send readers to a dictionary too often, but because it has more stability. The meaning of a technical term can sometimes be altered by an obscure monograph in an obscure learned journal, but not if the idea is expressed in the common language. In extreme cases, jargon conceals meaning, and the discipline of translating it into the common language often forces a writer to sharpen his grasp of his own topic. Jargon saves words, but squanders time. We prefer to print the extra words.

Letter to a distinguished scientist writing in English, an acquired language, for the first time.

I have now finished the extremely laborious and time consuming job of editing and rewriting your manuscript and I have sent it to Professor X for his expert advice. But the manuscript is far from complete and ready for the printer. Some things that must be done can be done only by you. A few of these things I have already written you about, and I urgently need your answers. You must go through the entire manuscript again and eliminate all modifying phrases such as "it seems" and "it appears" where they are not strictly required because the scientific evidence is inadequate. The constant use of these phrases makes the manuscript tiresome reading in spots.

Another point on which I have already written you is to request you to recheck your footnotes and references, some of which I have found wrong as to page number and in other respects. You should always refer to an English language edition where one exists, and if the book has been published in England and America, to the American edition, if that was the original one. It is imperative in the English language to use the full name of the author, not just the initial of his first name, as is the continental practice. It sounds terribly pedantic in English if you do follow the European custom. Furthermore I enclose herewith some guidance on the form of our footnotes which must include the title in full, as well as the city, the publisher, the date of publication, volume where necessary, as well as the page reference (see p. 11 of the enclosed guidance booklet).

All these points I have written to you about before, though in somewhat less detail. But what follows is new, and most important.

The first question concerns your quotations from the Bible. I have three versions at home, all different, and none corresponds with yours. I need most urgently to know which version you have used, and to be precise, you had better give me the complete title page or any other information about it, because it apparently is not enough to say "The King James Version" since that has been revised several times. On the whole, I prefer the King James version, because of the magnificence of its style, although the King James version of some of your quotations, particularly Joshua 11, 16, is much more obscure than the Revised version. I think the solution in this and possibly in a few other instances is to use the King James version throughout in the text, and add a footnote giving other, clearer versions, when necessary. It can be done here, later, as soon as you tell us which version you have used.

The next point concerns your description of pottery. I am afraid that you have relied entirely or almost entirely upon technical terminology, and that even the most interested general reader cannot follow to the point of visualizing the pottery you refer to. I believe that we ought to be able to visualize the pottery from your words alone, even if excellent illustrations are supplied. I have no objection to the use of the proper technical term if it is accompanied by a vivid description in the common language. This will be very important to the success of the book outside of purely scientific circles. I must ask you to review your own manuscript with this in mind at once.

The word "pebble" presents some difficulties. In English it suggests a stone no bigger than one that can be held in one hand. I am sure you use it correctly as far as eoliths are concerned, but when you reach the age of incipient farming, I am not so sure that you distinguish properly between pebbles, stones, rocks, etc. When you say that the neolithic basements were covered with pebbles, do you really mean rather round stones of the size one can hold in one hand, or smaller; or do you mean *stones,* which conveys to us a meaning of something slightly larger, and of any shape, including a flat shape? For even larger stone objects, the word *rock* should be used, as it should be for the raw material in its natural place, in the earth or on mountainsides.

I must also know at once whether the rock pictures of the desert were invariably carved, or invariably painted, or sometimes painted and sometimes carved. This makes a great deal of difference in giving your style more flexibility and grace, since the concrete active verbs "to paint" and "to carve" in their various grammatical forms ought to be substituted for the one or two terms you use rather stiffly and vaguely, such as "depict."

Another point of the utmost importance concerns only that part of the book covering the period after the invention of writing. I have had long experience in handling works in your field and I can assure you that perhaps the single most fascinating thing to the general reader is the question of primitive or early writing, the various scripts, what they looked like, whether we can read them, how their secret was cracked, if it was, etc. I am afraid you have neglected this point completely. I consider this subject so important and such a sales asset that I would like to urge you to prepare a whole special chapter on it, taking all the space you wish, and supplying line cuts illustrating the different scripts.

We are going to have acute problems with some of your technical terminology, but I have to wait till Professor X finishes the manuscript to write you in detail about this. For instance, I think your term "Indo-Aryan" is not correct in English. I think it must be either "Indo-European" for the language or Aryan for the people, but I am not sure about this; I am only sure that "Indo-Aryan" is a term not used at all.

As you will see, when I return the original copy of the manuscript to you for your approval of the rewriting, it has been so drastically rewritten that the carbon copy unfortunately is not going to be usable for anything at all except to convey my detailed questions to you. These questions will cover many things not mentioned in this letter, and I hope you will supply the most detailed answers you can in every case.

As to the book itself, I consider it a major scholarly achievement of which you should be proud. But it also is an extremely difficult book for the general reader in its first half. This raises some interesting questions. In the first place, I may have to go over the early chapters once again, now that I understand the weak spots in your English a little better, and see if I cannot make them a little easier reading for the intelligent layman without sacrificing any scientific accuracy. But there are two things that I would suggest you do in the meanwhile. I assume that you are going to write in English a great deal hereafter, and I must say that your English improves noticeably toward the end of the book. But it still lacks a certain richness and flexibility of vocabulary. It was easy enough for me to correct certain grammatical errors, but it was much harder, because it was risky, to try to inject a greater richness of vocabulary into your prose. I have chanced it in a few cases because you will have the opportunity of checking my revisions. But I think, *both for the purposes of this book and for the future,* it would be a most important investment of your time if you would read Lewis Mumford's new book, *The City in History,* immediately. I know it has been published in England as well as in America, so it should be easily available to you. Actually, it is an immensely long book, but you will only have to read the early chapters, taking the history of the cities through the neolithic. Mumford is not a scientist, and I am not suggesting that you will learn anything of a scientific nature from him. But he is a magnificent stylist, and since in the early chapters he deals with palaeolithic, mesolithic, and neolithic man, I think you will do well to absorb his vocabulary. You may then want to make some further revisions in your own manuscript. You may also find Lewis Mumford's psychological and philosophical speculations interesting, even though you don't agree with them.

Believe me, I cannot stress the urgency of your reading the early chapters of this book too much.

The second thing we must do to help the general reader, and to give us a better chance of publishing the book successfully, is to supply the book with a ten-to-twenty-page introduction, directed outspokenly to the general reader, and explaining to him what he will find in the second half of the book, and even suggesting to him that he may find it most rewarding to read the second half of the book first, and then to pick up the first half. When you describe what is in the second half of the book you should do so in general terms, omitting all references to sources and scientific proof. In the text itself you will of course have to supply the scientific proof, and this is what makes it such difficult going in spots. I have written you about this before, and I must say that you have quite literally done what I asked you to do in the first place—taken the reader by the hand and explained to him at all times what was going on. You have been somewhat repetitious at times, and I have deleted a few of these passages where I thought they were not necessary. But this additional help of an introduction is also now necessary.

On the other hand, I must tell you frankly that I do not like your "Conclusion" or epilogue at all. I think perhaps it is the result of the limitations of your English, but as it is written now, it sounds very commonplace and a bit banal; and also sounds quite repetitious. The place to tell the reader why your subject is important to him is in the introduction, not in the epilogue, where he has grasped the point long since, or he would never have read through to the epilogue. I have made some slight cuts here but I want to review the whole thing when you decide what you want to do about the introduction.

In successful books, the text and the illustrations should be more or less independent in the sense that they are independently comprehensible. I don't think you should rely on your photographs to elucidate obscurities in the text, but always try to be clear with your words. By the same token I think that the photographs will need much fuller, non-technical captions. I have made no attempt to cope with the photographs just yet, and certainly not to select them or place them. This is going to be a fantastic job, simply because I don't know with any degree of certainty which figure you are referring to in your figure references in the text, even though you have done a splendid job of organizing the photographs chronologically. No doubt we must allow double the usual time to publish your new book. I think that much of the material, including manuscript, proofs, illustrations, and captions, will have to travel back and forth between us several times, unless by chance you decide to come to the United States about four or five months from now, which will probably be the crucial period.

I have given an enormous amount of my time to this book because I think it is important. In return, I am and shall be quite perfectionist in my requests of you.

I'll write you again as soon as Prof. X has read the manuscript. He's a human dynamo, so I don't imagine he'll take very long over it.

Cordially,

I think you already know from X, a good friend of this house, that we are very much interested in your recent magazine article. It seems to us that this is very well done in itself, but cries for expansion into an 80,000 word book. You whet the reader's appetite. You touch on many dramatic moments that suggest full-scale descriptions. In fact the piece could be considered an outline for a book.

I am of course speaking of a trade book, a book for the general reader. A word about books of this kind. We don't think they should be written down for simple-minded readers. We think they should be just as scientifically sound as the author can make them. At the same time, we like to see technical jargon translated into the common language, and see no reason why sound books need be obscure or difficult reading. We hope that these books will be popular, but that does not require over-simplification. In the case of your prospective book, the inherent drama should create excitement enough to keep the reader turning the pages.

Do let me know what you think of all this. If you are interested in writing such a book for us, we probably could accept the magazine article as a general outline. We then would require from you a few sample chapters to show just how and in what style you would expand the material.

Cordially,

Letter to a very able author who fell short of his own standards. The manuscript was subsequently drastically rewritten and accepted.

You have written a good book—but not quite good enough. As I see it, you are a masterly teacher. Your writing is sober, informed, and wonderfully clear for the layman. You succeed in clarifying some very complex geological situations.

But then, why do we not offer to publish the book? I shall accept your own reference to Rachel Carson as the basis for what follows. You simply do not know how to paint word pictures. You do not know how to evoke vivid images of particular phenomena. You are not the master of what is called good sensory reporting. Now these qualities are not always necessary. But a "blind" nature writer is no nature writer at all, as far as the general public is concerned. I could give you literally hundreds of examples of what I mean. For instance, you say clearly and intelligibly that a (landslide) menaced a certain highway. Are you really going to leave it at that? It must have been an awsome spectacle—and perhaps terrifying to hear, also. Couldn't you spare a paragraph or two to say what it would have been like for a traveler to pass under it on the highway?

In your reference to mumified sheep, you merely tease the reader. A few more details of what it looked like (and possibly what it smelled like) and about its zoological characteristics, would have helped a great deal.

You quote a very dramatic description by X. This is very effective writing. But you don't do anything of the kind on your own. You are comprehensive, as you should be. But I should think it would be eminently worthwhile to paint the portrait, in the utmost detail, of a dozen or so particularly interesting natural phenomena.

From the layman's point of view, your writing is not at all bad, except that it is badly punctuated, and except that it is sometimes a little repetitious. However, I think your even, pedagogic tone becomes a little monotonous after a while. It is a question of emphasis, of excitement. Where the emphasis should be I leave to you, but it needs emphasis that will lead to more force and color in your writing.

If your book dealt with a major scientific field, it might be possible to work out these problems in detail. But the subject of this book, although it has its own learned journal, is only a fragment of geology, and therefore a portion of a science, as far as trade publishing is concerned. Much as I would like to be able to publish a purely utilitarian book in this field, I don't think we could do it successfully. To be successful, your book must give pleasure as well as information, as the books of Rachel Carson do. Under these circumstances, the best I can do is to write you these generalized criticisms, and return the manuscript to you with many thanks for letting me see it.

It is quite possible that some other publisher will wish to publish it as it is. But if you feel responsive to the comments I made in this letter, so responsive that you wish to rewrite the manuscript drastically with these comments in mind, I certainly would welcome the opportunity to reconsider it.

Cordially,

Letter to a foreign-born novelist writing in English, for him an acquired language. For clarity, the points are deliberately repeated in various formulations.

I have read your revised manuscript and on the whole I think you have done a splendid job. The ending is now very strong. As I told you, I want one or two more people to read it before coming to a final decision, but there is a more immediate problem than that. I think that Chapter XIII, when the young man makes love with the girl in the fisherman's shack, has to be entirely rewritten. I have discussed this with your agent and another reader here, and we all agree that through a series of accidents the scene has almost the opposite effect of the one you intended. Because you have been rather vague about all the physical details of the scene, details which I am sure you have visualized in your mind but have not presented to the reader, it ends up by becoming rather ludicrous.

The scene belongs in the book, and is very important in clarifying the motivation. But it has an entirely uncharacteristic weakness: it is not visual. Throughout the rest of the book you present wonderful visual images which enable the American reader to *see* your people and their land. Please don't misunderstand me. I am certainly not asking you to write an obscene chapter. Erotic, of course. Obscene, no. I don't know exactly how to make the distinction to you, but several of us here feel that it is more obscene to be vague than to be forthright. After all, this is the first sexual experience for both man and girl, a moment of deep emotion. This has disappeared almost entirely from the scene. What are the girl's feelings? This too must be added, and is perhaps *more important than anything else I have to suggest*. The way you handle the scene now, the girl is almost a piece of furniture.

The whole setting is very challenging. No doubt this will be the first time in literature that anyone has made love in a sardine cauldron. And for reasons too complicated to explain in a letter, please call it a *cauldron* throughout, and not a *pot*.

And this is not all. You further compound the ludicrousness of the scene by confusing two appetites: hunger and sex. It simply will not do to have the man and the girl eat leftover sardines out of the same cauldron in which they make love. Why shouldn't there be two cauldrons? one for each appetite? Or perhaps they could find some leftover sardines elsewhere in the shack.

Another point: You have had the young man light a fire under the cauldron a little while before they begin to make love! At that point the reader doesn't think of the idyllic moment, but worries about blisters on the girl's bottom. I'm sorry to be so coarse about this, but these are the reactions you arouse by vague writing. Even the physical positions and movements of the two inside the cauldron are not clear. Furthermore, the fact that the shack is in darkness, and that you don't describe the banked fire very clearly, nor the kind of stove (I believe the Japanese call it a *kamo-do*) being used, all adds to the confusion.

It would be a great mistake to delete this scene, because it adds greatly to the structure of the book. But it must be rewritten entirely, with great care and much more frankness, and very explicitly. I think you will have to provide some dim light from the fire in the shack, and give a much clearer visual description. Furthermore, you will have to prepare the reader carefully for the size of the cauldron. Unless you stress its size, the situation will seem impossible. It would help if the man failed to light a fire under the cauldron, and if it were still kept warm by the ashes underneath.

Ashes retain their heat for quite a long time. Then the girl could quite logically climb into the cauldron to keep warm, and the boy eventually, having found sardines elsewhere, could creep in to join her.

I have the feeling that you are rather uneasy about American standards of decency in sexual matters. I think you can be quite frank and detailed about some gestures, provided you maintain the mood of lyricism and purity.

One more detail: What kind of skirt is it that is fastened around the girl's bosom? If your people's skirts do indeed fasten this way, then I think you must lay the groundwork in some detail, explaining just why the boy reached for the girl's bosom to unfasten her skirt. This is part of the general vagueness in physical description.

Another detail: While most American readers will not be prudish about sexual details, some may be quite repelled by the bubbles of saliva on the girl's teeth. There is something particularly disgusting in the description of the saliva as frothy. We associate frothing at the mouth with madness and physical uncleanliness. Perhaps it is chiefly your choice of adjectives, but you do emphasize the saliva beyond all reason. A sentence such as: "With a slight groan of 'Ahoo' her lips parted, and he touched her warmth and saliva." just won't do. There is absolutely nothing wrong about writing such a sentence as "His lips touched the moist warmth of her mouth" or, in certain circumstances, if the man is quite sophisticated, his tongue instead of his lips can touch the moist warmth of her mouth. But when you inject the clinical word *saliva,* you immediately put yourself in a predicament.

I'm afraid a similar problem exists concerning the word *bottom.* Certainly the cauldron has a bottom, but so has the girl, and no matter how you handle your description of the cauldron, readers will inevitably associate the two bottoms. I am afraid you better do without the word *bottom* entirely, since there are many other words for both kinds of bottoms.

I hope you will excuse me for writing in such detail. Usually language problems are not that complicated, but when it comes to sexual overtones and the free associations that go with them, the problems become unusually subtle and need careful explanation. I have spoken with your agent about this, and we both agree that you simply have to rewrite these few pages before we take formal action on our option. Perhaps the scene should be expanded. Do you need my copy of the manuscript?

Cordially,

MAGAZINES

PART THREE: *The Editors' Role in Shaping the Character of His Magazine*

L. Rust Hills

L. Rust Hills is Fiction Editor of ESQUIRE. *He has a Kings Point BS and an MA and BA from Wesleyan. He taught English at Carleton College and in Europe, and story writing in Columbia's GS program. He was a founding editor of the little magazine* QUIXOTE *and in 1961 was Director of the NYC Writers' Conference. He's currently writing a book on the short story for The Macmillan Company.*

*Few young editors today are as articulate, candid and influential as L. Rust Hills. In the following article he reveals the manner of his working day and the substance of his working philosophy. What he has to say about choosing the fiction for one of the most widely-read quality magazines in America—*ESQUIRE*—will dispel many illusions about the "glamour profession" of editing but it will reaffirm many ideas and ideals about what an editor is and what he does in the exercise of his craft.*

EDITING: OR ARGUING, PROCURING, TINKERING AND SENDING THINGS BACK

This article was originally given as a talk, "The Writer and the Editor," at the Columbia University Writers' Conference in July, 1960. It appears here in a slightly altered form.

Two things usually are meant by the word *editing:* one is *editing* a magazine, choosing the material that goes into it, or being an editor in a book publishing company; and the other is *editing* a manuscript, working over it with a pencil and various perceptions. Let me distinguish a bit more between the two and then discuss each a bit separately.

One man will usually be doing both kinds of work at a book publisher and usually at a magazine. Insofar as the second sense of the word is confined to the use of the pencil—correcting punctuation, standardizing capitalization, "styling" the manuscript—the editor's function is really that of *copy*editing. Almost all magazines and book publishers will have one or more copyeditors to do this work, usually an intelligent middle-aged lady (ladies are thought to be more *careful* about this detailed sort of work . . . what's meant by this, of course, is that they're thought to have less imagination than men, and to be less likely to become bored with meticulous work; she on her part knows what fools the editors are, how careless they can be).

The first kind of editing, being an editor of a magazine, or being one of the editors of a book publishing company (let me stick pretty much to what I know better, magazine editing, and mention book editing only where I feel real differences exist), is helping to create a magazine rather than helping to create a story or a novel or an article. It is almost policy-making, although of course management (usually the ownership) is the real policy-maker. As a rule, management will hire the kind of editor they think will make them the kind of book they think they want.

As far as the writer is concerned, the main difference between these two functions of the editor is that the first brings him and his work to the magazine or the publishing company; the other then "handles" him and his work. But, as I say, one man will usually perform the two roles. It is the difference between worrying about a given article or story or book or about the whole magazine from issue to issue or the book firm's whole seasonal list. And it isn't (or shouldn't be) only the managing editor who worries about things as a whole.

An editor in his function as editor of a magazine can best spend his time in arguing. He must argue with other editors that his stuff is better than their stuff and deserves more space in the book. He must argue with advertising space salesmen that their policy of committing editorial coverage directly or indirectly so as to get more advertising in a given area will compromise the integrity and inhibit the vitality of the magazine. He must argue with the circulation and promotion men that their effort to get in more "boob-bait" cover-line articles to boost circulation is going to harm the prestige of the magazine and eventually drive away readers by disappointing them once too often. And he must argue a great deal with management, to convince them that his ideas as to what should go into the magazine form a policy that is not different from their own, or try to convince them to change their policy. A certain tension in all this arguing is healthy, but if his ideas keep getting turned down consistently, the editor has eventually to quit. Ultimately, policy at any magazine which is not obviously failing goes back to one person's ideas—almost always, but not always, the owner's.

The owner will decide whether it is to be a readers' magazine or an editors' magazine. I feel that all magazines tend to be one or the other. The first is designed to meet the readers' interests exactly, on a sort of one-to-one basis. *Redbook,* I believe, has been a classic example of this sort. There they know (from readership surveys) that their readers are couples twenty and one-half years old, with one and one-half children, one and one-half cars, one and one-half thousand dollars in the bank, and so forth. So all their articles have to be for, and all their fiction has to be about, people with one and one-half children, one and one-half cars, one and one-half thousand dollars in the bank.

The other type of magazine (and it is often more interesting, although not necessarily so to its readership) is edited not according to the readers' interests, but according to the editors'. *The New Yorker,* when it was edited by Harold Ross, is a good example; but just as good, probably (and much better known to me) is *Esquire.* Because Arnold Gingrich, the founding editor and now publisher of *Esquire,* is, say, interested in sports cars and jazz and literature, the magazine over the years he's been there shows a certain continuity. But the sort of one and one-half cars continuity that advertising media experts delight in in a magazine has always been absent. Because of Mr. Gingrich's wide interests *Esquire*'s interests are broad. He is probably the only person in the whole world who can read every single thing in every issue of *Esquire* with real interest.

This is what is meant by *editing a magazine.* At the higher level, it means an editor hiring himself a staff to get what he wants; at a lower level, it means going out and getting it. *Procuring* is a major function, and as in any sort of procuring, having contacts and sources so as eventually to build a stable (in this case, of course, of writers) is of great value. In this area, editors use writers like trading cards. A writer, out in, say, Minnesota, is overwhelmed when he is taken up by an editor, and writes him letters, damp with tears of gratitude, for recommending him to other editors, who in turn have passed the word along to others, saying, "This is a good writer; you should ask him to do something for you." Marvelous as this is for a writer, the editor shouldn't ever forget that he's living on this man's work, and by recommending him to others, he's getting other names in return, and he's getting the reputation, very important in this business, of *knowing who the good new young writers are*. It is very important that an editor seem to know what's going on, so that people will tell him things. By judicious collecting, an editor can find himself with one of the larger collections, and if he's got a large collection of good writers he should not only have a reputation as a good editor (which isn't as unimportant as it sounds), but he should also have a good magazine.

A lot of this trading is done at lunch, I suppose, on the expense account, just as everyone assumes it is, and it's not unpleasant. Less pleasant is lunch with cranky lady agents, but after a while a new editor will find he gets so cranky himself that he realizes the lunches are doing more harm than good and gradually discontinues them. At first he reads all the little magazines avidly, looking for new talents. More and more, though, as he's in touch with more and more writers, he becomes more and more buried in (or under) their manuscripts, and he has less time, energy, and interest to find new ones. He settles more and more into a shell, publishing more and more the same writers (who have by now become friends). The newest new writing begins to seem terrible to him—as for instance, the Beat Generations writing seems to me. The only hope is that he'll be promoted and can hire someone who'll bring in the new people and talk him into using them.

That's the life-cycle of a magazine editor, and few of them can stay in the business to see it through. It requires infinite flexibility and a sort of superior-grade butterfly mind. As a consequence, a good editor may seem glib or even foolish to an expert or to a real intellectual, for he'll often be satisfied with the superficial as long as it sounds at all knowledgeable. Nevertheless, editing requires a sustained appetite for what's new that only the rarest of men can maintain as they grow older.

Let me talk now about the editor in the other sense, *the editor of a manuscript*.

As a graduate student at Wesleyan University, I was early taken by the critical idea that came up-river from William K. Wimsatt and others at Yale, that a work of literary art somehow has an existence apart from its author or even apart from its author's intention. The idea is, that in evaluating a piece of writing, you judge its "whole actual meaning" (to use Wimsatt's term), which is a question of the relation of parts to whole, rather than of means to ends or of manner to matter.

This is a matter of aesthetic theory, more proper in application to the act of criticism (which I take to be inspection of already published—and hence "final"—writing) than to the act of editing (which in the sense I'm using it now refers to unpublished writing, which can still be tinkered with). But it was natural for me to carry over from teaching into editing this concept of writing as having a meaning or existence of its own.

I tend to confuse (in talking about it) the point or purpose of the work (not entirely what creative writing classes call "the theme") with the "whole actual meaning." In "unfinished" writing this confusion is, I guess, inevitable. But "whole actual meaning" is what I mean, and the important thing is the relation of parts to the whole. I used to advance the definition of a good story as one in which the point or purpose is inextricably bedded in all the other aspects of the story: in the plot, the mood, the setting, the characterizations, even in the style. This inextricably bedded purpose is the whole actual meaning—the *work's* purpose, so to speak—that controls in turn the selection of all the other parts. Well, good editing always seemed to me, by extension then, to consist in the ability to comprehend the work's purpose and in the ability to demonstrate to the author better ways to realize or fulfill that purpose. I suppose it's quibbling not to refer to this as the author's purpose, but in some strange way, in actual practice this works out to be more than just an aesthetic-metaphysical distinction. For my own self, it is the only theory of such matters that permits an editor to contribute at all to a literary work. For if you think of literary art solely as an expression or extension of the author, where is the editor's role?

This is a pretty high-flying role to set up for an editor—side by side creating along with a writer—and it's a role that few working editors ever have the ability or (more realistically) the time for. I used to be an editor of a little magazine, and I seemed then to have more time and inclination for careful manuscript revisions. Of course the little magazine writers are (in theory, at least) less skillful, haven't yet perhaps learned all the things that can be done "to realize the work's purpose." Little magazine writers often feel that if they aren't getting paid they ought to have the right to have their stuff appear as they wrote it, no changes or suggestions needed. But little magazine editors aren't getting paid either; and they're likely to feel that if it's their magazine, they ought to have the right to have what's in it appear the way *they* want it. Payment seems to make both authors and editors compromise standards.

At a commercial magazine, material by established writers is seldom tinkered with as much as it probably ought to be. A lot of the fiction by "name" writers will be novel chunks (nowadays few established authors write many short stories) and a useful skill in a national magazine's fiction editor is the ability to recognize a good self-contained chunk of a novel and to figure out with the author ways to extract it, drawing out the roots and severing the threads that connect it with the rest of the novel. It is mainly in ways like this that commercial editors get into manuscript work, except sometimes with new writers. Mr. Gingrich at *Esquire,* for instance, has always felt that he edits best who edits least, and with writers of the skill and stature that a magazine like *Esquire* ought to have, he's probably right. Besides, the lack of editing gives the magazine a certain *potpourri* vitality that highly edited magazines like *Time* and *The New Yorker* sacrifice in order to gain a unified editorial tone—such a tone being of course of great use in delineating the magazine's "image" to potential advertisers, as well as being reassuring to the readers themselves.

Somewhere between the two editorial roles we've been talking about—the editor of magazine and the editor of a manuscript—falls the job which is actually most important of all. It is the answer I give when people ask me what I actually do as fiction editor at *Esquire.* I send things back. Sending things back is what editors in *both* senses of the word do most of. There is no single more important function. Nor is sending things back so wholly uncreative as it may sound. An editor can get as much good stuff, I'm convinced, from constructive sending-back as he ever would from lunching with cranky lady agents. Editors are always being asked that tedious question, "What percentage of the stories you publish comes from unknown writers?" and I've found that the best way to answer this (and it's true of all such loaded questions) is with another question: "What do you mean by an *unknown* writer?" There are probably few writers wholly unknown to a good editor who could write a story that the editor would take. A good editor, for instance, follows the little magazines as closely as he can, and he probably makes some sort of effort to keep records on the writers he sees published there and elsewhere. Is a man who has published a story in *The Tamarack Review* an "unknown" writer? It seems to me he is so, thoroughly; but he is still known of by a lot of editors. Many quality magazines will publish a large "percentage" of writers just as they are ready to leave the little magazine circuit, where they are often fairly well known, but entirely *un*known to the general public. And consider a writer who has never published anything anywhere at all, but who has sent in a couple of stories to an editor who returned them with a letter explaining why they weren't right and asking to see more—is he unknown? Of course he is, but not to the editor who wrote to him. The third or fourth story he sends may be the one the magazine will take. This is what I mean by constructive sending back. The promising writer is not going to try the same magazine again and again unless he is encouraged. Constructive sending back can keep an editor in touch with a promising writer long beyond the time he'd normally go off somewhere else; it may get the editor a story eventually.

It is equally important actively to discourage writers who *can't possibly ever*. If an editor is to have time at all for the writers who *could possibly sometime,* then he's got to be viciously negative with the others. I hear from time to time that I've had a mean reputation with agents because of the acid notes with which I returned manuscripts. The notes were angry because I did what no sensible editor ever does: I read the agents' manuscripts right through to the foolish end because I thought that they must have had some good reason for sending them to me. Then, of course, I was furious at myself and at them for wasting both our time. This, of course, changes too. Just as enthusiasm for the pursuit of good stuff wanes, so does outrage at the bad.

Let me conclude now with just a very few speculations about *what makes a good editor?*

There are all kinds of reasons, I guess, why a writer would make a good editor: he can do it, so he can tell others how. This is what makes a writer a good teacher of creative writing (if there can be such a thing). I discount entirely the idea that a writer is too committed to his own methods to be able to help shape the materials of another writer. But a writer, as an artist, isn't usually sufficiently interested in anything beyond his own work, or shouldn't be. And a writer as an editor or as a teacher is usually just waiting for the time he can get all this work off his hands and get back to what he really wants to do.

As you know, book publishers (especially publishers of textbooks, but of trade books, too) always want their editors to have had some sales experience. A book editor who has been a book salesman has a great advantage over his fellow editors in any argument: he can say, "Your book won't sell; I know it won't, because I've had experience selling." But everyone knows of the great discrepancy between what the public buys and what the world thinks is good. Publishers can't go on forever providing just what the public has shown it likes. Sooner or later people want to move along to some new thing for publishers to run into the ground. A magazine, as *Collier's* showed, can founder while providing what appeals to millions.

A critic? A teacher as editor? He *should* make a good editor, for he's most used to studying that "whole actual meaning" of a work without any sort of overinvolvement. But both teachers and critics are more likely to have an idea of what the reading public *ought* to like, than of what that public can actually be made to take.

There seems to be no professional training for a good editor. The really great ones seem never to have been anything else. It seems to be an instinctual thing. It is not just knowing what the public likes, as you can get from some sort of selling experience. It is knowing what they *will* like, slightly ahead of them. Not so far ahead as the critic or teacher is likely to be, but just so far ahead as a magazine editor always is. Ears up, listening, asking what's new, not minding if his version of the new thing will seem slightly shopworn and shoddy to the intellectuals who've been talking about it for years, but feeling somehow that he's interested in it himself, so his readers will be too. Thus, of course, the better the man, the better the magazine.

Bernard De Voto

Bernard De Voto was noted as a critic of American letters, a sturdy conservationist and long-time editor of HARPER'S MAGAZINE. *His "The Easy Chair" column, a platform for his outspoken and often controversial opinions on various aspects of American life and literature, was one of the magazine's most popular features during the twenty years he wrote it: 1935-1955.*

From the one hundredth anniversary issue (October, 1950) of HARPER'S MAGAZINE, *one of its most influential editors writes a review of the kind of critical journalism that made that magazine one of the leading periodicals here in America and throughout the literate world. His remarks are pertinent, too, for the whole scope of American journals of critical comment —the magazines for intelligent readers who accept topics taboo elsewhere, as long as they are presented in a civilized, intellectually unfettered manner.*

THE CONSTANT FUNCTION

THE Abbé Sieyès amply summarized his achievements during the Revolution: *"J'ai vécu,"* he stayed alive. That terse eloquence is like an incantation uttered when thunder grumbles to the left of noon. *Harper's* has been published for a hundred years; it was the first quality magazine that circulated nationally and it created a type. The type flourished for a long time and during the last quarter of the nineteenth century it dominated monthly journalism. Thereafter it declined and with the first world war it began to disappear. Besides *Harper's* only one other member of what was once called "the quality group" remains. To have survived for a hundred years is an achievement impressive in itself, but that the first quality magazine is as vigorous now as at any time during the century is a fact so significant that it invites examination.

The circulation figures cause no uneasiness in the Luce offices but they stand for a national influence altogether disproportionate to their sum. That influence, which was not achieved by chance, explains why *Harper's* has survived. As American journalism developed in the twentieth century, it seemed to be abandoning one of its basic functions. But the function was not only basic, it was vital, it could not be abandoned, and one segment of journalism had to perform it. Natural selection, which produces specialized life forms in adaptation to the environment, shaped *Harper's* to the service of the endangered function.

Begin with the fact that the magazine meets the competition of the newsstand; it must make a profit. There may be ways of keeping a subsidized magazine from being a closed magazine but none has yet been found. No way of keeping it from being dull has been found, either. Such a magazine usually begins in dedication to a set of findings postulated before the search for them begins, some pattern of belief, some gospel. It exists to advertise dogmas, to hold truth to a test oath, and to conduct public arguments for the private comfort of those who agree with the arguments before they are made. The job it does may repeatedly be valuable but its detachment is circumscribed by a vested interest; it is slanted journalism and must work under suspicion that the end in view has made it selective with the evidence. The suspicion is frequently well founded, for the shortest way between dedication and dogma makes a wide detour round evidence that points another way. And such a magazine is usually querulous and always pontifical. It so loves virtue that it appeals to nothing but the love of virtue. True believers doubtless find it *gemütlich,* but to sinful people, who greatly outnumber them, its self-righteousness is aggressively dull. Periodically it calls on the sinful to repent and to throw a nickel on the drum for virtue's sake—how can you be indifferent when the gospel hangs in the balance? That is its sales talk; it asks to be bought as an act of faith. Since they are withdrawn from competition, its editors need not be competent but only devout, its writers not interesting but only orthodox.

But what counts more heavily is that their ideas are not subjected to competition, either. In fact, they are protected from it, for we must not question gospel truths. Theoretically, a magazine which need not worry about the payroll and the printer ought to be the best medium for unbiased inquiry but things have never yet worked out that way. The profit motive is the only warranty journalism has found for what Justice Holmes called "free trade in ideas." The best test of truth, he decided, "is the power of the thought to get itself accepted in the competition of the market." But all subsidies rig the market; they are in restraint of trade. If a magazine is kept, it does not matter in the least who keeps it.

So two things, equally important, *Harper's* has to interest the audience it addresses—educated people, people of supple intelligence, of persistent curiosity, capable both of pursuing ideas and of playing with them. Presumably these people too love virtue but they will not suffer boredom for its sake; as it grows in the shuck it is not worth fifty cents to them. A *Harper's* editor is a man trying to put together a magazine which will sell for fifty cents on its merits. His nightmare is ponderousness and his prayer is that tomorrow's mail may have a frivolous manuscript in it, or if that be crowding providence too hard, at least an amusingly written one. He wakes to resume his search for new *Harper's* writers, writers who know what they are talking about and breathe easily while they talk.

And also, the audience insists on determining for itself what virtue is. *Harper's* must guarantee its readers that no orthodoxy will interfere with the free competition of ideas. They will not be editorially weighted or skewed; they will have their say and submit their claim. Justice Holmes's principle holds that so long as the market is free and open, error will be corrected, competition will provide the essential tests. They are functions of competition and they consist of criticism and appraisal. The evolution of American journalism made *Harper's* a magazine of appraisal, of critical inquiry.

For both newspapers and magazines have steadily narrowed the range of inquiry. Modern journalism concentrates on reporting. The facilities of communication, incomparably swifter than those of the nineteenth century, are focused on presenting, describing, showing, picturing, stating. Size, expense, and the pressure of the speed-up, not to mention the tastes of the mass audience, all work to the same end: get the thing reported and get on to the next thing that is clamoring to be reported. But if journalism stops with reporting, then a necessary part of its job is left undone. There must be something that says, Wait a minute! and asks, But just what is this, just what does it mean, and how can you be sure? What is reported must also be examined, interpreted, criticized, and reconsidered. If large-scale publishing cannot perform this function, it cannot therefore be allowed to atrophy; someone else must take care of it.

Thus *Harper's* often has found itself reporting news, though not as the daily paper reports it. Its reporting is retrospective, to correct or to amplify the record. Its reporter has had time that the legman lacked and so has turned up among the facts relations or significance that he missed, or has dug farther into the setting than he was able to. Newspapers can do this once-routine kind of follow-up only as a special feature and usually when they are able to build fresh news on the old.

Harper's, however, is much less concerned with news than with comment on it. The forces that have produced the modern newspaper have incidentally enervated the editorial page. Even if they had not, it would not now be possible for a paper to exert such a national influence as several did seventy-five years ago. To compensate for what it has lost, daily journalism has invented the syndicated column to interpret the news, but it has rather opened a new field than plugged the gap. A columnist cannot qualify himself to cover all the news, though some try to. He is a specialist, usually a specialist in politics, and he has to work under the same pressure of haste that drives the city desk. His frequently expert competitor, the radio analyst, is under a double exigency, for his space is measured in time. What the news weekly offers, a compound in which reporting and editorial interpretation are pressed together in register, is not a substitute for critical inquiry. But there has to be comment on the news that escapes from the tyranny of haste and the limitation of space. *Harper's* has become a vehicle for comment by experts.

The evolution of monthly journalism left similar areas bare. A magazine whose circulation is in the millions is primarily an enterprise in popular entertainment and information, and its service of information has to ignore a great deal of the world at hand. Here too *Harper's* is an impresario of experts, and in two kinds of knowledge, that which leaves the mass audience cold and that which it avoids because of anxiety. Something is happening in science or technology, in philosophy or sociology; in some odd half-acre of the United States or the world at large a sign seems to have been given, and somebody who understands it finds it promising or ominous; a learned specialty has turned up something potentially significant or important to a few people but not as yet to a great many. The big box office, the mass-circulation magazine, cannot deal with such things, but educated people must be kept in touch with the advance of knowledge. So *Harper's* transmits the knowledge of specialists and makes it negotiable. And also there is the information which the big magazine must avoid because it is tabooed. It has to be put at the disposal of people for whom it is important or usable.

The same two functions are more important still in the inquiries that concern opinion. A big magazine can deal hardly at all in opinion that is at odds with popular belief or tolerance, or that goes to the roots of either. Popular tranquillity of mind may be questioned, but it can be challenged only lightly, to a point short of discomfort. And the box office cannot give costly space to marginal thinking, the minority opinion that offends no one. But there has to be some channel round the avoidances, compromises, and taboos of the big magazine. Inquiries must be made, opinions must be expressed, judgments must be passed—ideas must be got into the market place. Here is a pivotal function of journalism, to which we citizens have given a charter of freedom and immunity on the express condition that it will get them there.

For we are committed. The independent press is a mechanism of our society. In the relationships of men there are no final truths, our premise runs, and error of opinion may be safely tolerated "so long as reason is left free to combat it." There is no way of telling in advance: an opinion that offends popular belief may be inflammatory, it may be fallacious, it may be right, it may be worthless and incapable of turning litmus paper either way. You can only get it into the market and set conflicting ideas to work on it, in the belief that what emerges will be the most dependable approximation of the truth. And this applies not only to "the thought we hate" but to the marginal opinion which modern journalism has tended to let go by default. If it goes by default it has been suppressed as effectively as if someone higher up had censored it. Hence a continuing necessity for a journalism that will provide the utmost possible latitude of discussion.

The utmost possible—which necessarily sets a limit, though one exceedingly difficult to define. Freedom of speech and of the press does not mean, as naïve and zealous people long to believe, that what I write must be published, but instead that if someone does publish it the constitutional guarantee will protect me. What I write may be not so much dangerous—the thought we hate—as harebrained, but written to an important end nevertheless. Against the indifference of journalism, I and those whom conceivably I might affect used to have the recourse of pamphleteering, but that has become prohibitively expensive and impossible to distribute nationally. If Thomas Paine himself were alive today he could reach an audience only through established periodicals—and it is precisely the possibility that even the looniest, or the most dangerous, point of view may have a seed in it from which a Thomas Paine may grow that forces a magazine of inquiry to strain its abhorrences to the utmost. At any moment the entirely inconsequential may become urgent. So the channel must be kept open for use.

The function assigned to *Harper's* by natural selection, then, was that of assuring the expression of opinion. A magazine which undertakes the job is subjected to formidable hazards. It is a shining target for the most malign skills of our age, publicity and propaganda; if it were to be victimized by either it would promptly die. Sensationalism would kill it just as fast. It cannot be a magazine of controversy, which means either a magazine with a cause or one which stages an exhibition match that is only an elegant kind of box office. But the facts that produce controversy and the clash of opinion that arises from them are in the very center of its path. If controversy therefore follows, it must amiably abide the uproar. And at the core of editorial responsibility are the kinds of opinion just alluded to, the harebrained and the dangerous, together with a great variety of others that hinge on them, the eccentricities, manias, fads, fashions, and delusions in which the human race and its sub-species the Americans are so fecund. They are inexhaustibly interesting and at any time any of them may explode into importance. It is the delight of journalism to inquire into them and the duty of critical journalism to appraise them—but shall the columns of *Harper's* be open to their advocacy? The question is far from pellucid. There is the sovereign principle: the widest possible freedom of discussion. And there is a fact: sometimes they may have a legitimate claim. A magazine of critical inquiry has to pass on the legitimacy of the claim; there is no way of not doing so.

This is the upper ether of editorial skill and integrity, and the life of the magazine hangs in the balance. It undertakes to facilitate the search for truth. In doing so it may please or antagonize, it may arouse, it may catalyze, but it cannot crusade and no one can use it to crusade with. Its safeguard is the temper in which it works. However ardent the heart, the mind must be cool. The critical spirit is skeptical, resolved to find out, to test all things. It refuses to let the mind's edge be blunted by wishfulness or indignation. It is aware that there are no final truths, "that time has upset many fighting faiths." It is willing to criticize its own motives and to announce its own mistakes. There is no finer irony than that which makes a reluctance to believe the principal guarantee that ideas will be wholly free to fight for acceptance.

Beyond this—which could have been called liberal journalism until the adjective came into disfavor—there is the additional necessity of being civilized. The skeptical intelligence will be urbane. It will dread solemnity as much as it dreads inaccuracy or propaganda. It will have leisure to enjoy the altogether unimportant and it will insist on handling even the weightiest subjects with a light touch. It has got to be the old pro, the ballplayers' ballplayer. "I been watching him for eight years," a fan is supposed to have remarked about

Joe DiMaggio, "and nobody ever knocked him a hard fly yet." *Harper's,* too, has got to look that way to the stands.

Harper's, that is, serves a constant function and can serve it only on the highest level of journalism. At its century mark, it may fairly ask where is there better journalism, or more expert, or more reliable? It implies a reciprocal audience, the people for whom the best that journalism can offer is indispensable. There has never been a time when that audience was very large. *Harper's* cannot claim that it has been alone in serving this audience or that it has served them better than some other magazines which have tried. But it has never fallen below their standards, it has never offered them less than the best journalism. It has put itself at the service of inquiring minds. It has tried to get at the realities of the contemporary scene, to inquire into them, to appraise them.

For a hundred years *Harper's* has been offering expert journalism to the most intelligent audience. They must have found it satisfactory, for they have kept it alive. At the turn of its century it expects that satisfaction to continue and expects to survive as long as there is any sensible way of looking ahead.

Edward Weeks

Edward Weeks has been the editor of the ATLANTIC MONTHLY *since 1938. He is also a noted lecturer, critic and reviewer.*

Early days on the ATLANTIC MONTHLY *in the 1920's; the great writers of that era; insights into an editor's working day; perceptive comments on editors and editing, the craftsman and his craft are among the themes that comprise the following selection from Edward Weeks' important memoir* IN FRIENDLY CANDOR.

Every editor could profit much from a careful reading of the entire volume, but from the selection that follows, Mr. Weeks' admonition to continue "editing up" is worthy enough to be a First Commandment for all neophyte editors and veterans who are tempted to talk down to the reader.

I HAD never been a fast reader in college, indeed I could seldom travel at faster than thirty-five pages an hour with those solid volumes we were required to read in the Widener Library. But now I had to step up the pace. By narrowing my gaze to the center of the page and reading straight down, I found I could get a glancing comprehension at double the speed. What was equally important, I arranged the day's reading as if it were a diet. I would begin with the hardheaded articles, the papers on economics, foreign policy, the scholastic thesee, in the morning when I was fresh. At eleven I would switch to short stories. After lunch I would make penciled notes for those rejections which merited more than the printed slip. Sometimes I wrote just a single line of hope in pencil at the bottom of the rejection slip; sometimes I went into constructive detail in a separate letter, with the result that the manuscript would almost certainly be revised and returned to us in ten days.

No day's reading is ever the same. A cool perceptive essay by Agnes Repplier or Willa Cather could give a brightness to the morning very different from the feeling which overcame me if by bad luck I chanced on a succession of papers by cranks. Over a six-month period I kept a tally of the "nut" manuscripts and found that they divided fairly evenly between California and New York City. Theosophists, the writers who talked familiarly to God, and those who took themselves seriously as the New Messiah, gravitated naturally to the land of Aimee Semple McPherson. There they found supporters, founded their temples and held forth. Lower Manhattan, on the other hand, was at this period the homeland of free verse, much of it splintered prose which, as it was subdivided in short staccato lines, looked like what the Chinese student called "goggerel." Poems would begin like this:

COSMOS
out of the womb of Time
came forth the azoic globe
earth,
a spark in space

and run on for two more pages, single-spaced. I have always suspected that H. G. Wells's *Outline of History* was a formative influence here. Among the traditional versifiers were a surprisingly large number of women who belonged to "The Samarkand School"; these were possessed with the desire to wander off with "gypsy lads" and "open hearts" along roads which always led to Samarkand for the closing rhyme.

A first reader becomes hypersensitive to those words which are being overworked in the popular vernacular, and some which used to make me wince were "opalescent," "plashing," "realistic," "sensed," "convincing," "reaction," "intriguing"—there were times when it took forceful restraint not to check them. But we did not leave our marks on manuscripts that were going back.

As a veteran I felt no lack of confidence in judging the articles, personal documents, and stories that had to do with the war. For short stories I had an insatiable appetite, and on my own I wrote to those whose work I most admired. It was too late to try for Katherine Mansfield, but we did secure one of the last by Rudyard Kipling, and I was much excited by Rudolph Fisher, a Negro X-ray technician who wrote powerfully and most knowingly about the Harlem and West Indian Negroes and who would have done some fine books for us had he lived. F. Scott Fitzgerald's generation was mine, and I laughed at and partly resented the fussy, overly nice criticism which the *Atlantic* used to publish about our Flaming Youth (read, as a sample, "Cornelia Discusses an Eligible Young Man" by Stuart P. Sherman, in the *Atlantic* for September 1924). I noticed that there were three areas of controversy which kept appearing and reappearing: Prohibition, anti-Semitism, and the influence of Roman Catholicism in a democratic society. As a Wilsonian Democrat I welcomed material about the League of Nations. I read with respect what Dean Inge, Samuel McChord Crothers, and Rufus Jones had to say about the spirit. And I wondered about our poets, so many of whom were genteel and so few of whom were young. While I was at Liveright's we had published a long poem, *The Waste Land,* by an American in London named T. S. Eliot, but for reasons I have never fathomed he was neither invited nor published by the *Atlantic* of the 1920s.

There were certain unwritten laws in the *Atlantic* office which were conveyed to me either by Miss Converse or by our head proofreader, Miss Caroline Church. The word "nigger" was not to be used if it could be avoided nor were the four-letter words, and as for "bitch" or "bastard," they were suggested either by "b——" or by "S.O.B." Our fastidious readers, so the saying went, were "our permanent and valuable core"; they were swift to voice their displeasure, and they always had been. In 1869, when the magazine published Mrs. Harriet Beecher Stowe's spectacular article protesting the indignities endured by Lady Byron ("The True Story of Lady Byron's Life," September 1869), fifteen thousand of our most fastidious canceled their subscriptions within a period of twelve months, an example not lost on later editors.

I remember in the spring of my first year we received from Miss Amy Lowell a poem entitled "Fool o' the Moon," a poem which, as she explained to Mr. Sedgwick in the accompanying note, had been most warmly received when she read it aloud. In details somewhat explicit for a spinster it described the love affair between the poet and Lady Moon, ending with the curtain line, "I have lain with Lady Moon." Mr. Sedgwick accepted the challenge and the poem, but I noticed that it was held in the icebox for some months, in fact was not actually published until July, when the schools and colleges which used the *Atlantic* in their English classes were dispersed and there was small likelihood of protest from their professors.

We were the first magazine of national circulation to publish a story by Ernest Hemingway. "Fifty Grand" told of a professional boxer, the welterweight champion, who was training for a title fight. He is past his prime, and so sure he is to be beaten that he bets $50,000 with the professional gamblers that he will lose. The climax of the fight, when the professional gamblers try to double-cross him, is as rugged and punishing a piece of prose as we have ever published, and I was proud that we took it without question or change. None of us had any way of knowing that "Fifty Grand" had already been declined by Ray Long, the editor of *Cosmopolitan*, by the *Saturday Evening Post* and *Collier's*, and that Max Perkins had tried to cut it for *Scribner's* and had given up. No one would think of objecting to it today, and because the writing had such force and authority behind it, few did then. We accepted it in midwinter and printed it in July of 1927.

I knew when Mr. Sedgwick had the manuscript of "Fifty Grand" in his hands, seated as I was in my room with both doors between us closed, for he let out a crescendo of short explosions, "oh-oh-Oh-Oh . . ."—and whenever he did this it was a sure indication that he had found something exciting. But when some long-promised beauty turned out to be a lemon, he could be heard moaning, beginning on a low note and swelling in volume, "Ohoooo *Oh*," which told F.C. and myself what we had already suspected—that he had a dud.

Like every young editor I was keen to bring into our columns the work of my friends and of writers I admired, and within limitations I was encouraged to do so. The poems of Robert Hillyer, John Crowe Ransom, Theodore Morrison, Morley Dobson, and William Whitman; a paper on hunting, "The Ibex and the Elephant," by Douglas Burden, and another fine pair, "Tiger, Tiger" and "Elephant," by his white hunter in Indo-China, a Frenchman, J. M. Defosse; stories by Manuel Komroff, and essays from three Englishmen who impressed me at Cambridge, J. B. S. Haldane, H. M. Tomlinson, and Walter de la Mare.

As a book salesman in New York I had the chance to skim through some of the new volumes by our competitors, and one day at The Sunrise Turn, a personal bookshop uptown, I stood absorbed for forty minutes with a new book entitled *The Cabala* by an unknown named Thornton Wilder. Now I wrote to Mr. Wilder on *Atlantic* stationery telling him of my admiration for his first book and suggesting that if he had a new one in progress we might like to consider it for serialization. He replied that he was working on a novel about South America, was three-quarters finished, and that he would send me the carbon copy. So we were presented with a preview of *The Bridge of San Luis Rey*. It was beautifully episodic, and even without the ending—the bridge had not yet collapsed—it seemed to me clear that this would be a great attraction for new readers. My two superiors, however, thought otherwise and I was left to write a very difficult letter of rejection.

A first reader is no good unless he is outspoken, and I was not always tactful. The treasurer of the *Atlantic* was MacGregor Jenkins, a genial, loquacious gentleman with a streak of sentimentality a yard wide. His anecdotes ran on forever, and I found myself keeping away from his open office on the third floor, for once entrapped you had to listen. I had very little liking for his short bucolic essays, sometimes about Amherst, where he had spent his boyhood and seen Emily Dickinson over the back fence, sometimes about his barn and its inmates in Dover. It seemed to me that his cows and chickens had no place in the *Atlantic,* and I was too young to respect the generosity in the acceptance. Each time they presented themselves I denounced his manuscripts and two months later there they were in the new issue.

I chafed under such restraints but not for long; I was learning fast and I did not miss New York. To be a junior on the *Atlantic's* staff in those days was to be borne along on a powerful current. Sedgwick had a flair for social criticism, and he found those who could probe for him with authority, and deep. He found William Z. Ripley, the Harvard economist, who in three devastating articles, "Main Street to Wall Street," "Stop, Look and Listen," and "More Light and Power Too" (January, September, and November 1926), laid bare the malpractices of high finance, the fabricated reports to the stockholders, the interlocking directorates, the scandal in public utilities which were lazily winked at in the boom. In this case Ripley's probing laid the groundwork for the S.E.C. Sedgwick persuaded a New York lawyer, Charles Marshall, to write an Open Letter to Governor Alfred E. Smith questioning whether the Governor's faith as a Roman Catholic disqualified him for the Presidency. The issue was hot and sensitive, especially in the South, and it is greatly to Sedgwick's credit that the Governor took the challenge seriously and published his historic reply in the *Atlantic's* columns. Again, it was Sedgwick who diverted away from the *New Republic* and into the *Atlantic* the 16,000-word investigation of the Sacco-Vanzetti trial in which Felix Frankfurter, then a professor at the Harvard Law School, proclaimed the innocence of the accused. These were just a few of his ten-strikes, and they explained why, after twenty years, the magazine was solidly in the black and no longer a "kept" journal as it had been at Houghton Mifflin. We were a small team who assisted a great editor, and there were three in particular who contributed mightily to this transformation: Donald B. Snyder, the assistant publisher who came aboard the year after I did; Teresa S. Fitzpatrick, who under the signature of "Christine Lowell" invited the subscribers; and Daisy Zanck, who was our entire manufacturing department and who handled the costly details of printing and paper and advertising make-up with incredible economy.

"Don't overedit," Mr. Sedgwick once wrote. "By so doing you will estrange your writers and rob the magazine of its indispensable variety." But the temptation to overedit is insidious. One of our elderly proofreaders simply could not cope with profanity; left to herself she would have removed every word of it, and after one or two angry run-ins with young contributors we wisely shifted her to our textbooks. The genteel tradition of the *Atlantic* was what Henry L. Mencken had in mind when in the early edition of *The American Language* he wrote: "All the more pretentious American authors try to write chastely and elegantly; the typical literary product of the country is still a refined essay in the *Atlantic Monthly,* perhaps gently jocose but never rough—by Emerson, so to speak, out of Charles Lamb."

When Mencken took upon himself the editing of the *American Mercury,* I was surprised to learn that he was overediting in his way just as much as we were in ours. As a first step we always corrected the spelling and punctuation in accordance with "Atlantic usage," and our cutting and rewriting was the second step, depending on how much we thought the manuscript needed. In general our tendency was to lean down the material whereas Mencken fattened it. He had his pet glossary of adjectives and epithets, and these he imposed upon the text of his contributors: a professor was referred to as a "bunkum professor"; ministers were "high priests" and political commentators were "soothsayers"; for politicians "the Honorable" became a term of contempt; these and similar endearments were bestowed upon the other members of Mencken's "booboisie" even though it may never have occurred to the author to do so when he wrote his piece. I remember how surprised I was when I first saw a manuscript which had been accepted by the *Mercury* and then returned for the author's approval with such additions written in. If the *Atlantic* by its overediting achieved a genteel sameness, Mencken by his achieved a rowdy sameness. With his magnificent prejudices he himself was never at a loss for fresh satire—Billy Sunday, the revivalist, was "America's celebrated pulpit-clown." But when his habitual glossary was imposed upon his contributors they came to sound as if they were Mencken's younger brothers, and the magazine lost its difference.

For four years I read in that back office, and if my father's warning was accurate, my time in Boston was nearly at an end. Yet when the summons came I was not ready for it. I sat across from Mr. Sedgwick on that rectangular Italian chair on which so many contributors had squirmed with discomfort before me; I looked out at the Public Garden thinking "Here falls the ax"—but that was not exactly what he was saying. He was saying something about making a permanent place for myself in the organization, editing the *Atlantic* books which grew out of the magazine. He was saying that a contract had been drawn with Little, Brown & Company, who would manufacture and distribute our books, and that as the Director of the Press I should deal directly with Alfred McIntyre, their President, and Roger Scaife, who handled their manufacturing. I was to be on my own . . . I said I wanted to think it over.

I had seen Dick Simon regularly ever since that day in 1925 when he came to Boston to sell the first Simon & Schuster list. He used to dine with us in our apartment, and I remember his taking out of his suitcase the dummy copies of the first crossword puzzle book, and of a larger volume by a writer called Will Durant. "You remember him," said Dick. "He used to write the introductions for the Haldeman-Julius ten-cent books. He's cut down all their philosophers for them. Quite a man!" That, of course, was the beginning of *The Story of Philosophy*. With Dick I had talked over the possibilities of coming back to New York, but on the other hand, if I stayed on here in Boston, I would be my own boss, with my own list of authors to build up, and a staff consisting of one secretary, the loyal Frances Bates. Sure to be fun and it might pay off. I decided to stay.

It was a hurtful shock to me that we lost our most profitable author, James Truslow Adams, within months of my taking over the Atlantic Monthly Press. It could not have come at a crueler moment, for Mr. Adams's most popular book, *The Epic of America,* was at the top of the best-seller list when without a word of warning he decided to transfer his future writing to Scribner's. The reasons were human enough—and none of us had anticipated them. As an undergraduate at Yale, Mr. Adams had majored in history, and on his graduation he had confided to his favorite professor that he wanted to write, and as a first step should he take his Ph.D.? No, said the professor, not if you want to write history; go down to Wall Street, save just as much money as you can for fifteen years, and then if you still want to write get out on your own. Adams did just that, and fifteen years later he retired from the market with a competence which enabled him—as a bachelor—to research and to write about colonial America. The *Atlantic* published his essays in the magazine and it also published the early books, *The Founding of New England* and *Revolutionary New England,* which established his reputation as a historian. Mr. Sedgwick had given him the idea for his *The Epic of America,* and it seemed to me rank injustice that he should quit us in the high tide of his success. What had made the difference was his marriage. When Adams married in midlife, he wanted to be assured of steady royalties—his savings were no longer enough; and when Scribner's approached him with an editing and writing contract which offered him and his wife security for years, he took it without question. I felt he should have divided his books between the two houses, but I knew that we had been remiss in not gauging his concern for the future. I did not recognize it as such at the time, but this was my first lesson in underediting.

A second instance of underediting occurred in the following year and this had to do with a dear friend of mine, Walter D. Edmonds, of whose work I was intensely proud. Walt Edmonds in college was one of the most clearly developed young writers I have ever known. He spent the summers at Boonville, close to the Erie Canal country; he had sold his first short story about the Canal to Scribner's shortly after graduation, and the plans for his first novel, *Rome Haul,* were already in part on paper. Mr. Sedgwick had persuaded him to send his work to us, and in time we were to print all of his historical novels: *Rome Haul, Erie Water, Drums Along the Mohawk, The Big Barn, Young Ames,* and last but not least that superb collection of his short stories, *Mostly Canallers.* It had never occurred to us that these short stories which had been written for an adult audience could with a very few adjustments be converted into delightful illustrated books for children. When Dodd, Mead and Company invited Walt to turn one of his stories into a juvenile he politely declined and referred the suggestion to us. Alfred and I showed no enthusiasm—we felt it would distract him from his novels.

A year later Dodd, Mead renewed the offer and this time Walter accepted with the result that today they have nine of his books under their imprint, and young readers the country over have relished them. This again was a costly instance of underediting.

These two errors of omission coming so early in my experience as an editor of books made me realize, dimly at first but with increasing clarity, that the editor's relations with his author can never be the same year in year out. They must be resilient and subject to the swiftest change. At the outset the editor, the publisher, has the authority and the young author coming to him is eager for every bit of advice, every bit of editing, every bit of support that can be given.

But the moment that author has become established this relationship is altered. Now it is the author who has the authority and in many cases he no longer needs or wants the advice which had earlier meant so much. Thomas Wolfe, who accepted so eagerly all the editing which Maxwell Perkins devoted to *Look Homeward, Angel,* no longer had need for such close attention when he was writing *Of Time and the River.* Now it was Thomas Wolfe who had the authority, and this I suspect was something which Max Perkins overlooked.

Sinclair Lewis, who revered Alfred Harcourt as a publisher and loved him as a friend, wrote his best novels for Harcourt Brace and was eager to invest his small savings in that firm at its inception. But after *Elmer Gantry* and *Dodsworth,* somehow the old familiarity induced a complacency toward the new book that Lewis resented. The advertising wasn't enough, so the letters say, and by inference neither was the solicitude. Alfred Harcourt had been guilty of underestimating the perpetually new needs of a writer. He had been guilty of underediting.

In the years of editing that lay ahead of me I was to realize that whether I was editing books or the magazine, my relationships with every writer who was dear to us had constantly to be redefined. What is true of friendship is true of editing: the understanding must be continually refreshed. Over the years I have edited 317 different volumes for the *Atlantic,* and I hope there are more to come. Each has presented its individual problem, and in each I have tried to remember that it was my job to help when the author needed it, to reassure him, to call out of him his best, but always to bear in mind that the final decision was his.

An editor, like an advertising man, is always in search of new stimuli. With the antennae of his own senses he has to establish an identification, a kind of sensory intercom with his readers, and if he is an acute editor, he will expect that when a manuscript excites him it will have much the same effect on his readers. He is not infallible, but this intercom—what I have called his antennae—works both ways, and he learns to recognize very quickly what his people reject as well as what they accept.

The readers I serve have a loathing for ghost writers and those windy, vacuous generalizations which ghost writers propound for people who can't express themselves. Since so many American speeches today are ghost-written, my people have become very leery of speeches in print—and I know it. *Atlantic* readers are nonconformist; they expect the magazine to be nonpartisan and they would walk out on me in a body if I tried to confine the magazine to one point of view. They wish to be surprised, and they look for the unpredictable.

My readers are highly conscientious about education, about race relations, most of all about the threat of nuclear weapons. A young graduate of the Harvard Medical School doing his UMT was sent out to the island of Bikini, to help protect the army-navy personnel from radiation. He did his work with a Geiger counter, but during the tropical nights when he could not sleep he filled an old college notebook with his impressions of what that bomb test really portended. When we published those pages under the title "No Place to Hide," we knew that Dr. David Bradley was talking to our people about nuclear warfare as they had never been talked to before.

Our readers are eager for American history, and I suspect that they find courage in reading about those earlier Americans who stood up to crucial decisions. Catherine Drinker Bowen performed a great service for this country when she brought readers into close touch with that "Yankee from Olympus," Mr. Justice Oliver Wendell Holmes, and later when she performed the same function for the crusty, rugged, right-minded young John Adams. We drew on both of those books for the *Atlantic*. Biography is read today with avidity and it can be serialized with less internal damage than a novel: *The Years With Ross,* which my associate, Charles W. Morton, induced James Thurber to write for us, was our most popular feature since the war.

My readers have small appetite for the inbred, introverted short stories published with such dreary monotony by some of my more stylish competitors. As a change of pace I induced Peter Ustinov, who had never written a short story in his life, to embark on an exclusive series for the *Atlantic*. Peter is one of the most entrancing and original performers on TV. I felt he would be just as original, just as refreshing in his fiction—and so he is. My people like what is poetic and genuine, and they dislike what is synthetic and tired.

When I became the ninth editor of the *Atlantic* in June of 1938, a dinner was given in my honor at the St. Botolph Club in Boston. Present were a number of our distinguished New England contributors, including Robert Frost (who was later to read aloud a new poem provided I'd accept it "sight unseen"), such dear rivals as Fred Allen of *Harper's,* and my two immediate predecessors,

Bliss Perry and Ellery Sedgwick. As I entered the cocktail reception, I heard Bliss Perry remark: "Here comes the next victim," and I remember his saying to me during the dinner—he sat on my right —"There are really only two rules of editing I can give you. The first: pay your contributors on acceptance—the money will never look bigger. The second is more personal: remember how vulnerable we all are to fatigue and indigestion; when you feel bilious, try to postpone to the next day your troublesome decisions." Well, I was forty and full of cocktails at the time and the possibility that I should ever be a weary or dyspeptic editor seemed remote. I felt that the buoyancy of that evening would last me as long as I could see to read.

Early in my editorship I learned that editors work on a weekend to weekend basis. During the week they dictate letters; they talk on the telephone, and to those pregnant with manuscripts; and they attend what are called Conferences—the surest device for killing time known to industry. I learned that an editor's work week really begins on Friday afternoon when with his secretary's help he stuffs his briefcase with all the things he ought to have attended to during the week. Beginning Friday night and continuing through Sunday he reads his prizes and makes his discoveries, blueprints the next issue, and dreams up his big ideas for the future in that ancient Indian posture of sitting and contemplating his navel. No editor worth his salt can live without a minimum of contemplation and privacy.

By Monday morning he is at his peak: he has caught up with his reading; he feels confident of his decisions and eager to explore the new leads which came to him while he was not listening to the sermon Sunday morning. This will be one of those rare days when he has the world in his hand, when writers and agents say "Yes" and when the telephone is like a voice from Heaven. "Get me Senator X in Washington," he says to his secretary, "and after that I want to speak to Harold Ober, the literary agent." Then he begins leafing through the morning mail.

The Quill Club of Terre Haute will appreciate it if he will serve as one of three judges of its annual short story contest. Not more than seventy manuscripts are expected, and they hope he can complete his rating by October 1. The Harvard Dames would like him to speak on a literary subject any Thursday evening in November. Unfortunately their budget is a modest one and they can offer no fee greater than their appreciation. That nice, if persistent, couple he met at Breadloaf has a daughter, fresh from Smith, who wants an editorial job. She has typing but has purposely not learned shorthand since it might tie her down. A reader in Kentucky wishes to point out that the word "thoroughbred" can only be applied to a horse with a pedigree. The *Atlantic* contributor who wrote that his heroine "had the look of a high-spirited thoroughbred" was not paying the lady the compliment he intended—and never mind what Webster says about it. "Would you like to read my series on the Orient?" asks a hand-written card. "Seven articles averaging 9000 words. Will come in for an appointment." The query is not inscribed on a regular postcard, no, it is written in the white margins of the get-acquainted, cut-price subscription reply card which we so thoughtfully insert in our newsstand copies. No postage necessary.

You will see that I have discarded my disguise, and that the editor I am talking about is myself. No Monday mail is complete without a letter from a contributor who objects to the way we have edited his copy. The one before me comes from Raymond Chandler in Hollywood. I had asked Chandler to do a piece for us on Oscar night. He did it, and it was a beauty: full of the most penetrating little daggers. The trouble was, our Boston proofreaders were not familiar with Chandler's style, and when he described the crowd in the free seats "giving out" that awful moaning sound, they simply deleted the preposition. I had also changed the title to "Oscar Night in Hollywood." Mr. Chandler, having read his galleys, is now in a slow burn:

Dear Mr. Weeks:

I'm afraid you've thrown me for a loss. I thought Juju Worship in Hollywood was a perfectly good title. But you're the boss. I've thought of various other titles such as Bank Night in Hollywood, Sutter's Last Stand, The Golden Peepshow, All it Needs is Elephants, The Hot Shot Handicap, Where Vaudeville Went When it Died, and rot like that. But nothing that smacks you in the kisser.

By the way, would you convey my compliments to the purist who reads your proofs and tell him or her that I write in a sort of broken-down patois which is something like the way a Swiss waiter talks, and that when I split an infinitive, God damn it, I split it so it will stay split, and when I interrupt the velvety smoothness of my more or less literate syntax with a few sudden words of barroom vernacular, this is done with the eyes wide open and the mind relaxed but attentive. The method may not be perfect, but it is all I have. I think your proofreader is kindly attempting to steady me on my feet, but much as I appreciate the solicitude, I am really able to steer a fairly clear course, provided I got both sidewalks and the street between.

Kindest regards,

RAY CHANDLER

(To be tossed and gored by a contributor can be a good thing; individuality is the spice of life.)

Now I've about reached the end of my Monday mail. My secretary has a way of saving the letters of abuse till the last and here they are. There is an anonymous postcard reviling us for publishing a respectful article on Russian education and calling me "The Red Brahmin of Beacon Hill." And what are these, these multigraphed letters on paper of gray burlap? They are all identical and there must be more than a hundred. Slowly the meaning becomes clear. In our Washington Report we had referred to "the organized Polish minority" which might affect the elections in Michigan. Before me is a Polish demonstration. "Dear Sir: I the undersigned wish to deny indignantly the accusation in the September *Atlantic,* page 39, that there is an organized Polish minortiy in the United States . . ." One hundred and thirty-nine of them by actual count.

All this time of eager assimilation the phone has been ringing, a conference with the Advertising Department has been set for 11; it is now 10:30; Senator X in Washington has not returned my call, and how many pinpricks do you need to deflate a balloon?

I sometimes wonder why we do it, and of course the truth is we couldn't be paid to do anything else. Editing is in our blood and all this attrition I have been talking about is simply the gristle in our meat. We edit because, God help us, we think it is important. If we were committed to Bedlam we would edit a handwritten sheet for our fellow inmates, and if Russia took over this country, we would edit underground. We think we were born to do this and we believe that what we are doing is in the public good.

At rare intervals we are confirmed in this belief. There are turning points in the career of every magazine and those editors who made the turn will never forget it. Sometimes you see the high point a long way ahead, as we did in Boston when for eighteen months we built up the big issues which signalized our Centennial in the autumn of 1957. That November issue, on our birthday, was our dream book; it sold out on the Eastern seaboard in 36 hours, and for the only time in our history we went back on press. We are a spontaneous people and quick to recognize a warning. In 1934 De Witt Wallace had a fateful conversation with a garageman in Armonk Village, New York. The mechanic asked him if he had any idea of the murder that was being committed on our highways every day. Wallace went home and brooded; then got in touch with J. C. Furnas who was told to spare no detail in arousing Americans to the horror of wild driving. I don't know how many times the article was rewritten; I do know that "And Sudden Death" permanently changed the character of *The Reader's Digest* and that 4 million reprints were requested in the three months after publication.

Think of the audacity of Harold Ross in sending John Hersey to Hiroshima and of then devoting an entire issue of the *New Yorker* to his findings with no space reserved even for the advertisements. McCarthy was at the height of his intimidation when Max Ascoli had the courage to attack the China Lobby in two resounding articles in the *Reporter*. Think of the urgency of Norman Cousins in flying over to Lambaréné to persuade Dr. Schweitzer to speak out against the insanity of nuclear warfare. Think of the foresight of the editors of *Look,* particularly Dan Mich, when in 1956 they correctly forecast the Southern resistance to integration and went out to meet it in their lead article, "The South vs. The Supreme Court." Fred Allen of *Harper's* twice led the whole field with his exposure of the infuriating corruption in labor relations: first in 1948 in the blazing article, "The Blast in Centralia, No. 5," and four years later with Mary Heaton Vorse's unsparing account of the longshoremen and how those pirates were holding up the Port of New York. Again when Dr. J. Robert Oppenheimer was being demoted as a security risk, I like to remember that within a month three magazines, mine among them, sprang to his defense. This is the courage, this is the vigilance which the country expects of magazine editors.

The danger for us all is that we think too exclusively in terms of leading articles, newsstand sales and advertising revenue and far too little about our allies. We have bet our lives on the currency of the printed word, yet it doesn't seem to trouble us that reading—the habit and delight of reading—could be steadily diminished under the pressure of new competition. We have a powerfully hypnotic rival in television and there is no question whatever that television has seriously cut into the time once given to reading. In every college community we have a heavy competition in the long-playing record; undergraduates today spend as much money collecting records as they do collecting books. In this rivalry for attention we badly need the help of English teachers and librarians. They, too, are dedicated to the printed word and they tap the enthusiasm of the young, yet we hardly give them the time of day. What can we do? What awards could we give to show our appreciation of librarians and teachers and of all they do to make books and magazines desirable?

Why have we neglected radio, and why has radio neglected us?

Not since the death of Alec Woollcott have we heard a nationwide voice exciting people to read. "I have been going quietly mad," he would say, "over a new book called *Lost Horizon*" and the next day literally thousands went out to find that volume. Why not again? As for the booksellers and magazine distributors, not till the well-merited failure of the American News Company as a wholesaler did we ever worry our pretty heads about them. Evidently we are dangerously self-centered.

The summer of 1958 it occurred to me to thank the management of the American Telephone and Telegraph Company for their loyalty in advertising in the *Atlantic* uninterruptedly for fifty years. In his reply, Vice President Sanford B. Cousins wrote: "The *Atlantic* was one of the 52 magazines to carry our national advertising when it first appeared in 1908. Of them only 8 have survived the ravages of whatever diseases magazines suffer." Eight survivors out of fifty-two. The old *Life* must have been one of the casualties and the reason why the new *Life* is such a powerhouse is the decision, the turning point their editors took some years back, when they determined that pictures simply were not enough: they had to have prose too. Significant that they made their pitch in history—the history of art, of culture, a retelling with pictures of *The Outline of History* which appealed as nothing else could have done so surely to the American zeal for self-improvement. There is a clearly discernible trend here. The success of *American Heritage* is in direct response to the rising interest in history which has swept through the nation since the Second World War. Now that we have become the leader of the West, people want to catch up with the past; what can we learn from studying our earlier crises? No one but ourselves can pull us out of the next. So too in science. The transformation of *Scientific American* under the lead of Gerard Piel from a journal of technology to a magazine with a broad approach to physics, biology and scientific research paid off long before sputnik. And when those two bellwethers, the *Saturday Evening Post* and *Ladies' Home Journal,* discard fiction as their cover appeal and instead play up biography and adventures of the mind, you may be sure that a major change in American taste has occurred.

It is my guess that this swing to the serious will be accelerated and naturally I like this, for it means a greater opportunity for my magazine. So it does for others. The eager developing interest in the thoughtful, the scientific, the how-to-do-it material is traceable to what the census calls "professional and technical workers." In number they have been rapidly increasing; so has their purchasing power, so have their children in college. In the census age group of "65 and over" only 3½ per cent have a college degree, whereas in the age group ready for college today, white and colored, 17 per cent or five times as many are taking degrees. In the next decade that number will increase astronomically.

All editors have had to do with the young graduate and his college wife; we know their desire to have four or five children where we had two; their capability for doing things for themselves; the intentness they bring to their reading, their music, their homes, their travel and their use of leisure. This is the coming and dominant readership. Can you reach them and hold their loyalty? Certainly: not by talking down but by editing up.

Ellery Sedgwick

Ellery Sedgwick was editor of the ATLANTIC MONTHLY *from 1908 to 1938.*

In this all-too-brief selection from THE HAPPY PROFESSION, *Ellery Sedgwick, one of the greatest of the* ATLANTIC'*s editors, imparts his wise philosophy on the personal qualities and professional role of the editor, whether for the magazines or in trade book publishing.*

Wide travel, prejudices that are kept to himself, an open mind and taste "habitually exercised"—these are the hallmarks of the first-rate editor cited by a man who was one himself.

IT IS an editor's duty to have prejudices—and to keep them to himself. Indeed, although schoolteachers do not know it, the inculcation of prejudice is a vital part of education. Wrongful and stupid prejudice, of course, abounds, but prejudices at once wise and discriminating not only make for virtue, for friendship, for loyalty, they can be exquisitely adapted to individuality, most priceless of human possessions, which the fashion and manners of the modern world are doing their best to stamp out.

Prejudices stem from ideas, but it is not ideas which mould the modern world. It is words, and against the misuse of words every editorial prejudice should be fixed in concrete. The blind confidence of most Americans in the validity of words is a direct inheritance of the Declaration of Independence. We forget it was not God Almighty but Thomas Jefferson who declared all men born equal and free in spite of very considerable evidence to the contrary. Ever since that startling manifesto, politicians have attuned their long ears to the sound of words. Straight words, honest words, words that call up an accurate picture of any cause they advocate they consistently eschew, but instead twist to some alien meaning sweet and pleasant words which have hitherto borne an utterly different connotation. Their favorites are words which people have always associated with well-loved causes. In our political vocabulary these are the weasel words against which Theodore Roosevelt used to launch his choicest invectives. Call them rather jackal words, for they know no decency and hunt in packs.

Take the most threadbare of them all, "liberal," once a noble word. "Originally," says the dictionary, "the epithet for those arts which were worthy of a free man," it came naturally to signify an attitude favorable toward change in the direction of all the people. But it was slow and prudent change that the "liberal" favored. If it were swift and utter transformation the politician desired to express, a word stood by capable of its accurate expression. It is an honest word but "radical" has about it a certain sense of disruption, a complete break with the past. So the politician eschews it, and in its place slips the soothing syllables of "liberal." Any revolutionary change today is in the *liberal* direction. The closed shop is a *liberal* policy, sit-down strikes are expressions of *liberal* tolerance. And it goes without saying that all in opposition are classed as Tories, Tories such as fought against the American Revolution and have been at it ever since. Note for example any speech of Harry Bridges. Mr. Bridges merely desires to overthrow the Government of the United States, but never, never would he do it otherwise than by the advocacy of strictly *liberal* principles. And did you ever hear Mr. Hillman confessing to the prosecution of a *radical* design? Meanwhile Americans with some understanding of the past and reasonable hope for the future go on using *liberal* in its time-honored meaning, thus making it every day a more valuable prize for radicals to steal.

Prejudice has a bad name, yet what is it but suspended judgment? It is a brake on hasty action. Though it narrows the opinion it does not close the mind. When an untried idea is presented, it makes a man sniff—and perhaps the nose is a sounder guide than people think. When, in the agony of the First World War, our Secretary of State was outraged by the thought of Americans actually *fighting* for a cause, the British Ambassador said to me, "Your Mr. Bryan is an evil smell." Much as I esteemed the Great Commoner, I felt that the undiplomatic metaphor was correct.

My advice to beginning editors then is not to neglect prejudice but not to bear down upon it in too many directions at once. However strongly you feel, the important thing is never to *seem* to be intemperate. When your hopes are dim and your spirits dark, do not give vent to your own feelings but let some contributor speak his full mind for yours. Let him, if he can, paint the world blacker than it is. Let him take up the cudgels in behalf of your prejudices and exaggerate them to his heart's content. Remember that troops of readers whose bias runs counter to your own are always longing to have a go at you. Let the contributor draw their fire. Make him the editor's buckler and his stout shield. Once when my spirits drooped and the world seemed to be reaching an all-time low, the temptation came over me to break my own rules and be for once my own Jeremiah. Then it was, the Lord raised up a ram in the thicket and delivered me.

An open mind, says Chesterton, is like an open mouth, swallowing all that comes its way. But Chestertonian truth must be taken in a Pickwickian sense. To an editor open-mindedness is of the first importance. There is a point just below credulity and very far above skepticism where his mind should stick and open not one jot further. The so-called hard-boiled editor has none of the juices of life in him after the boiling is done. His role is to judge all that may be by what has been and to trim the possibilities of boundless experience to the metes of his own conventional mind. On the other hand there is the editor whose antennae are always a-quiver. This is an excellent characteristic for saints but not for editors. What the editor needs is imagination with tentacles on the fringe of it, in kind though not in degree such as faith has and science requires. If he meets a strange experience totally foreign to the probable, he should put on the brakes gently but let the motor run.

The editor is bade to make friends and given money to make them stick, but when was a friend ever bought in the "open market"? To make men friends and make them stick needs much more than money. It needs an editor's ideas; it needs his sagacious counsel, it needs his enthusiasm, it needs a store of human qualities such as authors are short of. Once an editor is an expert at this trade, he comes to understand how every man has a story locked inside him, and the puzzle is to pick the lock. The truth about this world is there are no absolutely uninteresting people in it. There are only people who seem depressingly uninteresting. Almost everybody has his little private "godown" where his treasure lies buried. Once you adopt this view of the universe, it makes a worth-while place of the planet. True it is that digging out the gold that lies in most of us is a hard and costly job. What was Emerson's message to young women who distrust their powers? "Oh discontented girl, take what you will, but pay the price." On the shop counters of the world goods are desirable but prices are high.

An editor should believe in his magazine. The trouble is many of them don't. You see all sorts of balderdash in the appeals they make to their readers. "Our readers edit our magazine. It is they who tell us what to put in." That is the sort of thing politicians say to their constituents. It is worse than nonsense. It is a lie. Every editor of quality gathers about his magazine readers who are in one way or another all of a kidney like his own.

A little magazine, as Bacon would say, maketh not a great fortune. But if it be conducted with enterprise and discretion, not as a multifarious catchall but as an intelligent and sympathetic extension of the editor's powers and interests, then shall he have his adequate reward. A corner mansion on the Avenue may not be his but that he would not value if he had it, and his comfortable house on a leafy if unfashionable street will lack no comfort. When I first took over the *Atlantic,* my wife and I expected to live on the modest scale of a professor's family. The magazine (now it can be told) was, in 1908 when I acquired it, selling some fifteen thousand copies a month. In the interests of solvency I consulted a friend wise in the devious ways of advertising, but even to him I dared not confess a figure which any self-respecting businessman would feel must be concealed. "Would you," I asked tremulously, "solicit advertising on the basis of a sworn figure, or would you go it blind, extolling the fame of your name and decrying the cheap argument of circulation?"

"If," said my mentor, avoiding my eye, "your sales are twenty-five thousand copies a month, I would boast of them. Otherwise, I would keep d——d quiet."

And d——d quiet I kept. I saw that a steep hill had to be climbed but two comforting thoughts came to mind. First, if the *Atlantic* had more subscribers and was losing less money, then I could not possibly have scraped up dollars enough to buy it. Secondly, I remembered that when Walter Hines Page had sat in my chair ten years earlier, the total circulation of the magazine had not exceeded six thousand copies a month; yet it was a poorly educated American in those days who had not heard of the *Atlantic.*

When in that first year of grace, MacGregor Jenkins and I took over the *Atlantic* and set to work with pencil and eraser, we scratched and scratched until the last drop of red ink disappeared from the books, and when we balanced them at the end of a year, the profit was four thousand dollars. Four thousand dollars! Here was a nest egg such as many a famous businessman has recorded with respect in the first chapter of his autobiography. So these figures are stamped on my commercial soul alongside one other unforgettable digit—the ten dollars which after college my father had given me to take me to my first job, thus marking the historic hiatus between paternal benevolence and the first gatherings of sweat on a man's brow.

The *Atlantic* prospered continuously, in its small way mightily, but the satisfaction of life bears scant relation to cash balances. My correspondence, increasing at compound interest, bore witness to the expanding influence of the magazine. People of notoriety, then of eminence, began to show a disposition to write for the *Atlantic* and through its pages unknown writers began to become very well-known writers indeed. In those days, it was my practice out of eighteen contributors in an issue to include at least eight who were making their first bows to the public. I remember the office jubilation when we were reliably informed that sermons on *Atlantic* topics were preached simultaneously in twenty churches. What the congregations suffered therefrom was beyond our caring, and we only rejoiced when, from London, the Dean of St. Paul's, the gloomy Dean himself, wrote that an *Atlantic* paper had been his text for three successive sermons. But not until the politicians began to notice the magazine did we feel certain the *Atlantic* had made a definite impact. Of his own will, President Wilson sent a priceless article—and received in return hundreds instead of the thousands he might have had for the asking from any big magazine. Al Smith, after an infinitude of consultation, decided that the *Atlantic* was the proper sounding-board for an article certain to have a crucial influence upon his career, and in later years Wendell Willkie testified that, though his advisers counseled some magazine of millions, he believed a more intensive influence would, in the long run, prove more effective in promoting his ideas—and after the event assured us he had been proved right. To inoculate the few who influence the many is the *Atlantic*'s perpetual formula.

In these meanderings I have not come on the question of taste. Taste underlies judgment. Often it is arbitrary and none the worse for that. In this world, it is quite as important to hate as to love. If you hate insincerity, if vulgarity has an instant effect upon the balance of your diaphragm, you won't go far astray. Like every other quality, taste grows from habit and, habitually exercised, it will become part of your fiber and bone. American education is apt to look on taste as an airy grace of life. In teacher-minds it is coupled with fastidiousness and gently laughed at. But I am grossly mistaken if the cultivation of a fastidious taste goes not closer to the root of the matter and accomplishes more in building what we call character than all the instruction in the curriculum and all the athletics of the campus. Once persuade a child to identify *bad* with *ugly* and you have made its instinct your strong ally. The homey motto on the wall has gone the way of the lambrequin and the antimacassar but it once taught a vigorous lesson. A threadbare distich, worked in worsted, hung over the piano.

> Vice is a monster of so frightful mien,
> As to be hated needs but to be seen

became a part of visual memory forever, in time to crisis to be thrown up large upon the screen. I remember a Scotch sailor telling me how, after a long voyage, he had taken his first shore leave at Vigo, thirty-five dollars in his pocket. His companions knew where they were going but he was daydreaming until he found himself in the parlor of a brothel. In one flash of lightning there came before his eyes the little oblong frame which for two generations had hung in the nursery of his home. In the crude reds and blues of the original he saw the words:—

> My God hath sent his angel, and hath shut the lions' mouths, that they have not hurt me: forasmuch as before him innocency was found in me.

That monition had fascinated his childish mind long before he knew what it meant. Now he knew.

Of course taste exfoliates into all sorts of ornamental arabesques of character such as most of us think of as belonging to the world of la-di-da. But the essence of it has structure and solidity, and enjoys an enormous advantage over moral lessons taught from without, in that it is instinctive. Taste is born in us. Education merely strengthens or smothers it. Sheep-headed people looking on this world as the Garden of Eden run to weeds since Adam ceased to cultivate it may think of the Ten Commandments as part of man's natural inheritance. But whether they are God-given or man-given, they are certainly practical regulations in a disorderly world. In keeping them, where precept fails, taste is a powerful support.

The great American sin is vulgarity and taste is its antidote. A curious vice this is to attach to a pioneering people but it did not come upon us until the pioneering stage was past, nor did it come flooding in with immigration. The Irish are beautifully immune to it. It is not characteristic of the Italian. Scandinavians are coarse, but not vulgar. But those who love America best feel how omnipresent vulgarity is amongst us. Hollywood is too tiresome an instance to cite, but look at a wedding breakfast on the screen, or the decoration of a room supposed to represent wealth and culture, and before a word is spoken you will see what it means to be vulgar. About vulgarity there is a self-consciousness which is the root of bad manners and bad taste. Compare the advertisements of our current novels with similar announcements in foreign papers. Our emphasis is always carried by notes at the top of the scale. Never the positive, the comparative never, always the superlative. Be blatant *and* be heard, is a rule of the trade. In writing, how rarely in America is realized the power of understatement. "Unique," which occurs once in a lifetime, has become a familiar quality of every novel, and "stupendous" is an everyday synonym for "large." How exaggeration defeats itself should be a lesson of earliest youth. I hear again the admonition of my uncle, Professor Child. His daughter had enjoyed an agreeable evening and reported her partner as "a fascinating young man." Professor Child sniffed fastidiously, giving his round nose a look of indescribable squeamishness: "Fascinating! Fascinating!" he repeated. "What you mean, Helen, is that your young man is honest—and possibly clean."

Of course superlatives do have their place. When a thing *is* best it deserves to be called so. Our famous painter, William Morris Hunt, had a word for masterpieces. They were "ultimates," and as his gift for profanity was on a par with his other talents, his "ultimates" became on occasions of appropriate commendation "those God-damned ultimate things."

At a certain famous dinner given by the Tavern Club in honor of Hunt's achievements, the artist was introduced by the Club president, Professor Norton. The exquisite propriety of Norton's speech, its gentle modulation and quiet resonance, had been a community tradition for fifty years. Now his peroration was indeed unique and roused a glorious shout of applause. Norton had been speaking of the testament of Beauty and how wonderfully Beauty was enhanced by its exceeding rarity. Finally he turned to the guest at his right: "And now, gentlemen, I have the pleasure of introducing to you one—of—those—God-damned—*ultimate*—things, William Morris Hunt."

Vulgarity is a total misconception of the values of life. Real values have not a touch of it, and these are the editor's everlasting lure. If he can find them under dramatic circumstances, so much the better, for drama is a very present help in the trouble of turning out an issue. There is no sharper barb to the editor's hook.

There is no editorial platitude so stale as "Trying to satisfy everybody satisfies nobody." Readers like you or they don't. They tag you as "lush" or "arid," "liberal" or "conservative," and let it go at that, but an editor is seldom one thing or another. This leads me to a bit of self-analysis. I am not sure whether it is the same with other people accustomed to a moderate degree of self-examination, but throughout my more reflective life, I have been conscious of certain settled differences in outlook between Myself and Me. Myself, so far back as I can remember, has been all for progress, always in favor of tinkering with the world machine, patching its weaknesses, and experimenting with new contraptions designed to increase its efficiency, while the more sophisticated Me keeps asking inconvenient questions as to which way progress, indeed whether progress may not be an illusion after all, and counseling a little salutary delay while we consider the matter. Philosophic friends tell me that in such cases Me is apt to grow a trifle more obstinate with the years. Myself certainly holds that Me does, but as the decades pass, I, the arbiter, incline to believe that progress is not a ladder, not even the spiral of Victorian hopes, but rather a meandering maze leading now up, now down, over difficult and hilly ground. If this be true, a certain quiescence which Myself calls "torpidity" and Me "caution" is scarcely a reprehensible attitude. The most congruous friend I can recall, Barrett Wendell, to whose consistency I have paid repeated tribute, maintained that change was invariably and indubitably bad. It must come, but it must be resisted. With that, arbiter I, cannot agree, and yet a bit of procrastination is not a vice.

Though reformers may chant with enthusiasm:—

> Truth forever on the scaffold,
> Wrong forever on the throne,

Truth, Right, and Wrong are rather shadowy characters. A definition with more reality seems to relate to the behavior of Virtue and of Folly. Too often these are inseparable companions, while over against Folly, Sagacity is prone to keep company, not so often with Vice but with a more elusive opposite of Virtue, Self-seeking. These get along swimmingly together and the result is not happy. The truth is, Virtue is much more reliable as an inspiration than as a guiding star. When trouble comes, it is Intelligence, not Virtue, which is most apt to point the reasonable way out. The Good (tell it in Gath) have their limitations. The mere phrase "unco guid" tells a story both of religious and of political reform. Perhaps the most profitable memorial in a democracy would be a gigantic model of a pendulum set up in the market place for all to see. The lesson a pendulum implies it cannot fail to teach.

What have memories like these to do with editing? My answer is that all experience goes to make an editor, and that the eye harvests memories, more accurate perhaps than the brain, and quite as penetrating.

A man lives by what he has been. Mistakes, failures, efforts, successes, aspirations, all make up the sum. He lives by what he has been, and we hope that, when his books are balanced, it will be recorded that he lived by what he might be. For the best part of a man's life is what he means to become. Forty-five years ago, when I was an ardent student of my profession, this was my substance of things hoped for:—

> To be honest. To be fair. To look with leniency on faults beyond one's own temptations. To cherish enthusiasms and to hate cant. To love friends well and books better. To be endlessly interested. To try to believe and to be reasonably credulous. To enjoy life and doubt its all-importance. To accept opportunity with gratitude. To hold good writing as the art above the arts, and to forgive him much who can write like an Angel.
>
> Amen.

Wolcott Gibbs

Wolcott Gibbs began as a copy reader on the New Yorker *in 1927 and by his death in 1958 at the age of 56, he had held many editorial posts on that magazine. He is probably best remembered as the* New Yorker's *acerbic, eminently quotable drama critic, a post he assumed in 1940. During his professional life with the* New Yorker, *Mr. Gibbs contributed fiction and articles to its pages, the best of which, in 1958, were collected under the title* More In Sorrow.

Much has been written about the so-called "New Yorker *style." With what is surely only a part of his tongue in his cheek, Wolcott Gibbs suggests the mechanics behind that style in the following selection from James Thurber's* The Years With Ross.

THEORY AND PRACTICE OF EDITING *NEW YORKER* ARTICLES

The average contributor to this magazine is semi-literate; that is, he is ornate to no purpose, full of senseless and elegant variations, and can be relied on to use three sentences where a word would do. It is impossible to lay down any exact and complete formula for bringing order out of this underbrush, but there are a few general rules.

1. Writers always use too damn many adverbs. On one page recently I found eleven modifying the verb "said." "He said morosely, violently, eloquently, so on." Editorial theory should probably be that a writer who can't make his context indicate the way his character is talking ought to be in another line of work. Anyway, it is impossible for a character to go through all these emotional states one after the other. Lon Chaney might be able to do it, but he is dead.

2. Word "said" is O.K. Efforts to avoid repetition by inserting

"grunted," "snorted," etc., are waste motion and offend the pure in heart.

3. Our writers are full of clichés, just as old barns are full of bats. There is obviously no rule about this, except that anything that you suspect of being a cliché undoubtedly is one and had better be removed.

4. Funny names belong to the past or to whatever is left of *Judge* magazine. Any character called Mrs. Middlebottom or Joe Zilch should be summarily changed to something else. This goes for animals, towns, the names of imaginary books and many other things.

5. Our employer, Mr. Ross, has a prejudice against having too many sentences beginning with "and" or "but." He claims that they are conjunctions and should not be used purely for literary effect. Or at least only very judiciously.

6. See our Mr. Weekes on the use of such words as "little," "vague," "confused," "faintly," "all mixed up," etc. etc. The point is that the average *New Yorker* writer, unfortunately influenced by Mr. Thurber, has come to believe that the ideal *New Yorker* piece is about a vague, little man helplessly confused by a menacing and complicated civilization. Whenever this note is not the whole point of the piece (and it far too often is) it should be regarded with suspicion.

7. The repetition of exposition in quotes went out with the Stanley Steamer:

> Marion gave me a pain in the neck.
> "You give me a pain in the neck, Marion," I said.

This turns up more often that you'd expect.

8. Another of Mr. Ross's theories is that a reader picking up a magazine called the *New Yorker* automatically supposes that any story in it takes place in New York. If it doesn't, if it's about Columbus, Ohio, the lead should say so. "When George Adams was sixteen, he began to worry about the girls" should read "When George Adams was sixteen, he began to worry about the girls he saw every day on the streets of Columbus" or something of the kind. More graceful preferably.

9. Also, since our contributions are signed at the end, the author's sex should be established at once if there is any reasonable doubt. It is distressing to read a piece all the way through under the impression that the "I" in it is a man and then find a woman's signature at the end. Also, of course, the other way round.

10. To quote Mr. Ross again, "Nobody gives a damn about a writer or his problems except another writer." Pieces about authors, reporters, poets, etc. are to be discouraged in principle. Whenever

possible the protagonist should be arbitrarily transplanted to another line of business. When the reference is incidental and unnecessary, it should come out.

11. This magazine is on the whole liberal about expletives. The only test I know of is whether or not they are really essential to the author's effect. "Son of a bitch," "bastard," and many others can be used whenever it is the editor's judgment that that is the only possible remark under the circumstances. When they are gratuitous, when the writer is just trying to sound tough to no especial purpose, they come out.

12. In the transcription of dialect, don't let the boys and girls misspell words just for a fake Bowery effect. There is no point, for instance, in "trubble," or "sed."

13. Mr. Weekes said the other night, in a moment of desperation, that he didn't believe he could stand any more triple adjectives. "A tall, florid and overbearing man called Jaeckel." Sometimes they're necessary, but when every noun has three adjectives connected with it, Mr. Weekes suffers and quite rightly.

14. I suffer myself very seriously from writers who divide quotes for some kind of ladies' club rhythm.

"I am going," he said, "downtown" is a horror, and unless a quote is pretty long I think it ought to stay on one side of the verb. Anyway, it ought to be divided logically, where there would be pause or something in the sentence.

15. Mr. Weekes has got a long list of banned words, beginning with "gadget." Ask him. It's not actually a ban, there being circumstances when they're necessary, but good words to avoid.

16. I would be delighted to go over the list of writers, explaining the peculiarities of each as they have appeared to me in more than ten years of exasperation on both sides.

17. Editing on manuscript should be done with a black pencil, decisively.

18. I almost forgot indirection, which probably maddens Mr. Ross more than anything else in the world. He objects, that is, to important objects of places or people being dragged into things in a secretive and underhanded manner. If, for instance, a profile has never told where a man lives, Ross protests against a sentence saying, "His Vermont house is full of valuable paintings." Should say "He has a house in Vermont and it is full, etc." Rather weird point, but it will come up from time to time.

19. Drunkenness and adultery present problems. As far as I can tell, writers must not be allowed to imply that they admire either of these things, or have enjoyed them personally, although they are

legitimate enough when pointing a moral or adorning a sufficiently grim story. They are nothing to be lighthearted about. "The *New Yorker* can not endorse adultery." Harold Ross vs. Sally Benson. Don't bother about this one. In the end it is a matter between Mr. Ross and his God. Homosexuality, on the other hand, is definitely out as humor, and dubious in any case.

20. The more "As a matter of facts," "howevers," "for instances," etc. etc. you can cut out, the nearer you are to the Kingdom of Heaven.

21. It has always seemed irritating to me when a story is written in the first person, but the narrator hasn't got the same name as the author. For instance, a story beginning: " 'George,' my father said to me one morning"; and signed at the end Horace McIntyre always baffles me. However, as far as I know this point has never been ruled upon officially, and should just be queried.

22. Editors are really the people who should put initial letters and white spaces in copy to indicate breaks in thought or action. Because of overwork or inertia or something, this has been done largely by the proofroom, which has a tendency to put them in for purposes of makeup rather than sense. It should revert to the editors.

23. For some reason our writers (especially Mr. Leonard Q. Ross) have a tendency to distrust even moderately long quotes and break them up arbitrarily and on the whole idiotically with editorial interpolations. "Mr. Kaplan felt that he and the cosmos were coterminus" or some such will frequently appear in the middle of a conversation for no other reason than that the author is afraid the reader's mind is wandering. Sometimes this is necessary, most often it isn't.

24. Writers also have an affection for the tricky or vaguely cosmic last line. "Suddenly Mr. Holtzmann felt tired" has appeared on far too many pieces in the last ten years. It is always a good idea to consider whether the last sentence of a piece is legitimate and necessary, or whether it is just an author showing off.

25. On the whole, we are hostile to puns.

26. How many of these changes can be made in copy depends, of course, to a large extent on the writer being edited. By going over the list, I can give a general idea of how much nonsense each artist will stand for.

27. Among many other things, the *New Yorker* is often accused of a patronizing attitude. Our authors are especially fond of referring to all foreigners as "little" and writing about them, as Mr. Maxwell

says, as if they were mantel ornaments. It is very important to keep the amused and Godlike tone out of pieces.

28. It has been one of Mr. Ross's long struggles to raise the tone or our contributors' surroundings, at least on paper. References to the gay Bohemian life in Greenwich Village and other low surroundings should be cut whenever possible. Nor should writers be permitted to boast about having their telephones cut off, or not being able to pay their bills, or getting their meals at the delicatessen, or any of the things which strike many writers as quaint and lovable.

29. Some of our writers are inclined to be a little arrogant about their knowledge of the French language. Probably best to put them back into English if there is a common English equivalent.

30. So far as possible make the pieces grammatical—but if you don't the copy room will, which is a comfort. Fowler's *English Usage* is our reference book. But don't be precious about it.

31. Try to preserve an author's style if he is an author and has a style. Try to make a dialogue sound like talk, not writing.

Harold Ross

Harold Ross was one of the editors of STARS AND STRIPES, *but he will be forever remembered as the first editor and guiding spirit of the* NEW YORKER, *a magazine which he brought to life in 1925 and with which he stayed on as editor-in-chief until his death, at 61, in 1951.*

Harold Ross was a complex man: unpredictable, erratic, mercurial, opinionated, ingenious and a complete individualist in all matters. But he, for all of these unorthodox qualities, was perhaps the most brilliant magazine editor of our time during the many years he ruled—and was—the NEW YORKER.

Few men knew him well. One who knew him better than most, though, was the late James Thurber, the great humorist who was one of Mr. Ross' young NEW YORKER *editors.*

In the following selection from James Thurber's THE YEARS WITH ROSS, *that "Siamese-twin": Ross-the-man and Ross-the-editor emerges . . . larger and more gorgeous than life, as is to be expected.*

YOU caught only glimpses of Ross, even if you spent a long evening with him. He was always in mid-flight, or on the edge of his chair, alighting or about to take off. He won't sit still in anybody's mind long enough for a full-length portrait. After six years of thinking about it, I realized that to do justice to Harold Ross I must write about him the way he talked and lived—leaping from peak to peak. What follows here is a monologue montage of that first day and of half a dozen swift and similar sessions. He was standing behind his desk, scowling at a manuscript lying on it, as if it were about to lash out at him. I had caught glimpses of him at the theater and at the Algonquin and, like everybody else, was familiar with the mobile face that constantly changed expression, the carrying voice, the eloquent large-fingered hands that were never in repose, but kept darting this way and that to emphasize his points or running through the thatch of hair that stood straight up until Ina Claire said she would like to take her shoes off and walk through it. That got into the gossip columns and Ross promptly had his barber flatten down the pompadour.

He wanted, first of all, to know how old I was, and when I told him it set him off on a lecture. "Men don't mature in this country, Thurber," he said. "They're children. I was editor of the *Stars and Stripes* when I was twenty-five. Most men in their twenties don't know their way around yet. I think it's the goddam system of women schoolteachers." He went to the window behind his desk and stared disconsolately down into the street, jingling coins in one of his pants pockets. I learned later that he made a point of keeping four or five dollars' worth of change in this pocket because he had once got stuck in a taxi, to his vast irritation, with nothing smaller than a ten-dollar bill. The driver couldn't change it and had to park and go into the store for coins and bills, and Ross didn't have time for that.

I told him that I wanted to write, and he snarled, "Writers are a dime a dozen, Thurber. What I want is an editor. I can't find editors. Nobody grows up. Do you know English?" I said I thought I knew English, and this started him off on a subject with which I was to become intensely familiar. "Everybody thinks he knows English," he said, "but nobody does. I think it's because of the goddam women schoolteachers." He turned away from the window and glared at me as if I were on the witness stand and he were the prosecuting attorney. "I want to make a business office out of this place, like any other business office," he said. "I'm surrounded by women and children. We have no manpower or ingenuity. I never know where anybody is, and I can't find out. Nobody tells me anything. They sit out there at their desks, getting me deeper and deeper into God knows what. Nobody has any self-discipline, nobody gets anything done. Nobody knows how to delegate anything. What I need is a man who can sit at a central desk and make this place operate like a business office, keep track of things, find out where people are. I am, by God, going to keep sex out of this office—sex is an incident. You've got to hold the artists' hands. Artists never go anywhere, they don't know anybody, they're antisocial."

He and I worked seven days a week, often late into the night, for at least two months, without a day off. I began to lose weight, editing factual copy for sports departments and those dealing with new apartments, women's fashions, and men's wear.

"Gretta Palmer keeps using words like introvert and extrovert," Ross complained one day. "I'm not interested in the housing problems of neurotics. Everybody's neurotic. Life is hard, but I haven't got time for people's personal troubles. You've got to watch Woolcott and Long and Parker—they keep trying to get double meanings into their stuff to embarrass me. Question everything. We damn near printed a newsbreak about a girl falling off the roof. That's feminine hygiene, somebody told me just in time. You probably never heard the expression in Ohio."

"In Ohio," I told him, "we say the mirror cracked from side to side."

"I don't want to hear about it," he said.

He nursed an editorial phobia about what he called the functional: "bathroom and bedroom stuff." Years later he deleted from a Janet Flanner "London Letter" a forthright explanation of the long nonliquid diet imposed upon the royal family and important dignitaries during the coronation of George VI. He was amused by the drawing of a water plug squirting a stream at a small astonished dog, with the caption "News," but he wouldn't print it. "So-and-so can't write a story without a man in it carrying a woman to a bed," he wailed. And again, "I'll never print another O'Hara story I don't understand. I want to know what his people are doing." He was depressed for weeks after the appearance of a full-page Arno depicting a man and a girl on a road in the moonlight, the man carrying the back seat of an automobile. "Why didn't somebody tell me what it meant?" he asked. Ross had insight, perception, and a unique kind of intuition, but they were matched by a dozen blind spots and strange areas of ignorance, surprising in a virile and observant reporter who had knocked about the world and lived two years in France. There were so many different Rosses, conflicting and contradictory, that the task of drawing him in words sometimes appears impossible, for the composite of all the Rosses should produce a single unmistakable entity: the most remarkable man I have ever known and the greatest editor. "If you get him down on paper," Wolcott Gibbs once warned me, "nobody will believe it."

Herbert Spencer was the only philosopher Ross ever quoted, and it was always the same quote: "A genius can do readily what nobody else can do at all," which precisely described the editorial genius Ross kept dreaming about.

"His mind is uncluttered by culture," said a man at the Players Club, during one of those impromptu panel discussions of Harold Ross that often began when writers and artists got together. "That's why he can give prose and pictures the benefit of the clearest concentration of any editor in the world." It wasn't as simple as that, for there was more than clear concentration behind the scowl and the searchlight glare that he turned on manuscripts, proofs, and drawings. He had a sound sense, a unique, almost intuitive perception of what was wrong with something, incomplete or out of balance, understated or overemphasized. He reminded me of an army scout riding at the head of a troop of cavalry who suddenly raises his hand in a green and silent valley and says, "Indians," although to the ordinary eye and ear there is no faintest sign or sound of anything alarming. Some of us writers were devoted to him, a few disliked him heartily, others came out of his office after conferences as from a side show, a juggling act, or a dentist's office, but almost everybody would rather have had the benefit of his criticism than that of any other editor on earth. His opinions were voluble, stabbing, and grinding, but they succeeded somehow in refreshing your knowledge of yourself and renewing your interest in your work.

Having a manuscript under Ross's scrutiny was like putting your car in the hands of a skilled mechanic, not an automotive engineer with a bachelor of science degree, but a guy who knows what makes a motor go, and sputter, and wheeze, and sometimes come to a dead stop; a man with an ear for the faintest body squeak as well as the loudest engine rattle. When you first gazed, appalled, upon an uncorrected proof of one of your stories or articles, each margin had a thicket of queries and complaints—one writer got a hundred and forty-four on one profile. It was as though you beheld the works of your car spread all over the garage floor, and the job of getting the thing together again and making it work seemed impossible. Then you realized that Ross was trying to make your Model T or old Stutz Bearcat into a Cadillac or Rolls-Royce. He was at work with the tools of his unflagging perfectionism, and, after an exchange of growls or snarls, you set to work to join him in his enterprise.

Ross's marginal questions and comments were sometimes mere quibbling or hairsplitting, and a few of them invariably revealed his profound ignorance in certain areas of life and learning and literature, while others betrayed his pet and petty prejudices. You had to wade through these and ignore them, as you did his occasional brief marginal essays on unrelated or completely irrelevant subjects. One or two of his trusted associate editors would sometimes intercept a proof and cross out the impertinent and immaterial Rossisms, but I always insisted that they be left in, for they were the stains and labels of a Ross that never ceased to amuse me.

The blurs and imperfections his scout's eye always caught drew from his pencil such designations as *unclear, repetition, cliché, ellipsis,* and now and then blunter words. He knew when you had tired and were writing carelessly, and when you were "just monkeying around here," or going out on a limb, or writing fancy, or showing off. His "Who he?" became famous not only in the office but outside, and ten years ago was the title of a piece on Ross written by Henry Pringle. Joe Liebling once had "Who he?" painted on the door of his office, to the bewilderment of strangers who wondered what kind of business Liebling could be in. Sometimes this query put a careful finger on someone who had not been clearly identified, and at other times it showed up the gaps in Ross's knowledge of historical, contemporary, or literary figures. (He once said that only two names were familiar to every reader in the civilized world: Houdini and Sherlock Holmes.)

I remember that Ross once told me, after reading a casual of mine, "You must have dropped about eight lines out of this in your final rewrite." The thing ran smoothly enough, it seemed to me when I reread it in his office, but I went back and checked my next to last draft. Ross had been wrong. I had dropped only seven lines.

When he worked on a manuscript or proof, he was surrounded by dictionaries, which he constantly consulted, along with one of his favorite books, Fowler's *Modern English Usage.* He learned more grammar and syntax from Fowler than he had ever picked up in his somewhat sketchy school days. He read the *Oxford English Dictionary* the way other men read fiction, and he sometimes delved into a volume of the *Britannica* at random.

Ross's opinion sheets, which must have run into millions of words during his nearly twenty-seven years as editor, were regarded as just a part of the day's work, and almost all of them were thrown away after the pieces they referred to had been put through. This is a pity, for there was more of Ross in them than any biographer could cram into two volumes. My wife has preserved, fortunately for this record, a couple of the editor's opinion sheets on pieces of mine, and I can see clearly now that turning them out was not mere drudgery but a kind of sanctuary, in which he could forget, for the time being, all his personal woes and worries.

In 1948 I wrote a slight casual called "Six for the Road," which I came to like so little that I never included it in a book. When the piece reached the *New Yorker,* both Lobrano and Mrs. White were away, and Ross sent his opinions direct to me. I set down here most of what he had to say about "Six for the Road" because it is Ross, pure and unalloyed:

"1. It isn't a typical party you're talking about here—doesn't include the kind of mild parties you've enumerated in preceding paragraph, but a party typical of this particular circle, the Spencer-Thurber circle. Also, suggest that these people here be pegged as suburban, as I have marked, or some such, for later in the piece, much later, it turns out that they live in places with stairs, which means houses, not apartments. You start a story like this off without a suburban plant and a reader assumes you're talking about metropolitan apartment house life, and is unfairly surprised when he comes to a passage about someone going upstairs.

"2. You might, if you want, clinch the suburban atmosphere by putting in here the name of some town in the region—Rye, or a Connecticut town.

"3. Above you twice call this function an *evening party,* in one instance saying it begins in the afternoon. Here you say the Spencers were asked to dinner. Now, even in the Spencer circle the dinner guests can't be asked to come in the afternoon, certainly. This mixing up of a dinner party and an evening party that begins in the afternoon baffled me for quite a while, and I have come up with the suggestion that the party be made a cocktail party with buffet dinner. I think this is a brilliant suggestion. You never later have the people sitting down to dinner, nor do you take any notice whatever of dinner. If you make cocktails and buffet dinner, there is no question in readers' minds at all, and it seems to me the kind of a function the Spencers would give—as I did in my younger days. This is the real reason I'm writing these notes direct. I think such a fix would help considerably.

"4. It seems to me that the *however* isn't right in this sentence, and that some such phrase as marked might be better. Please consider.

"5. This sentence won't parse as is. Needs insert such as marked, or *points out that* or some such.

"6. *June* will probably sound stale by time we get out. Can be changed later, I assume. (Am noting here so query will be carried.)

"7. There hasn't been more than one phase of this ailment, has there? (The second phase—itching knees—isn't mentioned until later.) Also, please give this point a thought: You tell the story of the party in the present tense, but you have this paragraph in the past tense. Shouldn't this paragraph be in the present tense? I suspect so, and with initial, to help with the switchover. Also, suggest that there might be more definite wording here to indicate this is the evening of the party. The transition here may not be quite right.

"8. If you don't make it a buffet dinner, or do *something,* it seems to me that these people are leaving awfully quick. I thought maybe all this happened before dinner, because you have *early in the evening* a paragraph and a half above (7) and you've accounted for very little time lapse; not much has happened.

"9. The sentence at (a) differs in nature from sentence at (b). In the (a) sentence you are writing from the viewpoint of the Bloodgoods, in the (b) sentence you're the omnipotent author, knowing all about it. Seems to me wrong.

"10. The *over their shoulders* phrase here give the right picture? Suggests to me *on their shoulders,* like a Greek maiden holding vase. (Small matter.)

"11. Very unexpected to learn at this late date that there's a bar in this place. Not mentioned before, and the definite pronoun has no antecedent.

"12. Is it consistent that Mrs. Bloodgood would be the repository for this confidence in view of the fact that she and her husband met the Spencers only two weeks before and have only seen them that once? And is it as clear as it should be *what* Dora whispered?

"13. And same question here. Remember, Mrs. Bloodgood has only met the Spencers that one time, when she asked them to the party. How could she know?

"14. A timid suggestion: Would phrase written in help point it, or would it over-diagram it?

"Pardon me for being fussy. Most of the foregoing not important, but I think that buffet dinner business is, and the locating of the story out of New York City. You'll see another proof of this, set in regular type. Some of the incidentals may be untimely by the time this can be used. Can check on these later.

"P.S. The only other complication I can think of is that the very next story we bought after this one was titled 'One for the Road.' My tentative stand is that you have seniority around here and the junior man will have to get another title."

Ken Purdy

Ken Purdy is one of America's best-known editors and free-lance writers. He was an Associate Editor of Look *from 1939-1941. Other magazines to which he contributed his editorial talents were* True *(editor-in-chief 1949-1954) and* Argosy *(editor-in-chief 1954-1955). Since 1955 he has been a free-lance writer. He has published three books, and articles and fiction by him have appeared in 40-odd magazines. At present he lives in England.*

There's all the difference in the world between being just another editor—a name on the masthead of the magazine—and a really top-flight editor, a man who gives the magazine the character, influence and success it has.

Ken Purdy, a man who Harold Ross of the New Yorker *once called "the most brilliant young editor in America," provides an utterly realistic examination of the practices and mal-practices of magazine editing in the article that follows, and a thorough examination of the qualities that make for a truly creative, first-rate editor.*

THE FRUIT OF THE BITTERSWEET

During the twenty years from 1935 to 1955 I worked as a reporter on three newspapers and as editor of one; as associate editor of three magazines and managing editor of one; as editorial consultant to two magazines and as editor-in-chief of four. During this time, too, I sold short stories and articles to 20-odd major magazines and published two books. I cite this only to demonstrate my right to my prejudices. I have viewed the battlefield from both sides and I have the wound-stripes and the hatchet-scars to prove it.

The relationship between editor and writer is, now and then, a happy one. Now and then, indeed. A warm, pleasant, long-standing relationship between an editor and a writer is a rarity. By the very nature of things it must be. These two people, the editor and the writer, do not begin to understand each other. I know, because I have been both editor and writer, and, if you want more, both simultaneously. Let me sketch the width of the chasm separating the two. Let me show you what they think of each other.

The writer sees the editor as a secure, well-paid executive, surrounded by eager and competent seconds-in-command who do all the work and let him have all the credit; buffered from harsh reality by a pretty secretary, or a pair of them, intent only on keeping him happy, bringing him his coffee in the morning, reminding him of his appointment with his masseur, ministering to his creature comfort in every way—or almost every way. Somebody else pays the rent for his office, somebody else meets his phone bill, and his lunches and his cocktail dates go on the expense account.

The editor's working day? In the writer's view, it's an eight-hour vacation. In the morning he looks at his mail, not all of it, naturally, his secretary has screened it thoroughly, keeping from him anything unworthy of his attention, or anything that might upset him. He dictates a few answers, or, more likely, scribbles notes on the letter: "Anne, tell him no." "Anne, ask Mike fix this." "Anne, if this legit. complain, let me know otherwise you tk. care."

Now the Art Director brings in a few layouts, the editor runs a blasé eye over them, OK's some, makes suggestions for minor alterations. He reads three or four manuscripts, all of them previously read and evaluated by associate editors. Nine times in ten he accepts their judgment. By now it's time for lunch, a good lunch, preceded by two or three Martinis. He's back in the office by three. He has appointments with a couple of writers. One has an idea which he turns down after a minute's consideration. The other has an idea which he says just might possibly work out, he'd be delighted to see an outline. He makes a few phone calls, picks up his brief case and leaves. He has to make an appearance at a cocktail party for Marilyn Monroe, it's a bore, but he really must, and then off to catch the 6:02 to Connecticut, or Westchester, or Long Island where he can relax on his country estate and prepare himself for the rigors of the next day.

Is this the way it really is? Not quite. There are a couple of things missing. One thing in particular is missing: Pressure. The editor, you see, has a publisher. Or, if he's his own publisher, he has a board chairman, a president, or whatever. This individual has not got where he is by being a nice fellow. He may be a nice fellow, but that isn't what made him publisher. He knows, or he wouldn't have the job, about the uses of Pressure. He knows, like a judoplayer, how to keep his subordinates perpetually offbalance. He leans on them. The editor can never get off the treadmill. Supposing he pulls a brilliant coup of some kind and drives his circulation up 100,000. Fine. The publisher congratulates him. He is a fair-haired boy. He is a hero. Great. But after he has been hand-clasped, praised, drunk to, the needle goes in: "Don't let it slide back, now. Be a pity to lose a nice chunk of circulation like that." For a few minutes the editor was thinking of that extra circulation as his own property. He pulled it in, it was all his. He has just received the message. He has just learned that it isn't his at all, it's the publisher's, and that if it drifts away in the next couple of months, the publisher's attitude will be that he, the editor, has stolen something.

Corollary to this the editor learns that the Basic Law of the little jungle in which he labors is that circulation must not be static; it must rise. Advertising revenue must rise, as well. And while increase in advertising revenue demonstrates only the brilliance of the head huckster, or advertising director, a drop in revenue proves conclusively that the editor is putting out an unattractive and uneffective magazine.

So the editor sits at his nice desk in his pretty office, and he rubs his head-bones hard together. I'd like to have a dollar for every hour I've spent at night in the various offices I can remember, sitting there with one light on, nobody else in the place, going through the magazine. You go through it page by page, front to back, back to front, then you do it over again. How could this title have been done better? Should this story have followed that one, or would it have been more effective farther back in the book? Is this a really funny cartoon? How in the name of God did our biggest competitor get onto the Dawes story before we did? Can't let that happen again. Can't, but how to prevent it? You turn off the light and look out the window and hope for an idea. It's August. What will be in the news in October? You must know what will make a good lead story for October. You read seven newspapers a day, 100 magazines a month, you try to know what's going on because that's the only way in which you can project a trend two or three months ahead. You've got to think of something, but you can't, not that night, anyway.

That's how it is with an editor—a good one; the others don't matter. What's going to be in the October book? That's what keeps him awake at night, that's what makes him seem, often, distant, rude, inconsiderate, hurried. He's doing a little work, too, on the side. If he's a good editor, he has read every word in the magazine three times over before the presses start to roll. The best editor of our day, Harold Ross of the *New Yorker,* would stop the presses and pull an entire plate in order to change a comma.

The man is making $20,000 to $50,000 or more a year if he's top man on an important book. He's earning it. He knows the meaning of the old Spanish proverb: "In this life, take what you want—but pay for it." Even if he's a fraud, and I could name a couple, even if he's getting by on charm, guts and the brains of a brilliant and selfless subordinate, still he's sweating for it, like a tightrope walker sweats for it. Nobody gives anything away.

A bleak, harassed existence? Certainly not. There are enormous satisfactions. Editing a magazine is a creative enterprise, after all, and all the satisfactions of creation can be taken from it. But, looking in from the outside, the writer cannot correctly evaluate either the satisfaction or the penalties.

How does the writer look to the editor? As we talked about top-bracket editors, we must talk about top-bracket writers. There are about as many in the one category as the other. Usually the editor is as envious of the writer as the writer is of him. It's a cliché, but it's true as true: most editors are frustrated writers. The editor sees in a writer a man, or a woman, who's making almost as much money as the editor is, sometimes more, and doing it, the editor thinks, much more easily. He has no boss and his time is his own. The pressure that is the bane of the editor's existence cannot be put on the writer. All right, the writer has to pay the butcher and meet the mortgage, but so does the editor. The editor sees in front of him a guy who gets up at 10 in the morning if he feels like it, and runs for nobody's commuting train. He can spend a couple of days in the library, write a historical piece and get $1,500 for it. He can visit some alleged celebrity for a few hours and write an article that will get him another $1,500. So now he's made a month's pay and he can sit in his backyard and think big thoughts for a week or so. If he has any enterprise at all, it's easy for him to get a free trip, everything paid, to almost anywhere in the world. Airlines, tourist bureaus, industrial outfits will be happy to freight him around while he picks up stories for which he will be well paid. The chances are he's better-known than the editor. Why shouldn't he be?

If Editor Zilch buys a piece from Writer Zounds, Zounds' name will be displayed with ten times the prominence of Zilch's in that issue. For every interesting or worthwhile contact that the editor can make, the writer, if he knows his business, can make five. And if the writer does fiction as well as nonfiction, the editor sees two more enviable facets of his profession: He can write where he pleases, he is tied to no one locality by the necessity of showing up at an office at 9:30 every morning, and, second, he may at any time hit the jackpot: a $100,000 movie sale, for instance, or a big book. It happens every week.

The editor sees in the writer somebody who wants to take something from him: money out of his budget, and space out of his magazine. He doesn't believe that the writer understands the importance of either of these items. He doesn't believe that the writer knows that there is, somewhere in the building, a gimlet-eyed treasurer-accountant type with the imagination of a given ape who thinks that writing-off an article that turned out badly is plainly and simply a criminal act. The editor doesn't believe that the writer knows that every page in the magazine must carry its own weight, must somehow contribute to the easing of the pressure that dogs him. He looks at the writer almost as he looks at a job applicant, saying to himself, "Wouldn't it be wonderful if one of these jerks, instead of trying to get something from me, would offer to help me?" His pride is in the way, though, and usually he won't say to the writer, "Look, things are tough all over. I've got to have a hot story for October. Think for a minute. I need help, boy."

He rarely says it. He must maintain his facade, or he thinks he must. So he sits there, not paying as much attention to his visitor as he ought to, and maybe they get together on an assignment anyway. The writer leaves and the editor says to himself, "I hope he pulls it off." And in the back of his head he's thinking what an easy thing it is for the writer to do: research and write one story, turn it in and be paid for it. He'd like to settle for one problem like that, instead of the fifty that are hounding him.

Is that the way it really is with the writer? Again, yes, in part. It's true that he has no boss—excepting himself, the toughest boss of all. For, being his own boss he is responsible for his own success, and if he fails he fails twice. It's true that he's working for himself and that nobody can write him an office memo with three carbons, pointing out his deficiencies in detail. He doesn't need it. He has a little book in which he keeps track of his income. If he has a bad week, it's a very bad week—he doesn't make any money. No ideas, no out-put, no money. The editor can have a sterile stretch in which not a single idea of any consequence occurs to him, but he'll be paid anyway. It's true that the writer has in his own hands the free disposition of his time, but he's likely to put in more hours than any 9-to-5 wage slave he knows. When the wage-slave's bell rings for freedom at five o'clock, he is legally and morally entitled to relax. The writer doesn't feel that similar privileges are his. The editor can spend an hour listening to a bore and convince himself that he's working, because, after all, something good may come of it. If a writer does the same thing he's cheating himself.

Strictly speaking, save only researching and the peddling of ideas, everything the non-fiction writer does that is not done at the typewriter is a waste of time. This realization is the slave who beats him, this is the monkey he carries on his back. If he steals time, he steals it from himself, and that hurts.

What else? If you're going to be a writer, you're going to be lonely. There's no way out of that one. Writing is like dying—you have to do it yourself.

Shall we leave on the down-beat ending? No, let us be commercial, and provide the up-beat ending so dear to editors and so necessary to the financial well-being of writers.

Well, then, was I happy as an editor? But yes. As a writer? Certainly. More as one than the other? Yes. I'd rather be a writer than anything else. If I couldn't be a writer I'd rather be an editor than anything else.

Advice? Counsel? Surely.

How to Be an Editor:

1. Having read everything and written much, having worked on small-town newspapers and bushleague magazines, you have been hired. You look at the magazine. You know it well, of course, because you've read it for a long time, as you have all other magazines of any consequence. You consider first how it can be improved typographically, how the layouts can be bettered, how it can be modernized and made brighter. This is easiest, so you do it first. There are ways to force the reader to look at a page, there are ways to force him to look at a certain part of the page first, another part later. You learned this years ago, it is one of the two or three secrets you have. You never tell anyone else.

2. You have an hour's talk with every member of the staff. You

are trying to separate sheep from goats, men from boys. You watch them all for two weeks. You will find one, two, or three people who are phonies and/or deadweights. You get rid of them at once, not by firing them, but by telling them that, alas, you will not be able to get on together, and urging them to find other jobs, which you will help them to do. Stubborn cases you tell, Go now, before I find out so much about you that I cannot in good conscience help you find another job. When you are sure you know the good ones you promise them that you will assume all responsibility for every mistake they ever make, and that you will personally deliver to your own superior credit for every good thing they ever do. This is an honest promise and you keep it to the letter from that day onward.

3. You look for, and find, stories with a high publicity potential. This is hard. Having published them, you personally see to it that the publicity is obtained. This is very hard.

4. You crawl into your readers' minds. You find out what they want, what they like, what they want in your magazine that they do not want in another. This is terribly hard. It is possible to learn how to do this, but no one ever learned it in less than 15 years, and some people could not learn it in 50. But without it you cannot be a good editor, although you can be a successful one.

5. You flog yourself until you automatically think about the magazine as soon as you wake up in the morning, and you think about it the last thing at night. This is hard, and burdensome, but unless you do it your mind will not produce ideas in volume.

Do these things and you can improve almost any magazine in the world, increase its circulation, add to its advertising. You can maintain this pace for about three years. After that you must slack off for a while, vacation, or accept a nervous breakdown. The choice depends on your temperament.

How to Be a Writer:

1. This is uncomplicated. Having read everything and written much, having studied techniques and methods, you cast off and declare yourself a writer. You need no legal permission. It is a unilateral action. You then resolve to write for eight hours a day. This is brutal, harder than anything else you have ever done. At first you will have to spend 16 hours a day to write for eight. Ultimately you will find that you produce a useful volume of work in five or six consecutive, not scattered, hours per day, six days a

week. You have arrived. You have made it. You are a writer.

What shall you write about? If you have to ask that question, do not, for the love of God, try at all, because you'll never succeed. Find a good job somewhere, and be happy.

INDEX OF NAMES

This index contains names of persons and firms and titles of literary works. Page references for the contributors to this anthology will be found in the Table of Contents.

ABOUT THE EDITOR

GERALD GROSS, born and educated in New York City, graduated from City College of New York in 1953 with a B.A. *cum laude* in English. Since his graduation he has held various positions as editor, and for the past six years has been reprint editor for one of New York's mass market paperback publishers.

Mr. Gross is the compiler and editor of PUBLISHERS ON PUBLISHING which was published by Grosset's Universal Library in the Fall of 1961. He is now working on a new book *The Edmund Pearson Reader* which will be published by Little, Brown & Company.

Mr. Gross is married and lives in Brooklyn Heights with his wife and infant daughter.

PUBLISHERS ON PUBLISHING

This is the first anthology — or, better still, compendium — of writings about publishing by the men who have known the profession best — the publishers. Gerald Gross has drawn upon the memoirs, recollections, articles and talks of more than thirty famous publishers to give the reader an unparalleled literary panorama of an exciting and unorthodox business. Among the publishers represented are Walter Hines Page, George Haven Putnam, Henry Holt, Frank Nelson Doubleday, Michael Sadleir, J. Henry Harper, Sir Geoffrey Faber, John Farrar, Donald Friede, Sir Stanley Unwin, Alfred A. Knopf and Bennett Cerf — just to mention a few. Much of this material has never before been available in book form, and some of it has only been available in limited private editions. As Frederic G. Melcher writes in his Preface: "Of all the records which may illuminate the nature and spirit of book publishing the most valuable and interesting . . . are those of the publishers themselves. . . . The book will be most welcome to any reader of publishing history, valuable and suggestive to the present or future practitioner."

PUBLISHERS ON PUBLISHING

This anthology of articles – all written by men who were or are actively engaged in book publishing – offers a fine, composite and always readable study of one of the liveliest of all businesses.

THE PHILADELPHIA INQUIRER

It is true, as Frederic G. Melcher notes in his preface, that "book publishers do not consider themselves as writers." Not in the general area of belles-lettres, certainly, but when they write about publishing they are usually fluent, cogent, forthright, and often masters of a crisp prose style that some of the names on their lists would do well to imitate. Gerald Gross had an abundance of material to choose from, and he has chosen well in assembling the units in this important anthology, which can be opened anywhere to profitable purpose and with high enjoyment.

THE NEW YORK TIMES

It is always fascinating to get a behind-the-scenes picture of the book publishing profession, which is supposed to be so mysterious and romantic. This book is almost a history of publishing – written by the men who lived it. It contains sixteen self-portraits by some of the most illustrious names in British and American publishing: Daniel Macmillan, Alfred Knopf, Horace Liveright, Frank Swinnerton, Charles Scribner, Jr., etc. . . . The fascinating anecdotes about such great men of letters as Dreiser, Maugham, and Lawrence make the book particularly interesting to writers.

THE WRITER

This is a unique portrait of the publishing industry as seen by publishers themselves. It begins with a letter by Daniel Macmillan dating from the early 1840's, and ends with a talk by Bennett Cerf less than a year ago. Anyone with any interest at all in book publishing should have this. And if you ever suffered the pangs of a rejection slip, John Farrar's "Letters to an Unpublished Writer" is worth the price of the books.

ALBANY TIMES UNION-KNICKERBOCKER

OCCUPATION: WRITER

By

Robert Graves

OCCUPATION: WRITER is not a how-to-write manual. It is more like a roller-coaster ride through one of the most astonishing minds of our times. But the title is accurate as far as it goes: Robert Graves has established himself at the top of his profession with a solid body of achievement in all literary forms over more than three decades. The general public knows him for his best-selling novels, which, though they deal with history, bear about the same relation to the genre of the "historical novel" as the "Iliad" might to the BOBBSEY TWINS. Scholars know him as one of the most penetrating searchers and fecund interpreters of man's past. Graves regards himself as a poet. Lesser poets may well regard him as a magician, for he seems to have an almost eerie familiarity with the Muse herself.

In this collection of shorter pieces are lusty humor, as in THE LOST ART OF SWEARING, erudition combined with wit, as in IMPERIAL INCEST, light satire, as in THE ANCESTORS OF COLONEL BLIMP, and "a selected number of theatrical pieces, short stories, and other elegant trifles calculated to delight the most discriminating of ladies and gentlemen."

UL-53

The UNIVERSAL *Library*

he Dance of Life *Havelock Ellis* . . 2
he Good Society *Walter Lippmann* . 3
he Late George Apley *Marquand* . 4
Ian and His Gods *Homer Smith* . . . 5
he Measure of Man *J. W. Krutch* . 6
Ielbourne *Lord David Cecil* 7
)scar Wilde *Hesketh Pearson* 8
he Puritan Oligarchy *Wertenbaker* 9
)uackery in Public Schools *Lynd* . 10
he Ides of March *Thornton Wilder* 13
Ioble Essences *Sir Osbert Sitwell* . . 14
Vhy Was Lincoln Murdered? *Otto Eisenschiml* 15
he Shock of Recognition *Wilson* (Vol. I; Vol. II) 17, 18
Iercules, My Shipmate *Robert Graves* 19
etters of Lord Byron *Barzun* 20
rish Folk Stories *Yeats* 21
outh Wind *Norman Douglas* 22
he Uprooted *Oscar Handlin* 23
ohn Adams and the American Revolution *Catherine Drinker Bowen* . . 24
he Longhorns *J. Frank Dobie* 25
ucrezia Borgia *Maria Bellonci* 26
tory of My Life *Clarence Darrow* . . 27
Vorld of Aldous Huxley *Rolo* 28
he Great Plains *Walter Prescott Webb* 29
merican Doctor's Odyssey *Heiser* . 30
our Plays by Ibsen 31
horter Novels of Herman Melville 32
he Star-Gazer *Zsolt de Harsanyi* . . 33
reud and His Time *Fritz Wittels* . . . 34
rimitive Religion *Robert H. Lowie* . 35
Iaupassant *Francis Steegmuller* . . . 36
he Green Crow *Sean O'Casey* . . . 37
1 Plays of the Greek Dramatists . 38
Selected Novels of Henry James . 39
he American Presidency *Laski* . . . 40
talin *Leon Trotsky* 41
J. S. Grant *Bruce Catton* 42
he Vanishing Hero *Sean O'Faolain* . 43
arl Marx: The Red Prussian *Leopold Schwarzschild* 44
)ecline and Fall *Evelyn Waugh* . . . 45
Iodern Woman *Lundberg & Farnham* 46
ndrew Jackson: Border Captain *Marquis James* 47

The Horse's Mouth *Joyce Cary* . . . 48
Green Mansions *W. H. Hudson* . . . 49
Myths of the World *Padraic Colum* 50
The Owl in the Attic *Thurber* . . . 51
Mrs. Eddy *Edwin F. Dakin* 52
Occupation: Writer *Robert Graves* . 53
The Tastemakers *Russell Lynes* . . . 54
With Napoleon in Russia *Armand de Caulaincourt* 55
Comedies of Oscar Wilde 56
Madame Bovary *Gustave Flaubert* . . . 57
Pride and Prejudice *Jane Austen* . . . 58
Nine Plays of Chekov 59
McSorley's Wonderful Saloon *Joseph Mitchell* 60
The Art of Love *Ovid* 61
Nijinsky *Romola Nijinsky* 62
Crime and Punishment *Dostoevsky* . . 63
Mister Jelly Roll *Alan Lomax* . . . 64
The Town and the City *Jack Kerouac* 65
50 Poems *e. e. cummings* 66
Herself Surprised *Joyce Cary* 67
Jane Austen *Elizabeth Jenkins* 68
Middle-Aged Man on the Flying Trapeze *James Thurber* 69
Frank Lloyd Wright on Architecture 70
Eyewitness *Eisenschiml & Newman* . . 71
My Life *Leon Trotsky* 72
A Pocketful of Wry *McGinley* 73
March of the Iron Men *Burlingame* . 74
Editor to Author *Perkins · Wheelock* 75
Speak, Memory *Vladimir Nabokov* . . 76
Let Your Mind Alone *Thurber* . . . 77
Disraeli *Hesketh Pearson* 78
Roosevelt & Hopkins *Sherwood* . . . 79
To Be a Pilgrim *Joyce Cary* 80
Churchill *Virginia Cowles* 81
D. H. Lawrence *Mary Freeman* 82
Leonardo da Vinci *Vallentin* 83
The Civil War Digest *Newman & Long* 84
The Seal in the Bedroom *Thurber* . . 85
The Murder of the Man Who Was 'Shakespeare' *Calvin Hoffman* . . . 86
Inside Benchley *Robert Benchley* . . 87
What's Ahead in Space *Select Committee on Astronautics & Space Exploration* . 88
Good Intentions *Ogden Nash* 89